Selling Your Handcrafted Art Jewelry

Kitty Piper
and
A. B. Petrow

**Published by CraftMasters™ Books
Sebastopol, California**

Copyright© 2010 By Craftmasters Books

All rights reserved. No part of this book shall be reproduced, stored in a retrieval system, or transmitted by any means, electronic, mechanical, photocopying, recording, or otherwise, except for the inclusion of brief quotations in review, without permission in writing from the publisher.

DISCLAIMER

This publication and accompanying software are designed to provide accurate and authoritative information with regard to the subject matter covered. It is sold with the understanding that the Publisher is not engaged in rendering legal, accounting, or other professional advice. If legal advice or other expert assistance is required, the services of a competent professional person should be sought.
--From a Declaration of Principles jointly adopted by a Committee of the American Bar Association and a Committee of Publishers and Associations.

Every effort has been made to make this book as complete and as accurate as possible, but no warranty or fitness is implied. Neither the author nor Craftmasters Books, nor anyone else who has been involved in the creation, production, or delivery of this product shall be liable for any direct, incidental or consequential damages, such as, but not limited to, loss of anticipated profits or benefits, resulting from its use or from any breach of any warranty. Some states do not allow the exclusion or limitation of direct, incidental or consequential damages so the above limitation may not apply to you.

Windows is a registered trademark of Microsoft Corporation. All other product and brand names mentioned in this publication are trademarks or registered trademarks of their respective holders.

Craftmasters Books
P. O. Box 1655
Sebastopol, CA 95473

ISBN-13: 978-0-9655193-7-3
ISBN-10: 0-9655193-7-6

Printed in USA by createspace.com
Photographs: A. B. Petrow (eagleab@aol.com)
Front cover booth: Andrea Frost, www.rabbitsandrainbows.com
Back cover booth: Albion Smith, www.absolutearts.com/portfolios/a/albion
Illustrations: Rhonda Libby (saint1276@yahoo.com)
Poetry: John Reiger (johnreigerpottery.com)

Table of Contents

Introduction 6

ART SHOWS AND CRAFT FAIRS 7
    Types of fairs 7
    First, you need a product 8
    Craft show myths 8
    How to find out where the fairs are 9
    Tips for finding a good show 9
    Local craft fair guides 9

LIST OF CRAFT FAIR GUIDES 10
    How to choose a good fair 11
    The application process 11
    Read and complete the application 11
    Slides 12
    What is the jury looking for? 12
    Photography 13
    Booth shots 16
    Zapplication 17
    Get the application in on time 18
    Tips for getting into the show 18
    Planning your booth 18
    Indoor booths 19
    Lighting 19
    Outdoor booths 20
    City streets 22
    Grassy parks 22
    In a large tent 23
    Weather 23
    More tips for outdoor shows, weights and weather 24
    Banners, booth signs, and photos 26
    More display tips 27
    Packaging 29
    Taking VISA and MasterCard 29
    Portable credit card terminals 30
    Tips for taking credit cards 30
    Selling tips 31
    On the road 34
    Travel tips 34
    Security on the road 36

- FLYING TO CRAFT FAIRS ... 37
- FLYING TIPS ... 38
- HOW TO INCREASE PROFITS ... 39

MORE CRAFT FAIR TIPS ... 40
- BEFORE THE SHOW ... 40
- SETTING UP FOR THE SHOW ... 41
- DURING THE SHOW ... 42
- AVOIDING THEFT ... 43
- HEALTH ... 44

LIST OF PROMOTERS OF MULTIPLE FAIRS AND SHOWS ... 45

SELLING TO STORES AND GALLERIES ... 50

WHOLESALE MARKETING ... 50
- TRADE SHOW PRODUCERS ... 51

WHOLESALE TIPS ... 52
- TRADE SHOWS ... 52
- DURING THE TRADE SHOW ... 52
- WHOLESALE BUSINESS ... 54
- WHOLESALE REPS ... 56
- MORE WHOLESALE TIPS ... 56
- TIPS FOR SELLING ON WHOLESALECRAFTS.COM ... 57
- OTHER MARKETS ... 58

SELLING ONLINE ... 60

INTERNET TIPS ... 61
- MAKING YOUR OWN WEB SITE ... 61
- TIPS FOR SELLING ON EBAY ... 63
- TIPS FOR SELLING ON ETSY ... 65

GENERAL BUSINESS AND MARKETING TIPS ... 67
- BOOKKEEPING ... 67
- TAXES ... 68
- COPYRIGHT ... 69
- PROMOTION ... 70
- PRICING ... 71
- MISCELLANEOUS ... 71

USEFUL ADDRESSES ... 73
- DISPLAY ... 73
- PHOTOGRAPHERS ... 74

BAGS AND BOXES 74
INSURANCE 74
CREDIT CARD PROCESSING SYSTEMS 75
COMPUTERS AND MICROSOFT™ OFFICE 75
INTRODUCTION 75
DIFFERENT MICROSOFT OFFICE CONFIGURATIONS 76
BASIC COMPUTER REQUIREMENTS 77
HOW TO USE MICROSOFT EXCEL 77
DOWNLOADING SPREADSHEETS 78
USING THE SPREADSHEETS 79
CRAFT PRICING (PRICING.XLS) 80
CRAFT FAIR APPLICATION ORGANIZER (ORGANIZER.XLS) 82
CRAFT FAIR EQUIPMENT LIST (EQUIPMENT.XLS) 86
CRAFT SHOW EXPENSE REPORT (EXPENSES.XLS) 88
CUSTOMER MAILING LIST (CUSTOMER.XLS) 90
TRADE SHOW COSTS (TRADE SHOW.XLS) 92
SALES REPRESENTATIVE AGREEMENT (REPAGREEMENT.DOC) 94
GALLERY DATABASE (GALLERY LIST.XLS) 96
CONSIGNMENT AGREEMENT (CONSIGNMENT.DOC) 100
MONTHLY ACCOUNTING SYSTEM (BOOKKEEPING.XLS) 102
INVOICE (INVOICE.XLS) 104
BUSINESS PLAN (BUSINESS PLAN.DOC) 106
INVENTORY (INVENTORY.XLS) 108
MARKETING PLAN (MARKETING PLAN.XLS) 110
PRESS RELEASE (PRESS RELEASE.DOC) 112
LETTERHEADS (LETTERHEADS.DOC) 114
HOW TO USE MICROSOFT PUBLISHER 118
HOW TO MAKE AN ARTIST'S STATEMENT 119

TOP 900 CRAFT FAIRS AND ART SHOWS 120

LETTER TO CRAFT FAIR PROMOTER FOR APPLICATION (FAIRLETTER.DOC) 121

TOP 1,100 GALLERIES IN THE UNITED STATES 151

CONCLUSION 175
INDEX 177

Introduction

Over the years at craft fairs and art shows, many people have approached us with questions about how to get started selling their own creative artistic creations. Frequently asked questions include: How do you find out about where and when the shows are? How do you get into the shows? Why are some people admitted and others not? Where did you get your canopy and tables? Can I make a good living doing this? How do I get stores to sell my work? Can I use the internet to make money?

With this book you have all the information you need to sell what you make, at art shows and craft fairs, to stores and galleries, and on the internet. With the 900 craft fairs, 1100 galleries, and a list of over 100 promoters, you are guaranteed to find people who will appreciate and buy your craft work. If you supply the necessary irresistible handmade products and lots of self-discipline, you will be successful.

The information contained in this book has helped us to sell over 1.9 million dollars worth of our handmade craft products over the last 30 years. Our intention is that you will have even more success, because now you have much more information than we had when we started.

Three Rivers Arts Festival, Pittsburgh, PA

Art Shows and Craft Fairs

Art Show or Craft Fair: An event that takes place usually during a weekend, where a group of people sell what they make; jewelry, woodwork, pottery, paintings, photographs, metalwork, etc. In addition to crafts, it may have music, or food and wine as an attraction. Every fair has a promoter who finds a location for the fair, secures permits, hires security, and determines which artists and craftspeople will sell at his or her show.

Types of fairs

Basically there are three types of shows:

- <u>The family show</u>

- <u>The craft fair</u>

- <u>The art show</u>

The family show may have carnival-type entertainment, chamber of commerce booths, a craft area, and music. At the craft fair there may be some music, but the emphasis is on art and crafts. The art show usually has only fine art and some fine crafts, with no other attractions for the customer. Many events overlap in other areas as well. For example an art show may have a music group as a lure, or a family show may have a small fine art exhibit. Shows may also specialize in traditional crafts like dried flower arranging and tole painting, or contemporary crafts such as fine handmade jewelry, pottery, fiber, and wood turning.

For your first show, you should pick a small local show. You probably won't make much money but you have to start somewhere, to learn what you need in the way of display equipment, comfort, product, etc. This is called "paying your dues." You can even start with a flea market. There are always a few shoppers shopping at a flea market that will recognize quality when they see it, and will give you some valuable feedback about your product, price, and display. Plus you can get rid of a few things cluttering up your garage. Flea marketing of your craft is usually only good for one or two trials, though. For one thing, the people who come each weekend to a flea market tend to be the same people over and over, and after two weeks your sales will drop dramatically.

First, you need a product

You have a product if:
1. It is something you like to make.
2. It is both useful and artistic.
3. It sells for at least five times more than the cost of the materials in it.
4. You can make a lot of them at a time.
5. You need a product that people want. If it has a function they will want it even more.

Craft show myths

If you are thinking along any of the following lines as you contemplate a successful craft fair business, forget it. You may be able to pull it off, but you will not be a success.
1. I will buy some imports and sell them as my own.
2. I will just show up at a fair without first applying, and they will let me in.
3. I will find a successful craftsperson and copy them.
4. I will make something that the stores have and sell it cheaper.
5. I will put my crafts on the Internet and won't have to do shows at all.
6. Being a successful craftsperson is easier than working at a job.
7. I will make only what I like. If the public likes it fine, if not, fine.
8. I can read and relax at a craft show, because I work all week.
9. I don't need to take Visa or MC, just cash.
10. I can sell crafts and avoid taxes.

All of the above are wrong!

Craft Fairs and Art Shows

How to find out where the fairs are

Visit a craft show advertised in your area and ask the artists who the promoter is. Also ask which shows they recommend, and which ones to avoid. Find out if the show is better for high-end crafts, or traditional arts and crafts, and how long the show has been going on. You can also search Google on the internet with some general keywords like "craft fairs (your state)." You will be surprised how many listings pop up.

Tips for finding a good show

☐ **Use www.festivalnet.com.**

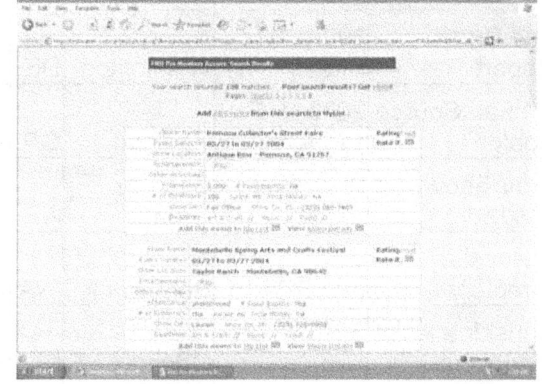

The membership fee is about $50 a year. Search the site by state and month, and you will see all the shows in that state for that month. One way to tell if a show has potential is by the booth fee. If it is under $100, it is probably too small of a show to make much money. One rule of thumb is that you should make 8 to 10 times the show fee.

☐ **Get the iphone app "Craft Fair"**

Only if you have an iphone or ipad, of course. The app has a list of 400 of the best shows in the country, as well as a useful "pricing your crafts" app, show profit app, and a list of things to bring.

☐ **Get the Art Fair SourceBook**

After you have been doing shows for a while, and if you want to travel to bigger shows in other states, this book is very helpful in telling you what to expect at a show. It gives you tons of information about each of the top 300 shows in the country. A subscription for one year is around $200.00. www.artfairsourcebook.com 800-358-2045

Local craft fair guides

Every area in the United States has one or more craft fair guides, magazines that report on fairs for several states in that region. A few guides specialize in fairs only in a single state, and some others try to cover all of the best fairs in the entire country.

List of Craft Fair Guides

NAME OF DIRECTORY	ADDRESS	CITY	ST	ZIP	CONTACT	PHONE	AREA COVERED
Crafter's Blue Book	P. O. Box 513	Kechi	KS	67067	DJ Wallace	888-206-6311	CO, KS, MS, OK, IL, MI, NE, SD, IA, MN, ND, and WI
Festival Network Online	P. O. Box 18839	Asheville	NC	28814	Kirt Irmiter	800-200-3737	United States and Canada
The Crafts Report	300 Water Street	Wilmington	DE	19801	Bernadette Finnerty	302-656-2209	United States
Art Fair Source Book	2003 N. E. 11th Ave.	Portland	OR	97212	Greg Lawler	800-358-2045	United States
Your Show Guide	P. O. Box 11795	Casa Grande	AZ	85230	Mary Davidson	520-836-8427	Arizona, Colorado, and Nevada
Festivals Directory	P.O.B 7515	Bonney Lk.	WA	98391	Carol Farer	253-863-6617	WA, OR, ID, MT
Sunshine Artist Magazine	3210 Dade Ave.	Orlando	FL	32804		407-228-9862	United States
The Network Marketing Guide	P. O. Box 1248	Palatine	IL	60078	Teresa or Nancy	847-604-3965	IL, MI, rest of the nation.
Extravaganza Craft News	160 Green Tree Dr.	Belgrade	MT	59714	Shasta McLaughlin	406-388-9883	Montana, Idaho, Wyoming, North and South Dakota
Art and Craft Show Yellow Pages	P. O. Box B	Red Hook	NY	12571	Betty Chypre	888-424-1326	Ct, MA, NJ, NY, PA, VT.
Wisconsin Art and Craft Fairs Directory	101 E. Wilson Street	Madison	WI	53702		608-266-0190	Wisconsin
Craftmaster News	P. O. Box 39429	Downey	CA	90239		562-869-5882	CA and other western states

How to choose a good fair

With so many fairs to choose from, it is a challenge to pick a good fair. My philosophy is to try almost any fair (if I have some indication that it might be good), and see what happens. If it is not good, I don't have to ever do it again. Sometimes a little-known fair will surprise you with a lot of sales. To try and minimize the bad fairs, I have a few basic criteria. Number one, I like to know a lot of people will be there. 10,000, 50,000, 120,000, 600,000 people. With enough shoppers I can make money at any show. Show me the people! If you have a more expensive product, then you might focus more on areas where the customers have more disposable income. This could be a smaller indoor art show that is sponsored by an art guild and has an excellent reputation, or a show in a very wealthy area. Again, experience counts. You have to be willing to try any well-reputed show at least once. That is the only way to know if your product and price is a match for that customer base.

- **Calculate the potential of the show.**

Multiply the attendance number by $30 (half of the people will spend $60 and half will spend nothing) and divide it by the number of artists. 50,000 people times $30 equals $1,500,000 divided by 250 artists equals an average of $6,000 per artist.

The application process

The first step is to get the fair's application. This doesn't cost you anything. Write to every fair that you might want to do, and ask for an application. I recommend sending a simple typed letter with your name and contact information. This enables the show producer to get your address right. The letter need only say "Please send me an application and any information about your upcoming shows, and put me on your mailing list. Thank you." Print fifty copies of the same generic letter, sign them, and mail them to the shows that you might be interested in. You don't have to impress the promoter in this letter. They will gladly send an application to anyone. Sometimes, if you waited until the last minute, the fair can fax you an application or you can get it online.

When you receive the application, the next step is to make a deadline list with the name of the fair, deadline date, and fair date on a sheet of paper, posted in a place where you will see it. There is a form for this in the spreadsheet section of this book. You then file the fair application in a folder with the name of the month on the folder that the fair is going to happen. When your deadline list shows that the fair application deadline is coming up, you go to the fair's folder, take out the application, fill it out, and mail it in.

Read and complete the application

Read the entire application when you get it. If you don't, you will often miss little details, such as "send in a resume," or "don't send anything in but the application," or even "include a slide of your workshop." It might be hard to get a good slide of your workshop at the last minute. Fill out the application completely and neatly. Many promoters have told me that they get a lot of incomplete and/or unreadable applications.

Slides

How important are your slides and images? Very important. **Extremely important!** Simply put, the better the show, the better your slides must be to get in. Although there are still a few good shows that are filled simply by the promoter looking at photos on her kitchen table, all of the best shows are juried.

A jury consists of 2 to 12 artists, promoters, art teachers, and local experts who sit in a darkened room while all of the slides or images are projected simultaneously on a wall or screen. As the three-to-six slides are shown, each judge gives points for design, creativity, craftsmanship, etc. The process often takes less than a minute for each artist, with the promoter reading the descriptions of each slide supplied by the artist if necessary. Often the acceptance of the artist is based solely on these points.

What is the jury looking for?

The jury is looking for good slides, first and foremost. This is the big hurdle. And of course, the jurors are looking for creativity and originality. Good slides won't necessarily get you into good shows, but bad slides are very likely to keep you out.

The first thing the jury notices is the quality of the slide. A poorly lit or badly composed slide might not look so bad under home viewing conditions, but when juried the slide is instantly compared with the expertly photographed slides already shown that day. So the first impression is important. A juror will be less impressed with unprofessional slides, and they will give fewer points. No matter how nice your jewelry is, you are wasting your time and money with poor quality slides.

All slides should be consistent. Each slide should show only one craft item, shown close-up, filling the screen, and well exposed. There is a strong desire in beginning craftspeople to show many items, five or six in each slide. They want to show the jury the range and variety of their design. But the juror will see only clutter. You have to pick your best pieces.

The same is true for the background. All of your slides should have the same background. Beginners love to put rocks, flowers, bricks, and other stuff in the picture. They also like to photograph on a fancy cloth or carpet background. They hope the attractiveness of the background will make their craft look more attractive. The opposite will happen. The juror will be confused, not impressed.

Photography

You can make your own photographs with either a 35mm camera or digital camera. You can have slides made from your digital camera images, or digital images from your film slides.

If you don't already have film camera experience, I would suggest that you go the digital route. Get a digital camera and have slides made from your images if and when you need them. You can also use your digital files for online applications, Zapplication, web galleries like etsy.com, and your cards and brochures.

Your digital camera doesn't have to be fancy. You can use nearly any digital camera made in the past three years with 3.2 megapixels or more. It might be more useful if it has manual settings so you can control your depth of field. Some digital cameras have scene settings that will provide you all you need for a good image. For example, Kodak has a flower setting that takes excellent photos. My Olympus SP-550 has a setting for auctions that works great.

The biggest advantage of a digital camera is that you can practice to perfection without it costing you a dime. You will need to learn a little about lighting. And you will need to learn about digital manipulation with a photo editing program.

If you don't want to spend the time and money to get good photo results on your own, hire a commercial photographer that specializes in craft or small product (table-top) photography. Some excellent photographers specializing in crafts are listed in the "useful addresses" section of this book. Always ask them for unmodified digital files or original film, unless you want them to make Zapplication files for you.

☐ <u>**Have slides made from your digital files.**</u>
You can correct your digital photos in Photoshop or Elements, and email the files to www.slides.com. They make slides from your digital files for around $2.50 each and FedEx them back to you. Slides are 3:2 ratio. The best resolution for making slides from your images is 4096 x 2730.

☐ <u>**Always use "Save As" when working with digital.**</u>
If you use "Save" the original is overwritten. Change the name with each modification step, so the original won't get lost. Always save the image at the highest possible setting, usually .tiff. Each

save to .jpg reduces the quality. If you have Photoshop, save to .psd until the final save, when you "save for the web."

☐ **Never use the digital zoom.**

Always use the optical zoom, somewhere in the middle of the zoom range. The optics are usually better in the middle. Move the camera, not the zoom.

☐ **Override the camera's light meter if possible.**

The built-in light meter in the camera will overexpose dark items, and underexpose light items. Use the lowest ISO setting in a digital camera. Always use the highest quality (resolution) setting in the camera.

☐ **Always use a tripod.**

Greater depth of field requires a slower shutter speed, and the longer shutter opening time increases the chance of camera shake. Use either a cable release or the camera timer so you won't shake the camera and get a fuzzy picture.

☐ **Use a neutral background.**

Don't use plaids, weavings, etc. Uncluttered is the key. Indoors use white, gray, or black (never use red), outdoors use white roll paper or a white sheet. Use a canopy in bright sun to provide even light. It will act as a giant soft box.

☐ **Use gradient paper.**

You can find gradient paper at Superior Specialties, 800-666-2545 **www.superspec.com** I like the #9, black to white, and the #37, blue to white.

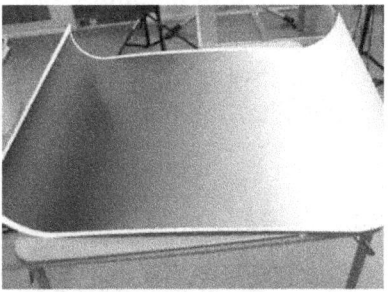

☐ **Use a commercial lens cleaning cloth.**

Anything else can and will scratch the coating on the lens.

☐ **Write down settings for every shot you take.**

Save your notes for future reference. If you keep notes, you won't have to relearn the entire process every time you take your photos. With digital, take a photo at every setting in your camera, take notes, then look at all the images in Photoshop or Elements. Then go with the setting that makes the best image.

☐ Use a light tent.
EZcube Light Tents provides even lighting. They are available on eBay for $45 to $90, depending on the size. Get a smaller one for jewelry and small items. For jewelry, use a Cloud Dome from Rio Grande. Even an old white lamp shade will even out the shadows.

☐ Use fluorescent bulbs and reflectors.
Use two or three T-2 Spiral bulbs for indoor shots with a smaller (18") light cube. Position one on each side and one at the top. Never use the built-in flash on your camera. Use the Photoshop levels eyedropper to bring a white or black background to normal color levels, which will make your jewelry the right color.

☐ Turn off all room lights.
You should turn off as many other lights as possible and close the curtains, so you control the lighting.

☐ Use a 50mm lens with a macro feature.
You can get one of these on eBay for less than $100. For close-ups, you will need macro capabilities. The macro feature will help you maintain focus with small items such as jewelry. You might have one built into your camera. To see if your digital camera with a built-in lens has macro, look for the flower symbol.

☐ Use f16 or f22 for depth of field.
Depth of field is the area of the image that is in focus, from front to back. If your camera has an "A" setting (aperture priority setting), set your f-stop at f22 and the camera will set the shutter

speed. Everything will be in focus. If you want to focus on one special detail of your work, or blur the background, use f4 for less depth of field.

☐ **Look at your images as a group.**

Put them together. They should have a consistency of vision. Check out the color relationships. Are they interesting? Do they grab your attention? Look for a theme.

Booth shots

When a show has two qualified applicants in the same media, and the jurors can't chose, they will go with the best looking booth.

☐ **Shoot your booth shot from a slight angle.**

Remove all clutter. Make your product stand out. Compare your booth shot to your product photos. They should be the same quality. People should not be in the booth photo. The top of the booth should not show in the photo. The jurors don't care what canopy you use.

☐ **Use a wide-angle lens for booth photos.**

A 28mm to 35mm lens will work best. Stand on a stool for a better angle, if necessary.

☐ **Overexpose outdoor booth shots.**

If you don't, the booth will look dark because the automatic meter in the camera will under-expose for the sky. Better yet, keep the sky and canopy out of the photo altogether. A cloudy day will provide even light, which is best. Spread a canopy wall on the ground in front of the booth (out of sight of the camera, of course) to reflect more light into the booth.

☐ **Use flash on indoor booth shots.**

Try to get light into the corners of the booth. You can use your photofloods, if you keep them out of the photo.

Zapplication

Many of the larger shows are using the zapplication process for online screening. Membership is free to artists. The show pays $1,500 to $4,500 for their services. You don't need any special software (except for photo editing), but you do need an email address and a credit card when you apply to shows. When you want to apply to a show, you simply go online, type in a brief description about your craft, select the photos you want to apply with, and pay the application fee with your credit card. Their web site, www.zapplication.org, is very helpful with detailed information. One nice feature is that they email you about upcoming shows by e-mail. Another is that you don't pay booth fees until you are accepted.

Photos for Zapplication must be square, 1920 pixels on each side, and under 1.8 mb in size. You can take your own digital pictures at your highest resolution, crop them square, adjust the levels to change the contrast, and resize them to 72 ppi (pixels per inch) by 1920 pixels x 1920 pixels with Elements or Photoshop. While any 3.2 megapixel digital camera will work, 6 to 10 mp is better. The photos should be saved to .tiff or .psd as you work on them, and when you are finished, saved for the web as baseline .jpg's.

If you use film, you can either have your slides digitized by your local lab or scan them yourself on a home scanner. Make sure they are saved as .tiff files. Since your photos have to be square for Zapplication, and 35 mm slides are rectangular, you can use Photoshop to add black strips on each side of vertical slides or the top and bottom of horizontal slides to make them square. Basically you make the canvas behind the slide square, and black, to provide the stripes. The zapplication.org web site explains how to do this. There are at least 15 professionals listed at the zapplication web site that will convert your slides for you for a small fee.

Artists can apply through ZAPP™ by following these steps :

1. Prepare your artwork images formatted to the Image Preparation specifications.
2. Create a profile by entering basic contact information and creating a username and password to ZAPP™.
3. Upload 6 to 40 digital images of your artwork and a booth photo to your image portfolio.
4. Select your choice of participating shows to apply to.
5. Pay the application fee online with a credit card, and submit the application online.
6. Receive e-mail notifications when your applications have been received, and jury results.
7. View your application status at any time on the "My Zapplications" page and choose to accept or decline show invitations on the site.

Get the application in on time

Another detail often overlooked when reading the application is the "must be received by' or "must be postmarked by" date. Don't wait till the deadline date to discover that the show wants the application in their office by that date, instead of merely postmarked with that date. At any rate, plan to get the application in the post office at least a week early if you can. That way you will have enough time (if you didn't read the application when it arrived) to get the required workshop slide, or price list, or photocopy of ID, etc

Tips for getting into the show

☐ **Apply to the show early.**
Some shows jury slides in the order they arrived at the office, or by postmark. Jurors might look at over 5,000 slides in a few days and they become bleary eyed after a while. You want them to be impressed with your slides while they are still alert.

☐ **Make your descriptions precise.**
If the show asks for a 25-word description for each image, don't write more or less. Your description will probably be read to the jury. If it is too long, it won't be read in full, and if it is short, you are missing an opportunity to tell the jurors what they can't see in your slides, such as process, texture, materials, use, etc. Zapplication allows only 100 characters.

☐ **You must grab the jurors attention with your slides.**
Use slides of your most colorful and interesting work, to get them noticed. Jurors are comparing your work to all the other work submitted. They usually have only 5 to 15 seconds to look at your slides. Sometimes there are several rounds of judging, with each round eliminating a group of artists. Jurors are looking for attention to detail, artistic mastery of materials, structure, concept, whimsy, originality, and how everything works together.

Planning your booth

One way to get up to speed about what kind of booth to use is to visit a craft show. Look around at the types of booths and the booth designs. What display looks simple, with the craft dominating, and what looks crowded. Which booths are attractive? Which artists seem busiest? The customer, when faced with a hundred booths and not enough time to examine all of them, will go to the most attractive and interesting looking booth.

Don't be afraid to ask other artists where they got display items or how they use them. Ask them how they hold down their canopies, where they got their display showcase, etc. Don't bother them

Indoor booths

If you are doing indoor shows only, a booth frame with drapes or other wall covering is required.

A workable combination indoor/outdoor booth is a white E-Z UP with the top off indoors (and the center top pole removed). This should have a Velcro-attaching top, as the bolt-on top is a real pain to remove, and you do not want a top in indoor shows. A lot of people will have much more elaborate displays, and scoff at this suggestion. However, I think the E-Z UP is good because:
1. It is very sturdy. It won't fall into your neighbor's ceramic or glass booth. (Note that I are talking indoors here.)
2. It has a lot of places from which to hang lights and drapes.
3. You can hang banners across the front to cover the lights and the frame. You can also make cloth socks to cover the legs.
4. It goes up in a flash, leaving you more time to work on the other parts of your display.
5. You don't have to keep track of a lot of corner pieces and rolling poles.
6. You don't have to rent pipe and drape, which adds $70 to $140 to your show fees.
7. You can use it for your outdoor shows as well.

Lighting

Indoor shows provide electricity. At some shows you have to pay extra, at others you don't. Some shows require a union electrician and $65.00 just to plug in and turn on your lights!

Most artists use track lighting with halogen bulbs. Office Depot has 24" light bars that have three bulb holders. You can get track in 4-foot lengths and light units for about $16 each. Attach the track with string ties to your booth poles. Make sure your booth lights don't shine in the customer's eyes.

Halogen lamps cost about $8 each. They give more light and show colors accurately. They also use less electricity then regular light bulbs. Halogen lamps are available in spot or flood configurations. Most booths have a 500-watt maximum. Ten 50-watt halogens will light a booth much better than six 75-watt incandescent bulbs. Gooseneck lamps look unprofessional. Use a three-prong extension cord, and grounded 5-plug power strips. Everything should be grounded. You should <u>never</u> use two-prong extension cords. If the electrician requires a grounded (three-prong) wire on your lights, and you have only a two-prong plug, you will have to add a ground wire. Have someone who is knowledgeable about electricity to help you with this before the show.

Outdoor booths

Economy--The best display for the least buck is again the E-Z UP canopy. It sets up in a hurry. You can usually find a quality canopy with durable walls and a carrying bag for under $600. If you do 25 shows a year for four years, your cost is $6 per show. If you get one with white-coated metal and a Velcro attached top, you can also use it indoors.

As for the top, make sure it is not a color canopy. A purple canopy will make all of your products look purple, a blue one will give them a blue tinge, etc. Don't use a canopy that does not have the legs straight up and down. The canopies with legs that point out look really out of place in a professional craft show.

If they are in season at Costco or Sam's Club, the Caravan (or EZ-Up Lite) is cheaper, around $200, and works for all but the windiest shows. They are lightweight and waterproof. They come with four sides, an awning, a bag with wheels, removable top, and a white coating on the metal parts.

E-Z UP frame used outdoors

Professional--The Light Dome, from Creative Energies, 800-351-8889, is very heavy duty. The cost is around $800.00 with 4 walls and carrying cases. The frame weighs about 35 lbs, and the walls about 8 lbs each. The top is 14 lbs, so the whole canopy weighs just over 75 lbs. You can use it anywhere, indoors or out, it goes up relatively fast, it is lightweight, and it looks good. It is also the most sturdy. I have been in shows with hurricane-force winds that had every tent flapping in every direction with the exception of one well-anchored light dome, which didn't even move.

Light Dome

You can use a Light Dome indoors. The large round cross-poles hold drapes and lights.

Other Canopies –Some artists get a Trimline Canopy for really bad weather. This is a different look than the E-Z UP, and takes about 20 minutes longer to set up. It is available from the Flourish Company at 800-296-0049.

Craft Huts are used by artists who sell in hurricane areas. They have steel legs and will not leak. Always use the top cross brace on a Craft Hut. If you don't, the arches can blow in toward the middle, and the top will fill with water during rainstorms and can collapse the entire tent. They are available from Flourish. Flourish also sells mesh panels for hanging art.

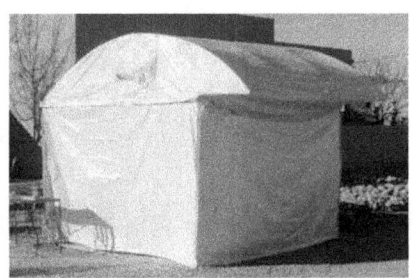

City streets

The best anchor for city streets is weights. Thirty five to fifty pounds per corner will usually be enough. Some craftspeople nail the legs of the canopy with concrete nails (or use screws with washers and an electric screwdriver) directly into the asphalt. Many shows expressly prohibit this (today's nail hole is tomorrow's pothole). The promoters may not mention it to you, but you might not get back into the show. I recommend weighting two or more corners with 50 pounds each, then have an extra 50 lb. weight in the middle of the booth, with a rope tied to the top (for E-Z UPs). Concrete blocks weigh 34 lbs. Any wind that can move this much weight can move almost any amount of weight, so if a storm is expected, and you don't have tall panels, lower the canopy to half-height overnight (another handy feature of the E-Z UPs and Light Domes).

Grassy parks

Tents in a grassy park are the easiest to tie down. Use dog stakes. A dog stake is a corkscrew-like device available at pet supply stores that is screwed into the ground. Put two stakes on the two corners that face the wind, and another in the middle of the tent. The middle one is screwed in before the show, but it is only used when the wind comes up. A rope is quickly tied to it and looped over the top of the canopy frame. This beats standing there holding your canopy as the wind blows it around. You can also use weights, if you brought them.

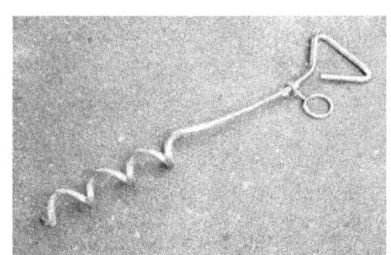

In a large tent

Some outdoor shows have huge big-top circus-type tents that everyone sets up their booths under. The Asparagus Festival in Stockton, California, Pink Palace in Memphis, Sunfest in Ocean City, the Columbus Arts Festival in Ohio, and the Jazz Festival in New Orleans have big tents. Some tents have room for your E-Z UP inside of the tent. Be sure to remove your top for more light, and remove your peak pole so you don't put a dent in their tent. Occasionally a tent show will not allow E-Z UPs or a full size 10 x 10 booth. You will still need something to hold your walls up and to keep them from flapping into your neighbor's booth. You might have to make or buy a conduit frame to make a booth nine and one-half feet on each side by seven feet high. Flourish sells these. You will need a wall for the front at night, unless they drop the tent walls.

Weather

You are going to have rain and wind at outdoor shows. The best protection from rain is a canopy with walls. Everything should be stored in Rubbermaids. If the corners of the top of your E-Z UP start to collect water, a large clamp on the top of the inside frame will usually prevent puddles. Wind will either blow your canopy away or blow things out from under it. The best tie-down is to something already there, a rail, a tree, park bench. If you are next to a really heavy booth, ask them if you can tie your canopy legs to theirs.

The worst scenario is when you have both wind and rain. This is one reason why a lot of craftspeople only do indoor shows. But they are missing a lot of opportunities to make money. All a windy <u>and</u> rainy show means is that you need a little more weather protection. The sun will eventually come out and you will make some money.

On hot days, bring an ice chest, ice, and lots of water. You can add an awning on the side of your canopy that gets the most direct sun, to shade your products and yourself. Portable AC or DC fans will help keep you and your customers cool.

More tips for outdoor shows, weights and weather

- **Always have a weight handy when you set up.**
You should tie your booth to a weight or immoveable object while you are setting up, in case of a sudden gust of wind.

- **Use 8-gallon plastic water cans for weights.**
8 gallons of water weighs about 65 lbs. Get the water cans with handles (sporting goods, camping stores, or RV stores). Fill them at a gas station or food booth when you get to the show and dump them at the end of the show. Carrying empty cans will save you gas, since less weight in your vehicle increases your gas mileage.

- **Make your own weights with PVC tube.**
Fill a 6" diameter PVC pipe, 36" long, with concrete, using an end cap and a 12" eyebolt with a washer on the other end. Some artists like as much as 100 lbs. on each corner of their display. Don't use 3" or 4" pipe—you'll be wasting your time with light weights. You can also fill a 5-gallon bucket with concrete and use an eyebolt in the same way.

- **Attach weights to the inside top of tent as well as legs.**
Attach the rope to the cross bar on E-Z UPs. When weights are used only on the legs, the tent can still twist in the wind.

- **Use metal stakes in hard ground.**
E-Z UP canopies come with 12" nail-like stakes. They are designed to be hammered into dirt, through the hole in each leg plate. Have a claw hammer available to get them out.

Craft Fairs and Art Shows

☐ **Use your spare tire for an emergency weight.**

It won't help much but might keep your canopy from flying until you get to Home Depot and get some heavier weight. Use a rope to attach it to the center or top corner of your booth.

☐ **Keep your electrical outlet dry.**

If you have an outdoor booth with electricity, make sure your outlet is in your booth at night. Raise it up off the ground. Don't wrap a plastic bag around the outlet; it might fill up with water. When unplugging lights, stand on something dry, like cardboard or a ladder.

☐ **Keep an ear on the weather.**

A weather radio can be purchased at Radio Shack for less than $50. You should ask a local at the show which county the show is in, as weather reports are given by county.

☐ **Make an awning for your booth with conduit.**

Use three eight foot pieces of 1" conduit. Clamp two on each side inside of your E-Z UP, extending out the front about 3 feet. Clamp one piece in the middle. You can fold up a wall or use a section of patio mesh from Home Depot, and hang it across the pipes. Put clamps on the ends. Use it in rainy weather or when you are facing the sun. Make sure it is 6' 6" tall or more, so no one bumps their head on it.

☐ **If it is really windy take your canopy down.**

This is what might happen if you don't.

Fountain Hills, Arizona

Craft Fairs and Art Shows

☐ **Get 12-volt accessories at truck stops.**
Truck drivers run everything on 12 volts. You can get 12-volt fans to keep your booth cool. They also have 12-volt coffee makers, coolers, TV's, vibrating seat back pads, hot plates, etc.

Banners, booth signs, and photos

A banner is a great help to people trying to find your booth who had promised to return (those customers are called be-backs.) It also helps them decide whether to come over to the booth in the first place, when there are so many booths to choose from. The banner should say something about the contents of the booth, not simply the name of the artist. Unless the artist is relatively famous, the banner should say "Handmade Jewelry" or "Jewelry by Dana Andrews," not just "Dana Andrews."

You might need two banners. One cloth, about one foot high by five feet long that hangs across the top of your canopy on a rope. It helps people find you if they came to the show looking for you. You can take it down at night, when you don't want anyone to know what is in your booth. The other is vinyl, 2 1/2 feet high and 9 feet long, with your product and signature on it. Use it for big outdoor fairs when a potential customer may be 50 feet or more away from the front of the booth. Have it made at Kinko's, with grommets on the corners. Attach it to 6' conduit poles, or plastic curtain rods, with bungees, and attach the poles to your canopy legs with clamps.

An artists statement is an 8 1/2" by 11" sheet of paper (see page 119) displayed in a clear acrylic stand on your table or hanging in your booth on the wall. It should have a photo of you working in your shop and your name and address at the top. The rest of the page should tell the customer a little about you, how your craft is made, what materials you use, and something about your motivation and purpose. Many fairs are requiring it in your booth. Some customers love to read it completely while waiting. Others might even want a copy, if you feel like handing them out. Send a copy of this statement with your show applications, unless the show specifically states that you should only send slides and nothing else. A few shows are requiring an artist's statement with your application.

Every booth should have a sign about 12" by 24" with the name of the artist and where the artist is from, hanging in the back of the booth. Some shows provide them, but I like to bring my own in case they don't. A sign that indicates the town and state you are from is a good conversation starter. Having your name in large print is helpful to the customer when writing a check.

Always have an 8x10 or bigger photo of your workshop somewhere in the booth. When asked, "Do you make these yourself?" point to the photo and say, "Yes. Here is a picture of my shop and the tools I use." This is also a great conversation starter. People are very curious as to how and where you make your product.

Many artists with small items have large photos of their jewelry hanging up in their booth. These are helpful for people who can't get quite close enough to see because of the crowd. You can get a slide or print blown up to a 20" x 24" poster at FedEx (Kinko's) for under $40. Kodak, through photo stores, offers 20" x 30" posters from your slides for $22.95.

More display tips

☐ **Use drop down bamboo rollups for walls.**

8-foot rollups attached to your EZ-up frame with shower curtain hooks will make your booth seem cozier. They allow air circulation on a hot day, while providing some privacy from the booth next to you. You never know who your neighbor is going to be. The only drawback is that 8 feet is too long for most cars without a luggage rack. 2 four-foot rollups can be used instead.

☐ **Have your product photos laminated on both sides.**

They will hang easier in your booth and won't be damaged by water. For indoor shows, mount them on foam core from an art supply store. Use grommets and strong thin wire to hang up your photos to keep them from ripping or falling down.

☐ **Use dark curtains indoors.**

The background should not be noticeable. If not black, burgundy and neutral colors are best.

☐ **Use white walls with light curtains outdoors.**

White will reflect light into your booth and brighten up your crafts in the shade of your canopy.

Craft Fairs and Art Shows

☐ **Hang a curtain over a back corner of your booth.**

You can use the space for a changing room or storage.

☐ **Fireproof your tablecloths.**

Fire retardant paints and sprays are available from Flamort. They will provide a certificate for the fire marshal. **www.flamort.com** (510) 357-9494

☐ **Use a portfolio or scrapbook.**

Take prints of your past creations and put them in a scrapbook along with pictures of your studio. Customers can browse this while waiting.

☐ **Display items at various heights.**

This increases the visual appeal of your booth. Small items in your booth should be closer to eye level. Makes your crafts easy to reach. Pedestals are available from Armstrong Products in Oklahoma-800-278-4279 www.armstrongproducts.com.

☐ **Make your table taller.**

Use PVC tubing to make leg extensions, so your customers don't have to bend over to see your products.

☐ **Have signs in your booth that communicate.**

Your artist's statement, credit card acceptance, discount policy, name of business, etc., are all signs that "talk" to your customers for you. They also give customers something to read while you are talking to other customers.

☐ **Uncluttered look:**

After you set up, step back and see if your booth looks cluttered. If so, simplify it. One way to spot clutter is to look at your booth through a camera lens. Hide boxes and carts. Some promoters require this, and it benefits you as well.

☐ **Use a tall chair.**

Every time you get up from a low chair you put stress on your back. You should be able to just slide forward off of it. The seat should be at least 30" high, so you are eye-level with the customer. I like Gold Medal canvas director chairs and the aluminum chair that www.dickblick.com sells.

Packaging

You should always provide gift boxes. If your product is useful as a gift, and a gift box is available, display a few boxes and offer them to every customer, especially around Christmas, Father's Day, Mother's Day, etc. If the customer is looking for a gift and sees the product already in a nice gift box, you have just provided a solution. The gift box may stimulate the customer to think of your product as a gift and then think about who to give it to.

Every product you sell should be put in an attractive bag. The customer appreciates it. You might need two sizes of bags, a small one that holds one or two products, and a big one that holds more. Offer to hold the customer's purchase while they check out the rest of the show.

Provide a hang tag with information about how the product was made, what it is made of, how to care for it, who made it, and how to get in touch with them. This tag should fit neatly in the gift box.

Taking VISA and MasterCard

You should try to get set up to take charge cards as soon as possible. At some shows your sales will be 80 or 90 percent from VISA or MasterCard sales. There are two ways to take credit cards:
1. Run the card through a portable imprinter at the show, and then key or call in the sales when you get home.
2. Run the card through a portable wireless terminal at the show, which clears the card through a cellular connection.

You will need a business account with a bank, and permission from them to take cards in your business. The bank is going to give you the money from the cards before it is actually collected by them, so you must have good credit. If your bank won't let you take credit cards, there are several choices:

1. <u>Get another bank</u>. If you have $2,000 cash to open a business account with, make it clear to the new bank that your opening the account is contingent on your being able to process credit cards. They will take you seriously if they want your business. You tell them that you will be taking the cards at trade shows or at shows in your home. They might visit your home to see if you really have a business. They may also want to see a business license or resale permit.

2. <u>Go directly to a credit card company</u>. Novus Services, a company associated with Discover Card, will set you up directly with them, and they send the money from the card charges directly to your bank. Their phone number is 1-800-347-2000. They will let you take MasterCard and VISA in addition to Discover. They give you a portable imprinter and sell you a Trans 330 terminal for about $300. You imprint a charge slip from the card at the show in the imprinter and give the customer a copy. Later at your motel or home, you key in the numbers from the card on the Trans 330, which is hooked up to a phone, and they give you an authorization number clearing the card. They charge you about 2.4 % of the sale amount. They are anxious to get more business, and more

likely to sign you up than a bank. American Express is a separate company, and their charges are processed separately. They too are actively looking for new businesses. They have a separate imprinter for their shorter charge slips.

Portable credit card terminals

Credit card processing fees are cheaper (1.8%) when cards are run through a portable credit card terminal and cleared immediately, than when run through an imprinter and called in by phone (2.8%). The reduction in fees and reduction in losses from bad cards will pay for the terminal in a year or two. The time you save by not calling in the cards after the show, and the peace of mind from having the card cleared at the show, make the cost of the terminal worthwhile.

One company I recommend with excellent service is Total Merchant Services. Their number is 888-682-4464. They, as most merchant service companies, sell the Lipman Nurit 8000 GPRS. It is completely portable, and uses either rechargeable batteries or can be hooked up to AC Power. Buy an extra battery. The 8000 can be connected to a phone line in your office, or connected by wireless when you are at a show. The cost is around $700. Some merchant providers will loan you the terminal and charge higher fees. Make sure you know how to use "store and forward" if you find you are at a show with no signal. You simply upload the charges when you have signal again. Select option 3 (Merchant Options). Then you have to scroll down to option 10 to see Store and Forward.

The customer's charge card is processed immediately by sliding the card through the terminal, and a charge slip is handed to them to sign. A copy of the slip is printed for a receipt for the customer. The terminal clears the card in about seven seconds. At the end of the day, the credit card company processes the batch of charges and in a few days deposits the money from VISA and MasterCard into your bank account. At the end of the month you receive a statement from the company detailing your sales by card type. Most companies charge an additional capture fee for American Express and Discover cards for clearing their cards. They may take a little longer to appear in your account. You have to set up the accounts with American Express and Discover separately, and then your terminal will take all of the cards.

Tips for taking credit cards

- **Put up "Credit Cards Accepted" signs.**

Some people are looking for this notice. They might have run out of cash at another booth, or simply didn't bring any. By the way, it is illegal to charge a customer extra for using a credit card. However it is not illegal to give a discount for cash.

- ☐ **Keep all credit card sales receipts.**

Put them in a separate envelope and write the name and dates of the show on it. If the charge is disputed, the signed original will be easier to locate.

- ☐ **Check the customer's credit card for their signature.**

If it isn't signed, have them sign it before you take it. If you are suspicious, ask to see their driver's license, and compare the signatures. Some customers prefer not to sign their credit cards. You can't force them to do so, but remind them that a thief could sign their name for them, and then the "false signatures" would match.

- ☐ **Bring a manual credit card machine and charge slips.**

If your electric credit card machine fails, runs out of paper, etc, you will still be able to take credit cards. When you use a manual credit card machine, try to get a phone number and address. It is illegal to require a credit card user's phone number, but you can ask them to put it in your address book for your mailing list. Then you will be able to call them if the slip is unreadable or lost (or if they left something in your booth). If you run out of charge slips when on the road, go to a local bank for more charge slips.

- ☐ **Always check the charge slip for clarity.**

Check to see if the number and expiration date is clear. Some cards have worn numbers, or the numbers have been tampered with (flattened). Sometimes the machine might not imprint the whole number (which you must check when you fill out the slip). When you get home to call the charges in, if you don't have the complete number you won't get paid.

- ☐ **Carry a portable battery pack.**

An automotive jump starter (from Kragen, Pep Boys, Wal-Mart) and a Radio shack 12 volt DC to 110 AC converter, along with your AC charger, will come in handy if your credit card terminal battery goes dead. The EverStart shown here is from Target and works as well with the AC converter.

Selling tips

- ☐ **Explain the benefits to the customer.**

People buy for personal benefit. Theirs. Not to do you a favor. Not because you are good looking or well dressed. They benefit from your product, or they pass it by. They might visualize how comfortable it will feel on their body the next day. Or they will visualize being perceived as individualistic because they have or give a one-of-a-kind object, or as an art lover who has actually met the artist who made the item, or as a meticulous person who buys well-crafted items. This is where the large photo of your jewelry being worn is helpful; it shows the customer how he or she will benefit. Then it is simply a matter of the price of the item matching the benefits of the item to the customer.

☐ Don't read a book in your booth.

It is too absorbing. A magazine might be okay, as the articles are shorter and don't require as much attention. A magazine about your craft, Metalsmith or Art Jewelry for example, is beneficial to both you and the customer. You learn some new techniques while waiting for a sale. The customer may believe you are up-to-date on your craft. If a magazine is prominently placed in your display, the customer might even infer that you are featured in the magazine. No harm there. Someday you will be. If you already are featured in a magazine, by all means, display it in your booth. Cut out the article, laminate it, and hang it on your wall.

☐ Avoid sales pressure

Give them a chance to look. Some customers might be reluctant to walk into a booth where the artist is staring at them and appears too eager to jump up and start trying to sell them something. Put them at ease. Always say a few words to the customer, such as "How are you doing today?," or "Feel free to look closely," or "You can try it on." After you get the product in their hands, give them time to examine the work, give them the details they ask for, and maybe a suggestion that the item would make a good gift, and that you have gift boxes. Then leave them alone again. People really appreciate feeling un-pressured in a shopping environment. Just imagine how you want to be treated when you shop. You want to be helped when you need it, but you don't want a salesperson hovering around you all the time. Do the same for your customers.

☐ How badly you need to make the sale is irrelevant

Whenever a customer asks how the show has been for you, tell them you are doing well, even if it is the worst show you have ever done. Even the bad shows have some benefits, such as learning frugality or humility, so you won't necessarily be lying. Never complain to the customers. There is nothing they can do about it.

☐ Always suggest the lower priced item

When a customer asks you which one you recommend, never suggest the higher priced item. They will always be suspicious and you will be scrambling to explain why it is better. Recommend a mid-range item, and they will immediately trust you. Of course, all of your products are of excellent quality and priced at exactly the right price. You did use the "pricing" spreadsheet on page 80, didn't you?

☐ Give them a reason to buy today.

Offer them a small discount (under 5%) if they buy it today. Say, "It is always good to have some gifts around in case you need them for an unexpected occasion."

- ☐ **Assume everyone has a credit card.**

They have the money to buy your jewelry, unless all of their cards are maxed out. Be sure that you tell them you take charge cards and they can see your VISA card signs or terminal.

- ☐ **Listen to your customers.**

They notice if you are not listening. If you are already dealing with a customer, and a second customer interrupts, ask the first customer if you can talk to the second one. Deal with the question politely, and then get back with your first customer.

- ☐ **Educate your customer.**

Art sales involve 50% education and 50% sales technique. Most people visiting your booth have no idea how you do what you do. Tell them why your work is worth the price and how hard it was to make. Be prepared to talk your head off. Don't let a few know-it-alls discourage you.

- ☐ **Mention environmental aspects of your craft.**

If you have an environmental angle to your product, describe it. Conservation of resources is very important to some people. Tell them how you use materials economically.

- ☐ **Tell people a story about your product.**

They want to know what inspired you to make it and how hard it is to make. Have photos of your shop to show them. Tell them about your lifestyle.

- ☐ **Maintain eye contact.**

If you are looking all around the show, they will too.

- ☐ **Never judge a customer by their appearance.**

Every artist has a story about the customer who dressed and acted like a hobo, but bought a very expensive item.

- ☐ **Remind people if it is the last day of the show.**

There are customers at every show who think the show goes on forever.

- ☐ **Use key words to make sales.**

Some comfortable key words are "warm, soft, clean, powerful, bigger, better, and yes." Yes, I have a gift box. Yes, I take charge cards. Yes, I have a trash bag. Yes, yes, yes.

- ☐ **Offer a guarantee to hesitant customers.**

Offer a full refund or replacement if customer is dissatisfied. You can warrant your materials and workmanship for a lifetime.

On the road

Many artists prefer to travel to shows in a van. A van is not much longer than a car when it comes to parking and getting in and out of the show set-up area. But if you ever need to nap or camp overnight, you may have that option with a van, and not with a car. Also, when you are driving a van, you have better visibility, and everyone on the road can see you better. And, of course, you can haul a lot more stuff. The drawback is are that you use more gasoline. I suggest that you not design a booth to fit in your car, but get a vehicle that fits a booth designed for maximum sales of your products.

I don't recommend sleeping in rest stops on the freeway at night. There is no security at a rest stop. If you are traveling and all rooms are booked up, park or nap in a truck stop. Almost every truck stop in the United States welcomes RV's (and vans). The bigger ones have 24-hour restaurants and free showers with a fill-up. More and more truckers are husband and wife teams, and truck stops cater to them. The restaurants at some of them (Pilot) have all-you-can-eat buffets for $9.00, and phones at every booth. Most have a security guard. The bathrooms are cleaner and safer then the ones at rest stops. The main drawback is truck noise. You either have to park as far from trucks as you can, or get earplugs.. You can hook your computer up at a booth and check your email. Just act like you own a big rig. ;-)

Travel tips

☐ **Never drive when sleepy.**
McDonald's coffee will keep you awake!

☐ **Keep a travel kit in your car.**
A travel kit contains a toothbrush, toothpaste, deodorant, floss, nail clippers, hairbrush, shampoo, conditioner, and vitamins. If you keep it in your car or van, you won't find that you have forgotten one of the above when you get to your show.

☐ Keep a small fire extinguisher handy.

Always carry a fire extinguisher in your car or van. Some shows ask you to keep it in your booth during the show. You never know when it might save your stock or someone's life. I know one artist who had an engine fire in a gas station, and the fire extinguisher saved both his van and the gas station!

☐ Use mapquest.com to get a map to the show.

Usually the show promoter will give directions to the show, but mapquest can also give you directions from the show to your hotel. www.mapquest.com

☐ Use an AAA or AARP card to save money on rooms.

Either of these cards will save you at least 10%. AARP cards are available to people age 50 and over.

☐ Always carry jumper cables.

You might accidentally leave your lights on, drain your battery, and need a jump-start. Get 12 gauge wire (not 14 or 16), and the longest ones they have.

☐ Check your tire pressure.

Carry a tire gauge. Fully-inflated tires can increase your gas mileage 15%. While the tire is cool, inflate to about 5 lbs less than the maximum pressure stated on the side of the tire.

☐ Check your spare tire for air.

You could be driving around with a flat spare tire, which will be no help at all if you have a flat.

☐ Learn to change your own tire; anyone can do it.

Sure, AAA can change it, in an hour or so. But you might miss the show. Carry gloves and coveralls to wear to change the tire. And keep a working flashlight in your vehicle. It is usually worthwhile to carry a small floor jack if you have room. They are much faster and easier to use than the pneumatic or scissor type of car jack. Check for a tire iron. Get the big x shaped tire iron. A woman can leverage one of these to loosen wheel nuts if necessary.

☐ Learn how to check your car fluids.

No one else is going to check them for you all the time. Learn how and where your oil, transmission, power steering, and wiper fluids are filled.

☐ Clear your gas line with STP water remover.

Available at Kragen or Pep Boys. Make sure the bottle says something about water removal from gas lines. Water buildup comes from condensation or fog, and will make your engine run rough.

☐ **Carry a spare alternator belt.**

The service station might not have the right one if yours breaks. Have someone show you where the belt is under your hood, so you can know if it is broken. Usually the alternator light will come on. A salesman at NAPA Auto Parts will tell you which one fits your vehicle. They are fairly easy to replace, with just a wrench and a screwdriver.

☐ **Carry extra keys.**

Keep them in a magnetic case under the car. Kragen Auto Supply sells the case.

☐ **Get the iphone app "craft fair"**

It has a list of everything you need to bring to a show. You can add or delete items, and place a check next to the ones you have or need.

☐ **Carry a first aid kit.**

Keep a well-stocked kit, in case you have to fix a blister, cut, or scraped knuckle. It should have band aids, Rolaids, Neosporin, ace bandage, ibuprophen, and aspirin

Security on the road

☐ **Have a tow service--Allstate, AAA, or Good Sam.**

The Good Sam Club Emergency Road Service is about $100 a year. This includes towing, gas, flat fixing, and lost keys. Good Sam Emergency Road Service for RV's phone number is (800) 234-3450. The number for AAA is (800) 922-8228, Sears Allstate Motor Club (866) 209-0394.

☐ **Get an alarm for your vehicle**

It should have an engine kill switch, remote, window stickers and a flashing red light visible to thieves when it is armed. Alarms cost less than $250 installed. I am always surprised that more artists don't have one.

☐ **If you have a trailer, get a lock for it.**

Also, paint a big number on the top and one on the street side. The one on top should be clear and big enough to be seen from a helicopter. Chances are your trailer will be found only a few miles from where it was stolen.

☐ **Don't tell the motel clerk you have valuables.**

Don't even ask if they have a lock box, unless it is an extremely reputable motel or hotel chain.

☐ **Leave a light and TV on in your motel room.**

A thief might think it is occupied when you are gone.

- ☐ <u>Don't ever leave your keys in your car ignition.</u>

Don't leave them in the ignition while you are loading in or packing up, or when your car is in your driveway, or at the gas station. Also, don't leave your cell phone on the dash. Thieves will sometimes smash a car window just for a cell phone.

- ☐ <u>Use a steering wheel locking device.</u>

If you don't have a burglar alarm, at least get a steering wheel lock. The Club (Le Club) costs about $30, and might save your stock.

- ☐ <u>Always park in a well-lit area.</u>

Park in front of your door at the motel, or in front of or very near the lobby. If you have a view of your vehicle, you can see by your flashing lights if the alarm is your car.

Flying to Craft Fairs

Flying to a craft fair has many advantages. You can do a show anywhere in the country and any time of year. Otherwise, if you drive to shows in another part of the country, you have to line up several in a row to make the trip worthwhile. Once you figure out how to fly to a show, you just pick the best ones around the country, fly there, and fly back. Plus, you get more time in the shop.

Jewelry is easier to fly with than most other crafts. The lighter and smaller your display, the easier it is. But don't let a heavier display stop you from the big shows. The trick for big displays is to ship your display by air cargo, rent a van when you get to the show, pick up the display with the van, and there you are, van, jewelry, and display, on the other side of the country, on the same day. The last time I checked, you could ship by Delta air cargo for $1.00 per pound. You can get help loading and unloading from Labor Ready, 4 hours for $60 (800-245-2267).

Yes, you can fly with your canopy. It must have a cover on it. Bring your jewelry with you in your carry-on luggage, and check the canopy with the rest of your luggage at the baggage counter. At the counter you may have to pay $30 for each additional bag and sometimes $100 for the third bag. The limit per bag without paying for excess weight is 50 pounds.

Some jewelers who fly bring a portable table and display (made from tubing from Abstracta or from postergarden.com) in a large suitcase, a Contico fiberglass trunk with 4 wheels attached on the bottom with selling supplies in it, and another suitcase with gift boxes and some clothes. The next trick is getting it all into a cab, your car rental, or the airport shuttle.

Flying tips

☐ <u>Book roundtrip flights with www.travelocity.com.</u>

At this time, they seem to be able to locate the best prices for round-trip airline tickets. Priceline is not good for flights because you can't choose your exact time of travel.

☐ <u>Use a travel agent if you need to book separate flights.</u>

Use a travel agent if you are flying to one city and returning from another. Sometimes they can tell you if you will need a car or not to get from your hotel to the show, and they might find you a room at a pretty good price. A good agent that we sometimes use can be reached at (800) 835-5090.

☐ <u>Book rooms with www.priceline.com.</u>

Offer a ridiculously low price; you just might get it. Start with four stars and $49.00. You might get bumped up to a four star hotel. Only ask for one area with your first offer. You can't change your price without changing something, so if you don't get your price you can add another area or reduce your stars and then slightly raise or lower your bid. Two star motels like Extended Stay America often have kitchenettes, and sometimes go for a bid of $35.00. You won't get them with a three star bid. Start early, because if your bids don't work, you have to wait 24 hours to bid again.

☐ <u>Print out your online airline and hotel reservations.</u>

Take them with you. Sometimes the hotel or motel computer doesn't get the information in time.

☐ <u>Use UPS to ship packages to your hotel.</u>

70 lbs. from SF to NY costs $70, less if you have daily pickup.

☐ <u>Use your frequent flyer miles to fly to shows.</u>

To find out more ways to get frequent flyer miles, go to www.mileageworkshop.com.

☐ <u>Keep your valuables in your carry-on bag.</u>

Never leave anything valuable in your checked luggage. Some planes on short hops make you put your carry-on in the baggage compartment. Put your most valuable jewelry in your handbag or day pack and keep it with you on the plane.

☐ <u>Make a lightweight table with Abstracta ½" tubes.</u>

You can use their tubes to assemble portable lightweight tables and cases with glass or plastic tops, that fit in a suitcase. Abstracta Structures (800) 223-7315   www.abstracta.com.

Craft Fairs and Art Shows

☐ **Use a collapsible water carrier for weight.**

You can get a 5 gal. collapsible water carrier by Reliance (Winnipeg, Canada, R3H-1A4, or Marin Outdoors). Five gallons of water weighs 42 lbs., but the container weights only two lbs empty. Fill at a faucet or with a hose (food booths), and borrow a hand truck to carry it to your booth.

☐ **Use concrete blocks for weights.**

If you rent a car, get concrete blocks (and rope) at the local Home Depot for $3 each, use them for weights, and after the show, give them to another artist, take them back to Home Depot, or leave them in a dumpster or construction site. Wear leather gloves when carrying them.

Concrete block covered with white tape

How to increase profits

☐ **Increase the price (improve the product).**

If your product has the right price, determined by your cost of materials, hourly wage, shop overhead costs, and retail selling costs, you can't raise your price too much without improving the product. Everything has a "right price" regardless of who you are selling it to. Use the pricing spreadsheet in this book on page 80. Many crafts at fairs are priced too low. If your price is the right price, and seems too much for the customers who visit your booth, then you have to find a show with more affluent customers.

☐ **Reduce material costs.**

Find a way to get your materials for less money. The Internet is great for this. Create less waste. Both buying too many materials, and throwing away scrap that could be sold, add up to increased costs.

☐ **Increase production.**
Work faster or make more pieces at a time.

☐ **Make more sales.**
Do more shows, better shows, or make additional sales to other outlets, such as stores and online.

☐ **Reduce overhead.**
Turn off the lights when you go out. One good helper is better than two not-good helpers. Keep the entire business production in your garage.

More Craft Fair Tips

Before the show

☐ **Make a checklist of show necessities.**
Check your list just before you leave home.
A sample list:
Gift boxes
Hang tags
Bags
VISA machine, thermal paper, and charger
VISA signage
Calculator
Sample of work in progress
Banner
Stakes
Booth sign
Statement of purpose (artist's statement)
Price stickers
Duct tape
Rope
Pocket knife
Clamps
Other handy stuff:
Phone charger
Camera, card, and batteries
Umbrella/raincoat

Mosquito repellant
String ties
Super glue
Rug or mat
Hand cleanser
Windex
Garbage bags (for end of the show clean-up)
Paper towels
Gloves (for tire changing, etc.)

☐ <u>**Call ahead if you are going to be late.**</u>

Otherwise, the promoter might give your space away.

Setting up for the show

☐ <u>**Use a hand truck with large tires for easy loading.**</u>

Big wheels roll over cracks better. Magline carts are the best hand trucks. They have big wheels, 2 or 4 wheel positions and hold up to 800 lbs. Priority Supply Company, 2127 Lake Lansing, Michigan 48912 (517) 374-8573.

☐ <u>**Never put tape on the legs of your E-Z UP.**</u>

The sticky residue left will prevent you from closing it down after the show.

☐ <u>**Raise your canopy to its full height.**</u>

Your booth will be more inviting and easier for tall people to get into. It lets in more light. If you roll up your walls, put them on before raising the canopy. Use a lower height when it is windy or raining. It will keep some of the rain out and offer less wind resistance.

☐ <u>**Use a combination stool/tool box for tools.**</u>

If you dedicate a set of tools for shows, and keep them in a combination stool/toolbox, you will always have the tool you need and the stool also helps you put up walls, curtains, and lights.

During the show

☐ Be in your booth early.
If you spend 60 minutes in your booth before the show is officially open, ready to help customers, and stay open a little longer in the evening, it adds up to four extra hours in a three day show. Or, one extra show for every six shows, at no extra cost to you. This applies to unfenced outdoor shows.

☐ Show your customers what you start with.
A raw material in the hand is worth a thousand words—show a glob of melted silver, uncut stone, carving wax, etc.

☐ Get a 50% deposit for custom work.
Full payment in advance is even better.

☐ Never charge extra for gift boxes, etc.
The customer will think you are cheap and resent the charge. Customers like the word "free."

☐ Never criticize other craftspeople.
Nothing looks more unprofessional to customers (or other craftspeople).

☐ Give a small price break for multiple purchases.
Customers think they can get a better price if they are buying directly from the artist. But you have to be firm. You might be dealing with a "flea market" personality, someone who never ever pays full price. Ten percent is a reasonable amount for three or more items. Don't offer it unless you think it might encourage them to buy. If your first reasonable discount offer is rejected, don't make another. Explain again why your product is better.

☐ Never sell seconds.
They will come back to haunt you, especially if your customer gives them to someone else, who doesn't know they are seconds, and brings them back to you to fix. It is better to have the "Everything I sell is perfect." mentality. People don't want flawed items for gifts.

☐ Don't use "Sale" signs at a fair.
The public expects that the price asked reflects the artist's time and materials. If items are on sale, you have to explain why. Some promoters forbid sale signs.

☐ Start a mailing list.
At shows, collect names, addresses, and/or email with a guest book, which could be a nice address book or notebook with large spaces for the customer to write big. Copy into a database all addresses from both the guest book and the checks you receive. Someday you will have a huge

mailing list. At least once a year, send a postcard or email to everyone on your list, with information about your shows, web site, or new products.

☐ **You can make your own guest book.**
Print headings for name, address, phone, email, and anything else you want to know, horizontally on a sheet of paper, and have Kinko's copy it and make a book for you, or put the copies in a 3-ring binder.

☐ **Keep your display out of the aisles.**
Don't put anything in front of your booth, and don't sit in the aisle, as it restricts the flow of traffic to the booth next to you.

☐ **Ask people what they think of your new items.**
Do they like the color, the price, shape, etc.? Pay close attention to their comments. This type of feedback is one of the great advantages of doing a retail craft fair or art show.

☐ **Floor coverings make everyone more comfortable.**
A 4'x 6' or bigger oriental rug in darker colors will make your booth look more elegant and make your feet less tired at the end of the day. Tape the front edge.

☐ **Always fill out the show survey.**
It is the best way to get the promoters to improve the show. Don't just write your complaints. Give helpful suggestions on how to improve the show. If they don't know what is wrong, how can they fix it?

☐ **Don't rush to pack up after a show ends.**
After 45 minutes, 75 percent of the other artists will be gone and out of your way. In addition, you might make a few more sales from latecomers. If you rush to get home after a show when you are tired, you are more likely to have an accident.

Avoiding theft

☐ **Keep valuables out of reach.**
Thieves look for a purse that is unattached and will reach under your table or in from the back of your booth to steal it. Put your purse or camera out of sight in a Rubbermaid or a large trunk. Attach your purse strap to a table leg, canopy leg, etc..

☐ **Don't use a cash box.**
Keep your money (at least all paper money) on your body, in a pocket, in a fanny pack, etc. Keep coins, but not bills, in a simple box for sales tax change. It will make noise if it is stolen.

☐ Separate large bills from small bills.

Keep large bills in a separate safe place that is harder to access, a different pocket, etc. This keeps you from accidentally giving someone big bills with their change, or spilling the money on the ground.

☐ You are more vulnerable to theft when packing up.

You are separated from your products when going to your vehicle, and again when the products are in the vehicle and you are back at the booth. Ask your neighbor to keep an eye on your booth. Lock your car doors anytime valuables are inside.

☐ Use a locked storage box or trunk.

A Contico fiberglass foot-locker can be locked in your booth with a padlock and bike chain attached to your table or something heavy. Put things like your credit card machine and calculator in it for overnight storage. If a drunk or prankster gets in your booth at night, they probably won't try to get into it.

Health

☐ At the first sign of a cold, take lots of vitamin C.

3,000 mgs a day should keep the cold at bay. Also take a multiple vitamin every day.

☐ Mercury vapor lighting can cause migraines.

These lights can also cause a green tinge in your booth. Use your own halogen lights to improve your lighting. Bring aspirins or Tylenol. Aspirin is also useful in reducing strokes.

☐ Drink lots of water during a show.

Dehydration will cause headaches and soreness. Water also helps to combat the low humidity of indoor shows.

List of Promoters of Multiple Fairs and Shows

Send all of the promoters in your area of the country a letter asking for information or an application. Many of them screen (jury) you only once, then if they like your products, you can do as many of their shows as you want without being re-screened for each show. Phone numbers and addresses change. If the number is wrong, google the promoter.

PROMOTER	ADDRESS	CITY	ST	ZIP	PHONE	# OF SHOWS
DeSoto Caverns Park	5181 DeSoto Caverns Pkwy.	Childersburg	AL	35044	800-933-2283	2 outdoor
Elise Blackwell	116 Al-Jo Curve	Selma	AL	36701	334-874-8044	1 indoor, 2 outdoor
Hillbilly Corner Arts, Crafts	22530 Deer Run Rd.	Hindsville	AR	72738	501-789-5726	2 indoor, 2 outdoor
Fourth Avenue Merchants Assoc.	329 East 7th Street	Tucson	AZ	85705	520-624-5004	2 outdoor
Magic Bird Promotions	P. O. Box 1803	Cave Creek	AZ	85327	480-488-2014	1 indoor, 8 outdoor
Mill Ave. Merch. Association	P. O. Box 53046	Phoenix	AZ	85072	480-967-4877	4 outdoor
Mountain Artists Guild	P. O. Box 12920	Prescott	AZ	86304	520-445-2510	2 outdoor
The Events Group	P. O. Box 328	Tempe	AZ	85280	602-968-5353	5 outdoor
Thunderbird Artists	15648 N. Eagles Nest Dr.	Fountain Hills	AZ	85268	480-837-5637	7 outdoor
Beckmans Gift Show	P. O. Box 2337	Los Angeles	CA	90027	323-962-5424	4 indoor
California Artists	P. O. Box 1963	Burlingame	CA	94011	650-348-7699	15 outdoor
Clovis Chamber of Commerce	325 Pollasky Ave	Clovis	CA	93612	559-299-7273	3 indoor
Custom Productions	P. O. Box 800524	Santa Clarita	CA	91350	661-297-0119	1 indoor, 5 outdoor
Eckerstrom Productions	5151 Cold Springs Drive	Forest Hill	CA	95631	530-367-4557	10 outdoor
Hartman Studios	P. O. Box 70160	Point Richmond	CA	94807	510-970-3217	4 outdoor
Harvest Festival	601 North McDowell Blvd	Petaluma	CA	94954	707-778-6300	15 indoor
Jan Etre Presents	P. O. Box 9188	Berkeley	CA	94709	510-526-7363	1 outdoor, 1 indoor

Craft Fairs and Art Shows

Name	Address	City	State	Zip	Phone	Shows
MLA Productions	1384 Weston Rd.	Scotts Valley	CA	95066	831-438-4751	3 outdoor
Pacific Fine Arts	P. O. Box 280	Pine Grove	CA	95665	209-296-1195	12 outdoor
Piecemaker	1720 Adams Av.	Costa Mesa	CA	92626	714-691-3112	4 outdoor
R.G. Canning Attractions	P. O. Box 400	Maywood	CA	90270	310-835-9370	24 outdoor
Ray Leier	3051 Via Maderas	Altadena	CA	91001	626-797-6803	6 outdoor
Sandpiper Prod.	P. O. Box S-3053	Carmel	CA	93921	831-620-1281	2 outdoor
Scenic Art Shows	P. O. Box 485	Chino	CA	91708	909-623-5977	4 outdoor
Show Biz Productions	16520 Harbor Blvd. #D-2	Fountain Valley	CA	92708	714-418-2000	4-6 indoor
Steve Powers and Company	P. O. Box 1610	Pismo Beach	CA	93448	805-481-7100	8 indoor
Village Artisans	P. O. Box 1448	Bakersfield	CA	93302	661-328-1943	2 indoor
West Coast Artists	P. O. Box 4389	Chatsworth	CA	91311	818-709-2907	22 outdoor
West Fest Productions	100 So. Sunrise Way #145	Palm Springs	CA	92262	760-321-2148	20 outdoor
Adams County Historical Society	9601 Henderson Rd.	Brighton	CO	80601	303-659-7103	3 indoor
Chun Capital Hill People's Fair	1490 Lafayette St. #104	Denver	CO	80218	303-830-1651	1 outdoor
Cortez Area C of C	P. O. Box 968	Cortez	CO	81321	970-565-3414	2 outdoor
Denver Merchandise Mart	451 E. 58th Ave. #470	Denver	CO	80216	303-292-6278	2 indoor
Downtown Denver Partnership	511 16th St. #200	Denver	CO	80202	303-295-6330	3 outdoor
J&J Promotions	8490 W. Colfax Ave. Box 33	Lakewood	CO	80215	303-232-7147	3 indoor
Keystone Art Festival	P. O. Box 38	Keystone	CO	80435	970-496-4570	1 outdoor
Howard Allan Events Ltd.	9695 W. Broward Blvd.	Plantation	FL	33324	954-472-3755	40 outdoor
Monticello-Jefferson C of C	290 North Jefferson St.	Monticello	FL	32344	850-997-5552	2 outdoor
The Handmade in America Show	251 Creekside Dr.	St. Augustine	FL	32086	904-797-2600	20-30
United Production	125 5th Ave. N.	Safety Harbor	FL	34695	727-725-1562	4 outdoor
Hilltop Productions	481 Millard Gainey Road	DeFuniak Springs	FL	32435	850-951-2148	20 outdoors

Craft Fairs and Art Shows

Andersonville Gld.	P. O. Box 6	Andersonville	GA	31711	912-924-2558	2 indoor
Blue Ridge Mountains Arts	P. O. Box 1016	Blue Ridge	GA	30513	706-632-2144	2 outdoor
Contemporary Crafts Market	575 Cooke St. Ste A PO 2820	Honolulu	HI	96813	808-422-7362	3 indoor (in CA)
Downtown Davenport Assn.	102 So. Harrison St.	Davenport	IA	52801	319-322-6268	4 outdoor
Festivals International	508 4th Ave. No.,	Clearlake	IA	50428	515-357-5177	2 indoor, 4 outdoor
Personalized Wood Products	P. O. Box 193	Amana	IA	52203	319-622-3100	2 outdoor
Buhl Chamber of Commerce	716 Hwy. 30 East	Guhl	ID	83316	208-543-6682	2 outdoor
American Society of Artists	P. O. Box 1326	Palatine	IL	60078	312-751-2500	12 indoor, 15 outdoor
Craft Show Promotions Inc.	302 Allen Ave.	West Chicago	IL	60186	630-293-3637	3 indoor, 9 outdoor
Bright Star Promotions	3428 Hill Vale Rd.	Louisville	KY	40241	502-423-STAR	20 indoor
Steinhauer Productions	16471 Hwy 40	Folsom	LA	70437	504-796-5853	15 indoor, 2 outdoor
Artisan Promotions.	83 Mt. Vernon St.	Boston	MA	2108	617-742-3973	3 indoor
Americana Arts and Crafts	15 Cypress Street	Hagerstown	MD	21742	301-791-2346	7 outdoor
Buyers Market of American Craft	3000 Chestnut Ave. #300	Baltimore	MD	21211	410-889-2933	2 indoor
Sugerloaf Mountain Works	200 Orchard Ridge Dr., #21	Gaithersburg	MD	20878	301-990-1400	8 indoors
White Oak Plaza Merchants	923 So. 7 Hwy.	Blue Springs	MO	64015	816-118-6620	4 indoors
Forest Grove Community Club	P. O. Box 16	Forest Grove	MT	59411	406-538-8348	2 indoors, 1 outdoors
Lewiston C. of C.	P. O. Box 818	Lewistown	MT	59457	538-5436	2 outdoor
Bele Chere Fest.	P. O. Box 7148	Ashville	NC	28802	828-259-5800	3 outdoor
High Country Art & Craft Guild	P. O. Box 2854	Asheville	NC	28802	828-254-0072	11 indoor, 1 outdoor
Downtown Comm	P. O. Box 962	Fargo	ND	58107	701-241-1570	1 in, 1 out
Huffman Productions Inc.	P. O. Box 184	Boys Town	NE	68010	402-331-2889	9 indoor
Kimberly Ann Kreations	RR1 Box 200	Hoskins,	NE	68740	402-565-4583	2 indoor

Craft Fairs and Art Shows

Name	Address	City	State	Zip	Phone	Shows
A. C. A. C.	P. O. Box 650	Montclair	NJ	7042	973-746-0091	6 outdoor
Rose Squared Inc.	12 Galaxy Ct.	Belle Mead	NJ	8502	908-874-5247	8 outdoor
Lovington Chamber of C.	201 S. Main	Lovington	NM	88260	505-396-5311	2 indoor-outdoor
Mill Museum	P. O. Box 287	Cleveland	NM	87115	505-387-2645	2 in/outdoor
The Walker Organization	3340 Wynn Rd. Suite D	Las Vegas	NV	89102	702-364-1174	3 indoor
Williams, Ltd.	4790 Caughlin Pkwy., #507	Reno	NV	89509	775-324-6435	5 indoor, 25 outdoor
American Arts & Crafts Alliance	45 Riverside Drive #15H	New York	NY	10025	212-866-2239	3 outdoor, 2 indoor
Amer. Craft Cncl.	72 Spring St.	New York	NY	10012	800-836-3470	7 indoor
Artrider Productions	P. O. Box 28	Woodstock	NY	12498	914-331-7900	8 indoor, 1 outdoor
Cord Shows, Ltd.	4 Whipporwill Lane	Armonk	NY	10504	914-273-4667	2 indoor, 2 outdoor
Designer Arts	114 Mill Road	Red Hook	NY	12571	800-660-1045	5 indoor
George Little Management	Ten Bank Street	White Plains	NY	10606	914-421-3206	5 indoor
Soho Antiques Fair & Crafts	P. O. Box 337	Garden City	NY	11530	212-682-2000	52 weeks a year
Washington Sq. Outdoor Art	115 East 9th St. #7C	NY	NY	10003	212-982-6255	2 outdoor
Raab Enterprises	P. O. Box 33428	N. Royalton	OH	44133	440-237-3424	30 indoor
Tom Danner Event Mgmt.	P. O. Box 1473	Marion	OH	43302	740-389-5707	2 indoor
Benton County Fairgrounds	110 SW 53rd St.	Corvallis	OR	97333	541-757-1521	6 indoor, 1 outdoor
Brookings Chamber	P. O. Box 940	Brookings	OR	97415	541-469-3181	1 indoor, 1 outdoor
Eugene Sat, Mkt.	76 W. Broadway	Eugene	OR	97401	541-686-8885	14 in/35 out
Jefferson County Fair	P. O. Box 237	Madras	OR	97741	541-475-4460	2 indoors
Oregon Homecrafters	P. O. Box 70333	Eugene	OR	97401	541-343-6856	5 indoors
Rogue Valley	P. O. Box 4041	Medford	OR	97501	888-826-9868	weekly
Sisters Area Chamber of C.	P. O. Box 430	Sisters	OR	97759	541-549-0251	1 indoors, 4 outdoors
Umatilla County Fair	P. O. Box 94	Hermiston	OR	97838	541-567-8115	1 indoors, 1 outdoors

Name	Address	City	State	Zip	Phone	Shows
Umpqa Valley Arts Association	P. O. Box 1105	Roseburg	OR	97470	541-672-2532	2 indoors, 2 outdoors
BJ Promotions Belle Shilling	RR#1, Box 1772	Union Dale	PA	18470	570-679-3670	40 indoors
Heritage Markets	P. O. Box 389	Carlisle	PA	17013	717-249-9404	15 indoors
Renaissance Craftables	541 Woodland Dr.	Radnor	PA	19087	610-687-8535	4 indoors, 4 outdoors
Country Fairs	6311 So. Canyon Rd.	Rapid City	SD	57702	605-343-8783	5 indoors, 1 outdoors
Festival in the Park	P. O. Box 648	Spearfish	SD	57783	605-642-2311	1 indoors, 1 outdoors
Esau, Inc.	P O Box 50096	Knoxville	TN	37950	865-588-1233	2 indoors
Tennessee Assoc of Craft Artists	P. O. Box 120066	Nashville	TN	37212	615-665-0502	3 outdoors
American Country Shows	P. O. Box 1129	Fredericksburg	TX	78624	830-997-2774	25 indoors
Art Promotion Counselors	P. O. Box 776	Alamo	TX	78516	956-787-6996	30-40 indoors
Events Mgmt. Group, Inc.	P. O. Box 8845	Virginia Beach	VA	23450	757-486-0220	3 indoor
Craft Producers	P. O. Box 300	Charlotte	VT	5445	802-425-3399	3 indoors, 9 outdoors
Jim Custer Enterprises, Inc.	P. O. Box 14987	Spokane	WA	99206	509-924-0588	4 indoors
Metro Parks, Tacoma	4702 So 19th St.	Tacoma	WA	98405	253-591-5484	3 outdoors
One Reel	P. O. Box 9750	Seattle	WA	98109	206-281-8111	2 outdoors
Showcase Northwest	P. O. Box 2815	Kirkland	WA	98083	800-521-7469	3 indoors
Wisconsin Indian Head Country, Inc.	P. O. Box 628	Chetec	WI	54728	715-924-2970	5 indoors, 4 outdoors

Selling to Stores and Galleries

Wholesale Marketing

If you just want to stay at home and work in your shop, you can get craft galleries and gift shops to sell your jewelry. This is called wholesale. If you make a product that sells for $40 at a craft fair, your wholesale price would be $20. The normal markup for a retail store is double the price they paid for the product. They would then sell it for $40, just like you do at shows. If the product cost you $5 to produce (in parts and labor), you would net $15 if you sold it wholesale for $20 and $35 if you sold it at a craft fair for $40. However, after you calculate your costs for doing the fair, you might only end up with a profit of $20 for your fair sale, but that is still more than the $15 you would make by selling wholesale. The reality is that most stores can sell your product for a little more than you can get it for at a show. The store might be able to get $50, so you could wholesale it to them for $25, and then you would net $20 profit either way.

Some store owners will be upset if you sell your product at a craft fair nearby for less than they are charging in the store. You often entice buyers at a fair by your presence alone – as the working artist – and also by selling your product to them a little cheaper than they might pay in a store. Customers know they can return your product to a store, but they might not be able to return it to you since the fair will not be there every week. So they might expect to pay you less, directly. If a store complains, you will just have to raise your price at the fair to match theirs for that weekend.

One way to get your product into a store is to call and set up a meeting with the buyer to see your craftwork. Many stores set aside a specific day of the week when they look at new work.

If you feel intimidated by store buyers, you can hire a professional sales representative to interact with them for you. Sales reps will take samples of your work, along with the samples of other craftspeople they represent, to all of the galleries and shops in their territory. The store will place their order with the rep, who will send the order to you. You ship the crafts directly to the store, and when you are paid by the store you send the rep a commission, usually 15% on a monthly basis.

You (or your sales rep) can also rent space at a gift show or trade show to sell your work. Some shows specialize in crafts, some have a handmade section, and some just mix you in with all the other products, whether handmade, machine-made or imported. These shows are only open to wholesale buyers from stores, and the craftsperson is only allowed to bring samples and take orders, but not to sell products at the show directly to the customers to take with them. The trade show seller displays the sample crafts, hands out business cards, collects business cards, and takes orders to be shipped at some date in the future. These shows usually charge about $20 per square foot for the booth displays, feature a thousand or more booths, and host anywhere from 5,000 to 80,000 buyers from retail stores around the country.

If you don't want to deal with the cost and hassle of presenting your work at a trade show, you can try to reach the store buyers by direct mail. Send them a catalog of your products and a pricelist, or a postcard directing them to your web site. You will need a mailing list of quality galleries.

You can produce your own list from the business cards you collected from doing trade shows, making personal visits, from ads seen in tourist magazines, and from the list in the back of this book. A mailing of 1,000 postcards will cost $170 for the cards and $230 for the postage. For less than the cost of one show you can have a photo of your best-selling craft product in the hands of 1,000 gallery owners.

Some craftspeople sell both wholesale to stores and retail at fairs, or they try wholesaling for a while and later go back to fairs. Advantages of wholesaling include less travel and larger orders at a time. Stores are open regularly, all year long, in all kinds of weather, and most have experienced sales people. Disadvantages include delays in getting paid because the stores expect to pay in 30 or 90 days, and having to make the same thing over and over.

Trade Show Producers

BMAC Buyers Markets of American Crafts/The Rosen Group, Inc.
300 Chestnut Ave., Suite 300, Baltimore, MD 21211 (410) 889-2933 Handmade in U.S.A.
2 wholesale-only only shows, February and August, in Philadelphia. 1600 booths. Medium to high quality.

GLM George Little Management, Inc.
10 Bank St., Suite 1200, White Plains, NY 10606 (914) 421-3200   Shows all over the country, with both imports and handmade crafts.

ACC American Craft Council Fairs/American Craft Enterprises Marketing
72 Spring Street, New York, NY 10012 (212) 274-0630 www.craftcouncil.org   Handmade only. One wholesale show combined with a retail show in February in Baltimore, just after the BMAC show. Very high quality.

Beckman's Gift Shows
Box 27337, Los Angeles, CA 90027 (213) 962-5424   Handmade crafts and imports. For the Chicago shows, call 800-677-6278.

ACRE American Craft Retailers Expo
One wholesale only show in Las Vegas in May and one in Orlando in January, www.wholesalecrafts.com. 604 Beaten Path Road, Mooresville, North Carolina, 28117. 888-427-2381

Wholesale Tips

Trade shows

☐ **Attend a show as a guest.**
Make notes about booth designs and price points of products similar to yours. To get in, you might have to register as if you have a store.

☐ **Make your booth interesting.**
When a buyer walks by, they scan your booth. They spend only about three seconds deciding whether to visit your booth or not. If nothing grabs their attention, they will keep walking.

☐ **Mail postcards before the show.**
Pre-show mailings will help you to have a good show. If it is your first show, you might be able to arrange for the promoter to mail your postcards to their mailing list of stores in your category.

☐ **You have to do a wholesale show several times for it to start to pay off.**
Gallery owners have to get to know you and trust you. Some gallery owners only purchase at trade shows.

☐ **Trade show displays**
Get portable lightweight tables and big folding banner stands from www.postergarden.com 800-707-2004

☐ **Use Zippy Mats for booth floors.**
Stacking interlocking floor rubber pieces, usually 24" by 24", make a comfortable floor in your booth for you and your customers. Wandix International, 800-385-6855 www.wandix.com.

During the trade show

☐ **Get to know more about the gallery.**
Ask the buyer about the gallery's location, style, owner's preferences. "Where is your store? Do you sell similar crafts? How long have you been in business? Are you involved in management?"

☐ **Hand out cards with your booth number.**
When there are hundreds of booths, buyers get confused when trying to find your booth again.

Wholesale

- **Make your own wholesale line sheet.**

Use 4 pages— one for a price list, one with a photo of your jewelry, one for an artist's statement, and one for terms, shipping information, and a warranty. Be sure your name, address, phone number, fax, and email address is on every page of material you give the customer. Place a copyright notice on each page (All designs copyright 2010 by Joe Artisan Design).

- **Recommend a starter order or show special.**

This will help the store to get to know your products. Offer a discount of 10% for purchasing the complete starter order. Have signage to describe the show special displayed in your booth.

- **Tell buyers what's new in your booth.**

They can always order the old products over the phone (even though they probably won't, waiting instead for you to call them!) Have a clipboard in your hand and start writing the customer's name and address on an order form, as you are talking to them.

- **Make customers ask for a brochure.**

Don't leave them within reach, but in sight. Get the customer's card for each brochure given out. No card or entry in your guest book, no brochure.

- **Pre-qualify your customer.**

Know who you are talking to. Some of the attendees at trade shows do not have stores and are just looking for a good deal. Authentic wholesale buyers usually have clipboards and are wearing comfortable shoes. Find out from the buyer which other craftspeople at the show they have bought from.

- **Wholesale buyers are drawn to presentation.**

They also like an artist who is well dressed and business-like. Casual dress is for craft shows.

- **Don't sit. smoke, talk on the phone, or chew gum**

If you act bored, you will be. So will your customers.

- **Make an information sheet for gallery owners.**

Gallery workers need knowledge about how you make your products. They can display it with your products so they don't have to think about it. Similar to an artist statement, the information sheet should have your photo on it, and information about what special techniques you use to make the product. Leave your address off of it. The store wants the customer to get more products from them, not you.

☐ **Write down buyer comments.**

Eavesdrop on people who are visiting your booth and write down comments they make. Also record comments made to you directly. Study them later, to learn what you can do to improve your sales.

☐ **Don't print too many catalogs.**

Even if a show has 20,000 attendees, only 300 might stop at your booth. You won't need thousands of catalogs.

☐ **Don't take more orders than you can handle.**

Before a wholesale show, calculate how many items you can make in the next six months. Never promise a delivery date you can't keep. Your goal is to ship on time.

☐ **After the first order, ask your customers to reorder.**

Call them three times a year. "Hi, I'm _____, from Company. I missed you at the wholesale show. How's your inventory? Can I help you out? Do you need stock? If you want product I have to get you on the production schedule. Do you have any old product to exchange?"

Wholesale business

☐ **Get cash for first order.**

The buyer can use a check or credit card. No C. O. D. Second order net 15 or net 30, after you check their three references. If the retailer wants you to make an exception, such as net 45, they will want exceptions later. If they need net 45, they can use a credit card. If they have a poor credit history, have them prepay with a check, and wait for it to clear.

☐ **Don't ship a new order until last order is paid in full.**

Tell the buyer of this policy when they place their first order.

☐ **Don't require huge minimums.**

Large minimum orders discourage small stores from trying your jewelry. You want to get your products in stores and keep them in stores. Selling to many small companies is also somewhat safer than selling to just a few large companies. If a large company goes bankrupt when owing you money, you could be in financial trouble.

☐ **Give area exclusivity on a trial basis.**

Tell your buyer that if sales are unsatisfactory in their store after three or four months, you will sell to other stores in their area. If you commit to exclusivity, the store must commit to making enough sales to make it worthwhile for you.

Wholesale

☐ **Put all terms on the order form.**
When buyer signs the order, it indicates that they have read the terms (whether they have or not).

☐ **Offer buyers a refund or exchange.**
Offer an exchange within one year for items that don't sell.

☐ **Buy or make a triplicate sales receipts book.**
One copy is for the customer at the show, one is for your files, and one either ships with the order as an invoice or is mailed separately. Make sure it has spaces for the delivery date, signature date, contact name, preferred terms, and the customer's signature. If you have a computer invoice program, you only need a duplicate sales book. You copy the order information into your invoice program when you get home.

☐ **Collect past due invoices by phone.**
Call and say, "My records show that you owe me x dollars. Will you send me a check for the full amount today?" Then send a letter, then phone, another letter, phone, letter. Ask for a credit card number to keep until you get the full amount. If you don't get paid, call a lawyer, and file suit.

☐ **Deliver the order on time.**
If you can't deliver the order on time, call the buyer, apologize, and reschedule. When order is late, you could say, "I put in a little extra effort to make sure that you got some unique items."

Wholesale reps

- **Find sales representatives at trade shows.**
Look for reps with handcrafted items that compliment (but don't compete directly with) yours.

- **Get a directory of sales reps.**
Directory of Wholesale Reps for Craft Professionals.
http://www.craftassoc.com/reps.html   800-715-9594

- **Get references from the sales rep.**
Be sure to call the references. Ask them if the rep is reliable, productive, etc.

- **Check your sales reps business contacts.**
Make sure he or she deals with the type of galleries that sell your type of products.

More wholesale tips

- **Check out American Style magazine.**
They have lots of ads for craft galleries, and you can add the gallery addresses to your mailing list.

- **Visit galleries when traveling.**
Get the business cards of craft galleries that could be a match for your products.

- **Don't just walk into a gallery with your craft products.**
Send photos first, with a cover letter, then schedule a meeting with the buyer. It shows that you are a professional. At the very least, call first.

- **Find gallery addresses at the library and on the internet.**
Your local library has every telephone Yellow Pages in the country on microfiche. Look for craft galleries, museums, or gift shops, and write down the address. You can also create a list of galleries from other artist's websites on the internet.

- **Set business hours for your home business.**
Self-discipline is the hardest part of being self-employed. Find out what wastes time. Use a message machine that says you are in the shop when you are working, so you won't be disturbed.

- **Track your shipping.**
You can track your packages online at **www.packtrack.com**. They track UPS, FedEx, and Airborne. UPS 800 PICKUPS www.ups.com. Yellow Freight 800-610-6500 www.myyellow.com.

Tips for selling on wholesalecrafts.com

www.wholesalecrafts.com is a web site for marketing to retailers. You can get a temporary ID and password to view the site by calling Nancy Vince at 888-427-2381 or email nancy@wholesalecrafts.com. She has more than 1,300 artists and 13,000 registered retailers. She charges $295 to $495 a year to have your photos on her website. The customer orders directly from you with no closing value fees.

- <u>Upload new work to your pages whenever possible.</u>

This will get you two items in the "New Work Last 90 days" showcase and also helps your placement in online searches.

- <u>Use a Logo and a Banner.</u>

It helps to have a professional looking page when the buyers come to look.

- <u>Utilize the detail image available for each item.</u>

Since the buyer cannot touch the items, use a close up or different angle to show the buyer exactly what they are buying.

- <u>Do a "Starter package' or "Best seller package".</u>

Entice first time buyers to try out your work by offering the same item in various sizes or colors, or a variety of items. Offer a discount on shipping or a display unit.

- <u>Try a special offer.</u>

Try free shipping for the month of ? or 10% off for the month of ?. Put this info in the price description box of an item and use it for a feature ad and as an announce in the classified board. Also apply for the free artists spotlight.

- <u>Check your Summary of Inquiries often.</u>

You might miss an order because you have a SPAM filter or bulk mail filter on your email.

- <u>Add more images.</u>

You can upload up to 280 images free of charge. You can tag them with a "New Work" logo and two of them will be shown in the New Work section for 90 days. When you add new work and use the new work icon your image will show up on the first pages of any keyword search done by the buyers for 30 days.

- <u>Consider adding a PDF catalog, price sheet, etc.</u>

You can have up to two of these on your page, and retailers get to see their options.

Wholesale

☐ **Check out the discussion boards.**

You may see a post where someone has asked for advice, and see all the responses. Also use the Announcements/classified section to let the buyers know of new work and specials and discounts you may want to order.

☐ **Buy a "Featured Items" ad at least once a month.**

With these $15 ads you are featured on the buyer homepage for 7 days and once in the weekly buyer newsletter.

Other Markets

☐ **Put your crafts in consignment stores**

One way to get your creations into stores is to place them on consignment. This means that the store does not pay you until they sell the item. If they don't sell it in a reasonable amount of time, you take it back. If they do sell it, they give you 60% of the amount they got for it. The reason you get more than the 50% you would get from a direct sale to a store is that you don't get your money right away, and risk having to take your product back (or not getting paid). The consignment store pays you more after the sale because they were able to place your item on their shelves, trying it out at no risk to themselves. Most artists and craftspeople don't do consignment unless they really like the store.

☐ **Sell to department stores.**

Contact the store nearest you and get the name and number of the buyer for your region.

☐ **Sell to museum gift shops.**

Museum Store Association has a trade show just for museum gift shop buyers. www.museumdistrict.com 303-329-6968.

☐ **Try home shopping networks.**

If you are set up to deliver quantities in the order of $20,000 (wholesale) at a time, you might want to contact QVC. Your product will reach 89 million homes simultaneously in 50 states. You only need to send a photo and description to get an appointment for an evaluation. Your product must retail for $15.00 or more. The entire $20,000 worth of products have to be in their warehouse before you go on the air. You can send a sample but it won't be returned. Contact: Guthy-Renker Corp, 115 Drummond Dr., Wilmington, DE 19808 1-888-NEW ITEM www.qvcproductsearch.com

☐ **Sell your products to catalogs.**

Lots of catalogs are listed at www.catalogsfroma-z.com and www.catalogcity.com. Check out "Secrets to Marketing Your Products to Catalog Companies," by Jack Briscoe Jr. (amazon.com)

☐ **Join a professional organization.**

It looks good on your artist's statement and your resume, and you can deduct the trips to the annual convention. They usually have a magazine that keeps you up to date about your craft. One example: Manufacturing Jewelers and Suppliers of America, 800-444-6572.

Afternoon by John C. Reiger

My eyes droop, the book slips.
"Yep, I made 'em," mumble lips.

Oh yes, I made them, every one.
Pitchers and bowls, by the ton.

And here I sit, in this fair spot,
Trying hard to sell the lot.

Or a few, or two, or even one.
To pay the rent, or just for fun.

This morning so full of hopes,
But by now I'm on the ropes.

It's four o'clock—the hours creep.
What will happen if I sleep?

And what will happen if I don't?
Nothing! But then… So I won't.

Oh, Oh, a customer. Look alive!
Sit up. Stand up. Speil that jive.

Nothing doing! There she goes.
Ease back, relax, time to dose.

And as my fair hopes decompose,
I seek relief in rhythmic prose.

No use, against the fates, to rail.
But, oh, she's back. At last a sale

Selling Online

In the past 10 years, shopping on the Internet has increased to the tune of billions of dollars a year. Selling your crafts on the Internet is easier than ever, but it is not the complete solution for selling craft for more than a very few people. The experience of holding a handmade creation directly from the craftsperson at a fair is not easy to recreate on the Internet.

The primary method of selling on the Internet is from your own web site. You have to make or have someone make you a web site, set it up to receive payments, and let customers know about it.

Making your own web site is not hard with products like Serif WebPlus (Serif.com). All a web site needs is text, images, an order form, and navigation buttons. WebPlus handles all of these needs in a very efficient way. Becoming good at using a web site creation program is like being good at using a word processing program. Once you learn the basics, it is just another skill to help you with your marketing. With WebPlus you will never have to learn html, java, flash, or animated gifs. I have created a complete web site with home page, product page, faq (frequently asked questions) page, and order form page, in less than an hour with this software.

You can always hire someone to make your web site, and try to get them to understand what you are trying to represent on your site. This works well for some artists. But what happens when the Webmaster decides not to work on your site anymore, or you loose track of them? It is better to learn the few skills needed to make your own web site, then you can modify it as much as you want whenever you want.

Receiving payments on the Internet is easy if you already take credit cards. The customer just emails or calls you with the credit card information. Otherwise, you can set your site up with PayPal buttons.

You let customers know about your web site by putting it on all of your correspondence, your email, your business cards, and your hangtags. You might even put a sign with your web site name in your booth. Contact the various search engines and tell them about your web site. WebPlus has a form for this.

Some artists are having some success with putting their products on eBay. The problem with eBay is that there are many people selling similar products to yours for much less money. You have to convince the potential buyer to buy your more expensive item by telling them how and why it is superior to the other jewelry on eBay. eBay is, after all, the world's largest flea market. It is not a craft gallery, but you can get a following of satisfied customers if you have a professional presentation.

Internet Tips

Making your own web site

☐ <u>Get your own domain name</u>

This currently costs about $70, which registers it for two years, and the cost is $35/year thereafter. When you control your own domain name with a legitimate provider, then you will be notified when it expires. To get a domain name, go to networksolutions.com. Do not use any other registrar, like GoDaddy.com, even though it costs less. They will take your name when you search for it, and then try to sell it back to you for a higher price

☐ <u>Find a good Internet Service Provider</u>

The ISP (web host) that I use is http://www.hostexcellence.com/ They charge $4 a month. They also have excellent and fast customer service.

☐ <u>Learn WebPlus by Serif.</u>

WebPlus costs under $100 and is very easy to learn. Get the Business Template package, pick a template, change the text and photos, add PayPal shopping cart buttons, and your jewelry is online!

☐ <u>Study good web design.</u>

Learn what make for bad web design, and avoid it. Go to www.webpagesthatsuck.com. Really!

☐ <u>Use a white background on your web pages.</u>

Have you ever tried to read white text on a black background?

☐ <u>Use Adobe Elements for your photos.</u>

Elements is free with some printers and scanners, otherwise it is available from Costco or CompUSA for under $100. It has all the features you need to retouch photos and size them for your web site or email.

☐ <u>Your web images should be 30K or less.</u>

Use Elements or Photoshop to resize your photos to 4"x6" at 72dpi, then "Save for the Web.".

☐ <u>Don't use fancy animation, Flash, or music.</u>

It takes too long to download for the millions of people out there who still have a slow phone internet connection. Flash doesn't work with iphones or ipads.

Internet

- **Get listed with search engines.**

Go to "add url" buttons on Yahoo, Google, or Exite to add your site. Most search engines use the first 12 or 15 words of text on your page. Make them relevant. Don't waste them on "Welcome to my home page."

- **Always use metatags.**

Use metatags on all of your pages. In HTML view, insert them after the title. Example: <META NAME="Keywords" CONTENT="silver, earrings, handmade, handcrafted, gold, gift, unique"> <META NAME="Description" CONTENT="Handmade earrings make excellent gifts for all occasions.">

- **Don't list all of your craft shows on your site.**

New craftspeople in your specialty might find your web site, apply to all of your shows, get in some of them, and either take your place or sell next to you and take half of your money in sales. This has happened to me twice. The huge loss of money hardly compensates for the occasional customer who went to your site to see where you were going to be next. You can send your best customers cards or email them about your upcoming shows. I recommend listing only your next couple of shows on your web site, and not showing all of your designs.

- **Use AOL for your email.**

There are lots of so-called free email providers, Yahoo, Google and Hotmail for example. But AOL has reliability, and some neat email tricks, such as being able to unsend your email after it has been sent, and saving mail both online and on your PC. We have used AOL since 1995 and have never lost any mail due to "box filled up," etc. AOL mail is now free.

- **Have a separate email address from your web site email.**

If your email is connected to your web site (info@yourwebsite.com) and your server goes down, you won't get your orders. You also get lots of junk mail, which sometimes fills your box, and then you won't even know you had an order.

- **Use PayPal's free shopping cart.**

At www.paypal.com, you can get either "buy now" buttons for each product, or a shopping cart for all of your products. It is easy to set up, and it is free when you create a merchant account. You just describe the item at the PayPal merchant site, then cut and paste the code in your html view to create a button next to the product (in WebPlus you just create a button). PayPal handles the rest, giving the customer a receipt and putting the money in your account. An alternative to PayPal is Google Checkout. The fees are the same.

Internet

☐ **Offer a money-back guarantee on your web site.**

The biggest problem with selling on a web site is credibility in the eyes of the buyer. A guarantee might ease their concerns.

☐ **Make a separate web page for wholesale customers.**

To put wholesale prices on your site, just make a page called yoursite.com/wholesale.htm, and tell your stores about it. Your retail customers won't know it is there if it isn't linked.

☐ **Get low-priced web site design from students.**

Contact a local college to find a student web site designer who needs exposure. They might be willing to help you for less money. Be sure to keep track of your user id and password if you need to change webmasters.

Tips for Selling on eBay

☐ **Use low-res pictures.**

Have a separate folder on your computer for your eBay photos or put them on an unlinked page on your website. You either can use a film camera and have your pictures delivered to you on a cd, or buy an inexpensive 3.2 megapixel camera with a macro lens for under $100.

☐ **Use your artist's statement for "About Me."**

You can cut and paste your artist statement to eBay's "About Me" page and help your customers get to know you better.

☐ **Be descriptive!**

eBay does not charge more for long descriptions. You can go into great depth about how you make it, what materials you use, and how successful you are at shows. Use testimonials. Not everyone will read it all, but interested buyers will appreciate it.

☐ **Use bulleted text in descriptions of your product.**

Customers don't want to or don't have time to read large blocks of text.

☐ **Use Turbo Lister for multiple listings.**

It is a free program from eBay. You can choose from hundreds of templates, use the same shipping information for all listings, and upload all of your listings at once. You can also schedule listings for later automatic uploading.

Internet

☐ **List on Thursday for 10 days.**

You will have two full weekends for people to see your product, for only a few cents more than a normal listing. The listing will end on Sunday, when people are home. If you list in the evening, more people will be home to bid as the auction closes.

☐ **Always use Delivery Confirmation.**

The customer cannot claim that he or she didn't get the package. It only costs 45 cents. If you buy your priority mail shipping online with "Click N Ship" at www.usps.com, or if you buy the postage with PayPal by clicking on the Ship button on your PayPal transaction list, delivery confirmation is free. Otherwise you have to go to the post office. If the item is over $50.00, always insure it.

☐ **Sell your extra supplies on eBay.**

This is a good way to get rid of unused tools and extra parts that you bought too many of. It helps your cash flow and makes the workshop easier to clean. Start these auctions at $ .99. There are thousands of craftspeople checking eBay every day.

☐ **Take PayPal for faster eBay sales.**

You have to get set up for PayPal, at www.paypal.com. This service is almost indispensable for internet transactions. Now that eBay owns PayPal, the service is even more reliable (and accountable)! Don't forget that cookies on your computer must be active to use it.

☐ **Use your 55 characters wisely.**

Keywords are the best way to attract buyers to your listing. Be sure to use common search words like "Jewelry" and "Silver," when appropriate. Then use homemade, color, medium, style. You can also search current and completed eBay listings to see what other sellers include in their titles. USE ALL CAPS TO GET ATTENTION!

☐ **Upgrade your listings.**

Create bold section headlines, bulleted lists, and restate the information featured in your title. Make your description easy to read. Add details about dimensions, condition, estimated value, interesting features. You can note if the item was made in a smoke free or pet free home. The more information you provide, the more likely the buyer is to bid on your item.

☐ **Use great photos.**

Use a contrasting, solid backdrop. Black or white draws the buyer's attention directly to the item. Cover all angles and zoom in on important details. Avoid using your flash.

☐ **Use a Gallery photo.**

You can attract attention to your item with a photo next to your listings in search results. In addition, when a buyer uses "Picture Gallery" to look at search results, your listing will be shown.

☐ Use a low starting price.

Your starting price should be the least (wholesale) price you would take for the item. Don't use a reserve price. Always have a "Buy It Now" price for impatient buyers.

☐ Calculate your shipping costs.

Specify reasonable shipping and handling cost in your listing. You can put a shipping calculator in your listing. You can add $5 to your listing price and then offer USPS Flat Rate Small Box Priority Mail shipping for free. Listings with free shipping sometimes come up sooner in searches. Offer to pay for shipping insurance if needed.

☐ Pack your jewelry securely.

Use lots of cushioning such as bubble wrap or peanuts. If you use newspaper, protect the item from ink rubbing off of the paper. Make sure you don't hear any rattling. By the way, you can order free USPS Priority Mail boxes right on eBay, and the Postal Service will deliver them for free. Use strong tape designed for shipping.

☐ Build your reputation.

Communication is the key. Answer any question promptly. Put a thank you note in your package. It will encourage your buyer to leave you positive feedback. Always leave positive feedback for your buyers. Use your About Me page and My World. Add pictures and tell the community abut your interests and collections. Write Reviews and Guides. You can use eBay Giving Works in your listings to donate some of the listing price to benefit a nonprofit.

Tips For Selling On Etsy

200,000 registered users watch 40,000 art and craft sellers that have set up a shop online here. Sellers join free, pay 20 cents to list each item, and etsy.com takes 3.5% of each sale. Other web sites for artists include artfire.com, www.lov.li, and www.dwanda.com in Europe.

☐ Fill out all fields.

Include a banner, a bio, a store announcement, a location, good descriptions with measurements and products, products with multiple views. Fill out your profile. Calculate shipping costs accurately and include them in each listing.

☐ Put in info your customer wants.

Does your jewelry tarnish? How long are your necklaces and bracelets?

Internet

- **Post store policies.**

What happens when you ship and the buyer says they didn't get it. What if they want to return it? What if it was a custom item or they say it was damaged.

- **Add personality to your listings.**

Include a personal touch. Use a picture of yourself for your avatar. Allow the customer to make a connection with you, the artist. Maybe share your inspiration for the work. Never copy anyone else's description, format, etc. Find a way to do something different from your competitors.

- **Spread out your listings.**

List a few items at a time. If you list all your items at once, you reduce your exposure on the category pages.

- **Post in the right category and use all your tags.**

Where would the shopper look for your product? Think like a buyer for a minute.

- **Use your thumbnail well.**

You need to create an image that is interesting. Your first image should be 75 px by 75 px so the entire item will show. Your other images can be bigger. You can make your photos stand out by using different angles, expressions, etc.

- **Promote your listings.**

1. Join forums and put your Etsy store URL in your signature, if the forum rules allow it.
2. Find people to link to your Etsy store, and do the same for them in return.
3. Put your Etsy URL in your e-mail signature
4. Advertise in free bulletin boards
5. Do business card swaps with other Etsy sellers.
6. Vistaprint.com - free business cards and give them away like crazy.

General Business and Marketing Tips

Bookkeeping

- **Use a Dome Simplified Monthly Bookkeeping Record.**

You can get a Dome book by calling (800) 432-4352, or a cheap copy by Adams at Office Depot or Office Max. It meets all IRS requirements for record keeping. You simply enter monthly expenditures on the left, income on the right, and add up the totals at the end of the year or tax time. There are two extra pages for expenses for each month. Just tear them out and write the name of the month in the space provided on the income side for each month.

- **You don't need separate account numbers.**

Accounting programs separate all deductions into categories. If the item is deductible, simply write it down in your Dome book. All that is needed for a deduction is a date, item, and amount (and a receipt).

- **Use commercial receipt books for wholesale orders.**

Use a rubber stamp with your company name and address, phone number and email. Gallery buyers are not as impressed with your sales forms and invoices as they are by timely delivery and fast turnover.

- **Fill out your phone orders by hand.**

You will never again have to hate your computer for not booting up in time to take the order. And, you won't have to hate your printer for not working when you need it.

- **Back up your mailing list.**

Keep duplicates (including account information) in a place separate from your workplace or office. In case of fire or theft, you won't have to re-create everything.

Taxes

☐ You have to pay taxes if you have a business.

The IRS considers a business as any activity that makes a profit in 2 out of 5 years. If you don't make any profit with your crafts, it is considered a hobby and you can't deduct your craft-related expenses.

☐ Find out what is deductible.

The Schedule C tax form has a list of deductions. A Dome book also has a list of everything that is deductible. The bottom line is, if you use it to assist your business, deduct it.

☐ Get tax information free direct from IRS.

Get IRS publication 334 "Tax Guide for Small Business" to get the facts about your taxes.

☐ Deduct credit card interest.

Your business credit cards don't have to be in your business name, just earmarked for business use. All of the interest on a business credit card can be deducted on your Schedule C. You should use your credit card for materials only if you can pay it off in three months or less.

☐ Don't deduct for business use of your home.

Since this is the most abused tax deduction, it is a red flag for the IRS, and the deduction (usually a percentage of the rent or mortgage for your house) is usually not large enough to be worth it.

☐ Check if a "Home Occupation" business license is required.

In some cities, even if you don't have employees, you may still need a business license to work out of your home. If you have employees, or the public comes to your studio, you might need to have your studio in a commercial zone. If you live in the country you usually don't need a business license but you still need a state sales tax number. Your bank should accept the state sales tax number instead of a business license. If they don't, find a different bank.

☐ Get an employee identification number.

If you have employees, you need an employee identification number (EIN) from the IRS. 1-800-829-4933. If you don't have employees, you can use your social security number for business purposes whenever an EIN is asked for.

☐ Keep track of your bank deposits.

In a field audit, the IRS will add up your bank deposits for the year and compare them with your stated gross income.

Business and Marketing

☐ **Get a state sales tax number or ID.**

Write, call, or go to the state office of taxation in your state. This is different from a fictitious name statement, which you get from your county offices. This is where you send the sales tax you collect.

Copyright

☐ **Copyright your work.**

Copyright costs $20.00 and protects the graphic or sculptural works for 70 years after the artist's death. Copyright forms are free and available from Library of Congress, U. S. Copyright Office. 202-707-9100. Their general information number is 202-479-0700. www.lcweb.loc.gov/copyright.

☐ **Use a design patent to protect your work.**

A design patent is good for 14 years. You can't get a design patent for anything that has been in public view for over a year. www.uspto.gov 202-707-9100

☐ **Copyright your catalog with a "Visual Arts" form.**

All of your designs will be protected for your life plus 70 years. www.loc.gov/copyright.

☐ **Use a "TM" after your company name.**

Do this even if you haven't registered the name yet, but intend to.

☐ **Always put a copyright notice on your work.**

"Copyright 2007 by Bob Smith". The date refers to the first use of your product. Put it on your printed materials and your products.

☐ **If someone is copying you, let him or her know.**

Tell them that under the law, you are entitled to their profits. They might not even know they are copying you.

☐ **Protect function with a utility patent.**

You can't copyright function but you can protect it. Utility patents are good for 18 years. www.uspto.gov.

Promotion

☐ <u>Pick up newspapers at every show you do.</u>

Take one home with you. Next year, send them a press release. People will come up to your booth and say they saw you in the paper.

☐ <u>Make your own press release.</u>

A press release is one or two pages of information. Tell who, what, where, why, when, etc. Explain why your method or style of craftsmanship is unique or what you are doing to save the planet. A press release is always double-spaced. Write "For Immediate Release" at the top, then put your contact information.

☐ <u>Send a cover letter with your press release</u>.

Tell the editor why their readers need to know about you. Include a glossy black-and-white 5x7 or 8x10 photograph of you and your shop and a photograph of your craft. You should take the photos in color in case you ever need color, then print them in black and white. (You can't print color from a black and white photo.)

☐ <u>Never write on the back of a publicity photo.</u>

It can't be reproduced, as the writing will show through. Write or use a rubber stamp on a label, <u>then</u> put the label on the back of the photo.

☐ <u>Use Microsoft Publisher for brochures.</u>

Microsoft Publisher is very useful for artist statements, postcards, stationery, catalogs, brochures, hang tags, etc. Some online printers such as www.printing4less.com can use your uploaded Publisher files. There is a Publisher lesson in this book on page 118.

☐ <u>Use first class mail for mailing your cards and brochures.</u>

Bulk mail only saves you about ten cents a letter and it is more likely to be unread. After you spend $125 for a bulk mail application, $125 for an annual fee, and all the time to separate your mail by zip code, have you really saved any money? Bulk mail rates are at <u>www.usps.com/directmail/</u>

Business and Marketing

Pricing

Pricing is one of the biggest problems for beginners. There is a pricing form in the computers section of this book on page 80, and with the "craft fair" app for the iphone. Pricing is simply adding the cost of materials in each piece to the labor cost (how many hours to make it times how much you want to make an hour), then multiplying by 2.5 for your retail price. Wholesale is half of that.

☐ **Never under-price your work.**

You might make more sales, but you will be broke at the end of the year. Never reduce your price unless you can cut your costs (both materials and labor). Selling out at a show is not always a good thing. If your product sells out at a show the first day, it is priced too low.

☐ **Find your best market.**

If your product price is too high for your market, find another market. Sell your one-of-a-kind pieces through a craft gallery, where your product is not compared to products at Target or Wal-Mart.

☐ **Have multiple price points.**

If you have products priced for low income, middle income, and high-end customers, you will always make money at a show.

☐ **Put price labels on every product you have for sale.**

You don't want the customer to think you are making up the price. And, you won't waste time with a customer who couldn't afford the item. Plus, you don't have to remember all the prices.

Miscellaneous

☐ **Write down where you want to be in 5 years.**

Make goals for 3 months, 1 year, and 5 years. The simple act of writing it down programs the subconscious to take actions that help you with your goals. See page 107.

☐ **Test market every new product.**

Craft fairs and wholesale trade shows are very helpful for product research. Don't make a hundred of one design until you have sold a few.

☐ **Write down a goal for production each day.**

You can do this last thing in the evening before, or first thing in the morning.

Business and Marketing

☐ **Save 10% of the gross from every show.**

This adds up. Don't spend it on anything. Save it for your house or retirement.

☐ **Set business hours for your home business.**

Self-discipline is the hardest part of being self-employed. Find out what wastes time. Use a message machine that says you are in the shop when you are working, so you won't be disturbed.

Strawberry Festival, Oxnard, California

Useful Addresses

Display

Dealer's Supply
P. O. Box 717, Matawan, NJ 07747   (800) 524-0576
(Free 20-page catalog)   Fire retardant, showcases, fitted table covers, booth signs, alarms

Abstracta Structures, Inc.
Consort Display Group, 2129 Portage St. Kalamazoo, MI 49001. 800-545-6424
This is where you get your lightweight table structures when you want to fly to shows. Tubular steel structural systems for displays, exhibits, store fixtures, and furniture. They make lightweight displays out of ½" tubing and supply the connectors. info@consort.com

O'Brien Manufacturing
2081 Knowles Road, Medford, OR, 97501   (541) 773-2410
Oak and glass cases of many shapes and sizes for wall, table, and countertop. Excellent quality, and fast delivery. I have been using their 12" deep by 24" wide by 18" high oak cases for years.

Daniels Display Co., Inc.
1267 Mission Street, San Francisco, CA 94103   (415) 861-4400
Power track lighting and tempered glass case systems. These are the glass display systems with the chrome metal connectors that are repositioned with a wide blade screwdriver. You can make your own shelves from clear plastic. Useful for transporting when space is at a premium.

Flourish Co.
RT. 1, Brashears Jct., Combs, AR 72721 www.flourish.com   (800) 296-0049
Arch top canopy, Promaster indoor booth frames (with both tabs and screws at the corners for better stability), and flame-resistant drapes. They also have metal mesh walls for hanging art.

Creative Energies, Inc.
1607 N. Magnolia Ave., Ocala, FL 34475   (800) 351-8889
Makers of the Light-Dome, the most stable canopy I have seen in windy shows. Useful indoors too.

DMG Products
(215) 393-8701 Fire Retardant -- fabric spray, wood spray, specialty cloths

International E-Z UP, Inc.
1601 Iowa Avenue, Riverside, CA 92507   (800) 45-SHADE
They are the distributors for the E-Z UP canopies. Call them for the numbers of your local dealers. One California dealer is Made in the Shade, P. O. Box 231, Cool, CA 95614 (916) 888-7970.
Another is Hawaiian Sun, Inc., Box 5447, Louisville, KY 40205 (502) 458-5066
The strongest heavy duty E-Z UP is called the Eclipse, 70 lbs, best for outdoor shows. The Express is the lighter version (51 lbs), with the removable top, best for flying or indoor shows.

Addresses

Photographers

Hap Sakwa
403 Taft St., Sebastopol, CA 95472 (707) 823-5787
Craftspeople all over the country send him products to be photographed. www.hapsakwa.com

Jerry Anthony
Excellent craft photography.   3952 Shattuck Avenue, Columbus, Ohio 43220 (614) 451-5207
info@jerryanthonyphoto.com

Bob Barrett
4 Julia Avenue
New Paltz, NY 12561
845-430-8599
www.bobbarrettphoto.com

Azad
Azad Photography
Specializes in jewelry   660 Laramie Blvd. Boulder CO 80304 (888) 258 0657 www.azadphoto.com

George Post
George Post Photography. 5835 Bouquet Avenue. Richmond CA 94805 (510) 237-0197
gpp@gpostphoto.com   www.gpostphoto.com

Bags and boxes

Uline
2105 South Lakeside Dr. Waukegan IL 60085 (800) 958-5463   Every size of box, bag, shipping label imaginable. Fast shipping. www.veripack.com (free catalog)

Rio Grande
7500 Bluewater Rd. N. W. Albuquerque, NM 87121.   (800) 545-6566. They have quality packaging and display for small products.

Insurance

Northwest Insurance Agency, Inc.
P. O. Box 1180, Santa Rosa, CA 95402 (707) 573-1300
They sell a Home-Based Business Owners policy from RLI Insurance Company (9025 North Lindbergh Drive, Peoria, IL 61615). Their policy for $1,000,000 liability, $5,000 medical expenses, and $50,000 fire liability costs about $295 a year. For an extra $100 you can get Personal Property coverage, which covers loss of stock or business equipment while on the road up to $5,000. They will add a name of any craft show that specifically requires it for $18 (prices are subject to change.) Also check out homebased –business insurance from the Hartford Co. (thru AARP).

Credit Card Processing Systems

Novus Services, Inc.
1641 North First Street, Suite 260, San Jose, CA 95112 (800) 347-2000
This is the one with a Trans 330 ($300), where you key the numbers in after the show.
Total Merchant Services
(888) 682-4464 They can set you up with a free wireless card terminal such as the Nurit 8000. This is the one we use.

Computers and Microsoft™ Office

Introduction

When you sell your handmade creations to the public, you have to deal with accounting, planning, inventory, invoices, and show scheduling. You might be thinking that computers can run your business, leaving you more time to create. Well, the bad news is that a computer can't run your business and it can waste a lot of your time. But the good news is that you can use a computer for your email, or to surf the Internet, put up a web site, sell on ebay and etsy, and actually use it to help you from time to time to organize various aspects of your business, such as your mailing list, inventory, pricing, or bookkeeping.

Most artists and craftspeople don't have enough time between doing shows and making products to wade through a lot of thick books about Microsoft **Office** or computers in general. You just want a few simple solutions. That is why this section includes:
1. Basic beginner lessons for using **Excel.**
2. 15 ready-made forms, databases, and spreadsheet templates.
3. Tips for using computers and software.

If you are totally new to computers, I recommend you try sitting at the computer with a friend who has some experience. You can learn more about **Windows** in one hour that way than in 20 hours reading a book about computers.

Hopefully you already have Microsoft **Office** installed on your computer. If you don't, **Office** comes with a user's guide to tell you how to install the software.

We have included a basic **Excel** lesson, which, if you need it and you follow the directions carefully, will get you started using spreadsheets. The design work of the spreadsheets has already been done for you. Once you learn how to use and change the spreadsheets and forms we have provided, you will be able to create your own templates as needed.

Different Microsoft Office Configurations

The most popular word processing program worldwide is Microsoft **Word**. The spreadsheet most used for **Windows** computers is Microsoft **Excel**. All of the forms and spreadsheets in this book can be used and modified with **Word** and **Excel**. Microsoft **Office** consists of these two programs, plus other programs depending on which version you buy. It is estimated that 80% of the computers in the world have Microsoft **Office** installed.

If you already have **Word** and **Excel** on your computer, you basically have **Office**. To check, click on Start, then Programs, and look for Microsoft **Word** and/or Microsoft **Excel**. If the installed **Word** and **Excel** is version 6.0 or newer, you are set. To check your version of either program, start the program and click on About under the Help drop-down menu.

If you don't have **Word** or **Excel** already, your best bet is Microsoft **Office, Small Business Edition** Upgrade* Version for about $240. It has **Word** and **Excel** (but not **Access**), and programs you probably don't need. It also includes another program you might find very useful, Microsoft **Publisher**.

Separately, **Publisher** costs under $100 and is well worth the price. I use it quite often for signs, flyers, information sheets and hang tags..

Microsoft **Office, Standard Edition**, consists of Microsoft **Word, Excel,** and **Powerpoint** (but not **Access** or **Publisher**). It usually retails for $400. The upgrade can be found for $190 at Office Depot. You need a previous version of **Office** or **Works** on your computer.

Microsoft **Office, Professional Edition** includes **Access**, a powerful complex database. This version retails for $500. Since you can record your mailing list in **Excel** and then print the labels with **Word** (I will show you how), you don't need **Access**. If you decide you want it later, **Access** can be purchased separately for about $100.

If you have **Excel** but not **Word**, Microsoft has **Works Suite**, consisting of **Word, Works, Encarta, Internet Explorer** and other programs for under $100.

Spreadsheets

Basic Computer Requirements

The <u>minimum</u> hardware requirements to use Microsoft **Office**, **Word** and **Excel**:
A personal computer with a Pentium 500 MHz or faster processor (Pentium 4 recommended)
Windows ME Operating system or newer
500 MB of Ram memory
40 GB of hard-disk space
SVGA Video
An ink jet printer to print out the forms and letters

A used PC computer with a Pentium chip that runs at a speed of 500 mhz, with 256 MB (megabytes) of RAM, a color monitor, and a 40 GB hard drive can be found for under $150. It will run **Windows ME and XP,** older versions of **Office**, and all of the templates mentioned here. It will also be SLOW.

If you are buying a new computer, get the most computer you can comfortably afford. Just keep in mind that a fast Pentium chip is not absolutely necessary to run Microsoft **Office**.

Your printer should be purchased new. Used printers offer too great a risk of faulty performance, for inconsequential savings. Office Depot has ink jet printers starting at $80 and laser printers for under $400. I use an HP Officejet 5610xi ink jet printer. I think the new Kodak printers use cheaper ink.

If you increase the memory in your computer to 1 Mb or more, your programs will run much faster.

How to use Microsoft Excel

Start **Excel** by clicking on the Start button, point to Programs, and then click Microsoft **Excel**. Or click on **Excel** on the **Office** Shortcut bar if you have one.
If the spreadsheet does not fill the screen, click on the middle (Maximize) box in the upper right corner.
Place your cursor on the cell A1. A is on the top row, 1 is a number to the left. Type "5" (don't type the quotation marks). Press enter.
Place the cursor on B and left click. Type "6". Press enter.
Use the right arrow key to go to cell C1 (or move the cursor, then left click). Type "+A1+B1" (without the quotation marks), then press the enter key. The number 11 will now be in cell C1.
Place the cursor on A1 again, and type "3". Press enter. The number 9 will appear in cell C1. The formula in C1 adds the numbers in A1 and B1.
Place the cursor on D1. Type "+sum(a1:c1)", then press enter (make sure it is a colon, not a semicolon.) The number 18 will appear in D1. The sum function in this formula added the numbers in A1, B1, and C1.

Place the cursor on E1. Type "+(A1*D1)", then press enter. The number 54 will appear in E1. The formula reads the * (asterisk) as a multiply command.

Place the cursor in B1. Type "4". Press enter. Now the number in C1 changes to 7 (the formula in C1 adds A1 plus B1). The number in D1 changes to 14, and the number in E1 changes to 42 (A1 multiplied by B1).

Select or highlight cells A1 through D1 by placing the cursor on A1 and holding down the left mouse button as you drag the cursor over B1, C1, and D1. Then select Format>Cells. Click on Alignment; click on the down arrow next to the horizontal box for more choices. Click on Center. Now the numbers are centered in their cells.

Select Format>Cells, then Number and Currency. Click on Okay. Now the numbers will have dollar signs in front of them. To get rid of the zeros to the right of the decimal place, change decimal places where you selected Currency to 0 by clicking on the arrows.

Put the cursor on A1. Select Insert>Rows. Now A1 is empty. Type "March". Move the cursor to B1 and type "April". Move the cursor to C1 and type Total. Press enter, then highlight A1, B1, C1 and click on the Bold Button.

To save this spreadsheet, click on File>Save As. Type a name in the file box, and click the Save button. To print this spreadsheet, chose File>Print

Downloading Spreadsheets

- All of these spreadsheets can be seen and downloaded at www.craftmasters.com/templates.html.

- Just click on the spreadsheet to open it. Excel (if you have it on your computer) will start and the spreadsheet will appear on your screen. You can also chose to download it to your computer and open it later while running Excel. in your computer memory.

Using the Spreadsheets

1. Click on the filename of the spreadsheet you wish to use. When you click on an .xls template, **Excel** will automatically start.
2. You can start Excel first, then open a spreadsheet by clicking on File>Open…from the drop down menu, then finding the spreadsheet.
3. Click on the yellow file folder with the left arrow, until you see Drive C in the window.
4. The examples in this book demonstrates what the form is designed to do and shows you, by example, where to insert your own information. All of the formulas are already in place on the form. To see what they look like, click on the cell, and the formula will appear in the contents window. Don't change the formula.
5. Save the document file with your info under a new file name using the File>Save As command. Save the document file in a different folder (the My Documents folder will work nicely.) This will ensure that any modifications you make will not alter the original form or any other forms you might have open. For the new file name, use a name you can easily remember, such as my prices, 2008 deadlines, 2008 calendar, the name of the customer, etc.
6. Fill in the form using the instructions in this book and save again (using the File>Save command this time, not Save As). Enter data in green or black rectangles. Results (calculations) will appear in red rectangles. <u>Don't enter data in red rectangles!</u> That is where the formulas are. If you accidentally type over a formula in a red rectangle, you can start over by reloading the template from the original directory or disk.
7. Print the form using either the print tool Icon or the File>Print command.

Lincoln Center, New York City, NY

Craft Pricing (pricing.xls)

Use this form to automatically calculate the price of your craft product. It is very simple and useful. Discount and Markup calculators are also included.

Step-by-step instructions:
1. Enter your numbers in column F only. Results appear in column G.
2. Calculate how many pieces you can make in a day. Put that number in the first box. If you take two days to make a piece, put .5 in this box. If you can make 50 pieces from start to finish, put 50 in this box. The spreadsheet will divide this number by 8 to determine how many you make in an hour.
3. Next you enter the salary you want to make a year. Be realistic here. Somewhere between a teacher and a doctor, depending on what you really expect to be able to make. If you have been doing this for a while, enter the amount you made last year. The spreadsheet will divide this number by 1920, which is the number of hours in a working year with 40 hour weeks and 4 weeks off for vacation as a basis.
4. Now you enter the total cost of the materials in each piece. For a jeweler, for example, this would be the silver plus any mechanical parts. Press enter.

The spreadsheet will now calculate your hourly rate, divide it by the pieces per hour, and add materials cost. It will add 15% for overhead, 10% for profit, and show the results in the box next to Distributor price (G7). This is your <u>absolute minimum price</u> for the craft product, out the door of your shop.

The wholesale price is the absolute minimum price plus 15% for a sales rep or other costs of getting your work into a retail store, such as mailing brochures or selling at wholesale trade shows.

The retail price is the wholesale price times 2, which would be the price you sell it at a craft show or the price a store would normally sell it for.

When entering a percent number in the Discounts and Markups section, always use a decimal first. For example, enter .40, not 40 for percent discount in F15.

Spreadsheets

	A	B	C	D	E	F	G
1					**Craft Pricing**		
2							
3							
4	Number of pieces you can complete per day:					40	
5	Amount of salary you want to make per year:					$75,000	
6			Cost of materials per piece:			$3.20	Results:
7					Distributor price:		$13.77
8					Wholesale price:		$15.83
9					Retail price:		$31.66
10							
11							
12					**Discounts**		
13							
14				Original price of item:		$39.00	
15				Percent discount:		40%	
16					Sale price:		$23.40
17					Amount of discount:		$15.60
18							
19				Original price of item:		$39.00	
20				Sale price:		$25.00	
21					Amount of discount:		$14.00
22					Percent discount:		36%
23							
24					**Markups**		
25							
26				Cost of item:		$19.00	
27				Percent markup:		110%	
28					Markup is:		$20.90
29					Selling price is:		$39.90
30							
31				Selling price of item:		$39.00	
32				Cost of item:		$19.00	
33					Percent markup is:		105%
34							
35				Selling price of item:		$39.00	
36				Percent markup:		125%	
37					Cost of item:		$17.33
38							
39							

Craft Fair Application Organizer (organizer.xls)

The purpose of this form is to avoid missing deadlines. When the information you input is sorted by the computer, you will have a list of upcoming deadline dates in the correct order.

Step-by-step instructions:
1. When you receive a brochure or application for a fair in the mail, immediately enter the fair name and deadline information on a printout of this form as shown. You don't have to boot up the computer each time, though. Write the fair information on this form by hand, and every two weeks or so, enter and sort the information on your computer, and print a new updated form. Keep this form in plain sight (not in a drawer!) on the refrigerator or bulletin board where you will see it often to check for approaching deadlines.
2. Enter deadline dates in column C. You don't have to type in the whole date. You can type au 10 and the computer will insert August 10 for you because the column is already formatted to show dates. Type the actual show dates in Column D, July 3-7, for example.
3. Check whether you need photos or slides. The time to check whether the show requires a photo of your booth, or a workshop slide, is when you first get the application. When the deadline is tomorrow, you may not have enough time.
4. After you have put in all of the fairs you are considering, sort the list by the deadline date. To do this, highlight the entire list that you want to sort by dragging the cursor from the upper left of the first entry to the lower right of the last entry. The click on Data>sort, then select deadline (or column C) in the sort by box, and click on the ascending button. Print out the form and post it where you will see it.
5. After entering the information on this form from the application, file the application in the folder for the month the fair takes place. When you apply to the fair, cross it off of this list.
6. When you find out that you are accepted, enter the fair in bold letters on the "Craft Fairs at a Glance" form on the next page.
7. The total of the upcoming show fees is shown at G38.
8. Change headings and columns as needed. Change the heading for Promoter to Motel Reservations, Income, or anything else you would like to note about the fair. You can delete a column by right clicking on the letter at the top of the column and selecting Delete.

Spreadsheets

	A	B	C	D	E	F	G	H
1		Craft Fair Organizer						
2					Photos or	Applied		Accepted?
3	Fair	Promoter	Deadline	Date	Slides	for? y/n	Show Fee	(y/n)
4	Park City	Kimball	2/4/2006	August 3-4	Slides	y	$350	y
5	Ann Arbor	State St.	2/28/2006	July 20-23	Slides	n	$450	
6								
7								
8								
9								
10								
11								
12								
13								
14								
15								
16								
17								
18								
19								
20								
21								
22								
23								
24								
25								
26								
27								
28								
29								
30								
31								
32								
33								
34								
35								
36								
37								
38							$800	

Craft Fairs at a Glance (fair year.xls)

This form shows the fairs for an entire year at a glance, and alerts you to weeks when you don't have a fair. This form is very useful in showing the big picture and helping you get organized.

Step-by-step instructions:
1. Print out this form and tape it up in a conspicuous place.
2. Write in names and dates of all fairs you are considering doing. Write in the dates and name of a fair when you get the application, if you haven't already. You don't need to write the entire name of the fair, just enough so you know which fair it is.
3. When you have some extra time, open this form in the computer and enter the names you had hand written on the previous printed form. Print this out to have a neat yearly calendar of all of your fairs. Indicate any fairs you are accepted in with Bold Type. To do this on the computer, highlight the name of the fair you typed in, then click on the **B** button in the button bar at the top of the page.
4. You can designate fairs applied to but not accepted yet with a question mark (?), fairs you are on the waiting list for with a "w", fairs that you are considering but haven't yet applied for with parenthesis ( ), and fairs you are in with **bold** type.

Utah Arts Festival, Salt Lake City, Utah

Spreadsheets

	A	B	C	D	E	F	G	H	I	J	K
1	**Craft Fairs at a Glance**			For:		Year:					
2	Month	Date	1st Weekend	Date	2nd Weekend	Date	3rd Weekend	Date	4th Weekend	Date	5th Weekend
3											
4	Jan.										
5											
6	Feb.							24-26	Fountain Hills		
7											
8	March										
9											
10	April										
11											
12	May										
13											
14	June			8-12	**Three Rivers**						
15											
16	July							20-23	AnnArbor		
17											
18	Aug.	3-4	Park City								
19											
20	Sept.										
21											
22	Oct.										
23											
24	Nov.										
25											
26	Dec.										
27	Notes:										
28											
29	**Bold type indicates Accepted.**			Normal type indicates applied for			( ) indicates "considering, not applied yet".				

Craft Fair Equipment List (equipment.xls)

Use this list to keep track of what to bring to a craft fair. It will certainly dampen your spirits to drive 500 miles to do a fair and discover that you have left something important behind. Glance over this list just before leaving for every fair.

Step-by-step instructions:
1. Change or delete any of the items in column A just by typing over them. Add other items as needed, such as different displays, kinds of stock, etc.
2. Print out a copy of this form, with the "Packed" and "Need" columns either filled out or blank, to be filled in by hand.

If you are interested in the value of what you have or need to get, or for planning or insurance purposes, insert the value in the Cost columns. The combined totals will appear in I35.

▫ Spreadsheet Tip

Do you have unexplained information in Excel cells? If a spreadsheet cell shows #####, it means that the cell is not wide enough to show the whole number. You can select the cell, click Format>Cells, Number to change the way the number is formatted. Or you can use Format>Column, Autofit Selection to adjust the column's width. Or you could just use the mouse, click on the line at the right top of the column, and drag to make the column wider.

Art in the Park, Boulder City, Nevada

Spreadsheets

	A	B	C	D	E	F	G	H	I
1				Craft Fair Equipment List					
2									
3	Item	Packed	Need	Cost		Item	Packed	Need	Cost
4	Canopy	x				Stock	x		
5	Walls or Backdrop	x				Calculator	x		
6	Stakes	x				Sales Tax Certificate			
7	Weights					Tax Chart			
8	Banner					Receipt Book			
9	Tables	x				Pens			
10	Chairs	x				Charge Machine	x		
11	Table Cloths	x				Charge Slips	x		
12	Display Cases	x				Bags			
13	Display Boards	x				Change			
14	Duct Tape		x	$4.00		Price tags			
15	Hammer					Business Cards	x		
16	Screwdriver	x				Brochures			
17	Pliers					Signs (pre-made)			
18	C-Clamps	x				Marker	x		
19	Push-pins					Sign materials			
20	Nails					Mailing List Book			
21	Safety-pins					Hang Tags	x		
22	Glue					Order Forms			
23	Extension Cord	x				Cooler	x		
24	Lighting					Thermos			
25	Extra Bulbs					Food			
26	First Aid Kit	x				Snacks			
27	Fire Extinguisher					Fair Information			
28	Fire Retardant Cert.					Parking pass			
29	Bungee Cords					State Map			
30	Rope	x				Fair Map			
31	Mirror								
32									
33				$4.00					$0.00
34									
35							Total Value		$4.00

Craft Show Expense Report (expenses.xls)

This form will show you how much you <u>really</u> make at a craft fair. It will also help you record business trip expenses for later deduction on your Schedule C at tax time. There are limits on the deductions allowable for costs of meals and transportation.

Generally you must be away from your hometown to deduct travel expenses on business trips. Craft fairs and trade shows are considered temporary business locations and your necessary expenses in getting to and from the fairs are considered business expenses and not commuting expenses (which are not deductible). You must keep records and receipts to support your deduction of these expenses.

The following expenses of a business trip away from home are deductible:
Plane, railroad, taxi and other transportation fares
Hotel and lodging expenses
Meal costs (50%)
Tips, telephone, and fax costs
Laundry and cleaning expenses
Excess baggage charges (including insurance)

Your tax home is your place of business, regardless of where you maintain your family residence. This tax home includes the entire city or general area of your business premises. Your residence may be your tax home if your income is dependent on craft fairs at widely scattered locations, you have no other fixed place of work, and your residence is in a location economically suited for your work.

Step-by-step instructions:
1. Enter your headings as shown and enter your physical location for each day in row 7 (traveling to or from, or at show).
2. Enter all expenses for the show as shown. Enter booth fee or deposit in B29, and put commission paid (if any) in row 29.
3. Net income shown at I33 is equal to show income minus expenses and show fees.
4. In this example the show fee is shown on Wednesday and the 20% commission given to the promoter at the end of the show is shown on Friday.
5. This form is set up for a weekend craft fair. For a trade show during the week, change the days of the week at the top to begin with Sunday instead of Wednesday.

Spreadsheets

Show Expense Report

Show Name: Tempe   Artist: _____
Starting Date: 4/1/2006   Ending Date: 4/3/2006
Comments: _____

	A	B	C	D	E	F	G	H	I
6	Date	Wednesday	Thursday	Friday	Saturday	Sunday	Monday	Tuesday	Totals
7	Location								
8	Lodging		$32.00	$32.00	$32.00	$32.00			$128.00
9	Breakfast			$5.40	$6.30	$3.95			$15.65
10	Lunch			$3.00	$3.50	$6.00			$12.50
11	Dinner			$11.50	$18.00	$7.40			$36.90
12	Phone								$0.00
13	Laundry								$0.00
14	Baggage								$0.00
15	**Sub-totals**	**$0.00**	**$32.00**	**$51.90**	**$59.80**	**$49.35**	**$0.00**	**$0.00**	$193.05
16	Airfare								$0.00
17	Train								$0.00
18	Cab								$0.00
19	Tips								$0.00
20	**Sub-totals**	**$0.00**	**$0.00**	**$0.00**	**$0.00**	**$0.00**	**$0.00**	**$0.00**	$0.00
21	Gas/Oil		$105.00				$121.00		$226.00
22	Parking			$15.00	$15.00	$15.00			$45.00
23	Tolls								$0.00
24	Rentals								$0.00
25	**Sub-total**	**$0.00**	**$105.00**	**$15.00**	**$15.00**	**$15.00**	**$121.00**	**$0.00**	$271.00
26									
27	Total Exp.	**$0.00**	**$137.00**	**$66.90**	**$74.80**	**$64.35**	**$121.00**	**$0.00**	$464.05
28									
29	Show Fees	$550.00							$550.00
30									
31	Show Sales			$521	$794	$336			$1,651
32									
33	Signature: _____					**Net Income from Show**			**$636.95**

Spreadsheets

Customer Mailing List (customer.xls)

This is a list of your current and past customers. All you do is enter the address from every check that you get at a craft fair or show. In addition you can use a guest book to get addresses. You have the customers enter their name and address whenever they buy something using a credit card or cash instead of a check.

Your list should consist of actual satisfied customers who know your work. Notify them of new products and upcoming craft fairs where they can buy from you. When you send them a brochure, ask them to pass it along to someone they know who might like to buy your products.

Step-by-step instructions:
1. In **Excel**, open customer.xls. Select Data>Form to see the database format. Enter information as shown. If you don't need information in a specific blank, just skip it.
2. Use the Tab key to move from field to field.
3. Use Enter or arrow keys to move to the next record.
4. The example shown on the next page is for the database view in **Excel**.
5. To print labels, use the envelopes and labels function in **Word**. (See below for information how to do this).

▫ <u>To print mailing labels in Microsoft Word:</u>
1. Open Word, select Tools, Mail Merge.
2. Under 1. Main Document, click on Create, Mailing Labels, Active window.
3. Under 2, Data Source, Get Data, Open Data Source.
4. In the Open Data Source window, select Files of type (at the bottom)—MS Excel Worksheets (*.xls). Then browse file up or down to find your listofgalleries.xls and open it. Ignore the first window that says something about asap utilities (click OK), then in the little Microsoft Excel window, select Database.
5. A window opens that says Set up main document.
6. Select Avery standard, then select 5160 address labels. Click okay.
7. In the Create Labels window that opens, click on Insert Merge Field, and put the name on the first line.
8. Press enter to go to the next line and click on insert merge field again and put the address on the second line. Put the city, state and zip on the third line.
9. Click okay, then click on #. Merge. In the Merge window that opens, click on All, then Merge again. Your labels will appear. Put in mail label (1x2 5/8 paper 5160) and print your labels.

Spreadsheets

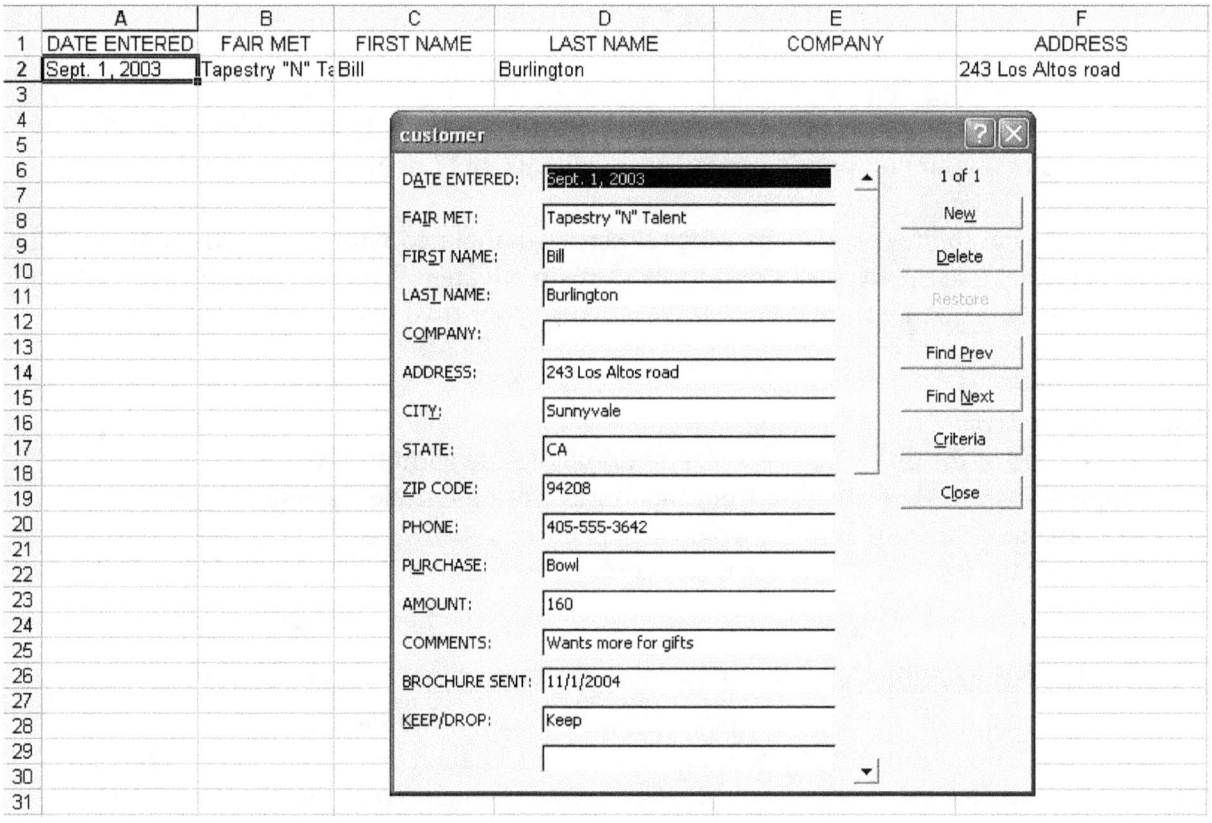

Trade Show Costs (trade show.xls)

Trade shows can be expensive, and may not produce immediate profits. However, they are a great way to meet distributors, your competition, retail store owners and buyers, and even sales reps.

Beside the cost of the booth, there are many other expenses associated with doing a trade show. This form will help you calculate the expenses of a trade show in advance. You may find areas in which you can cut some costs. You might save money if you build your own display and shipping cartons for it.

Step-by-step instructions:
1. Enter the names of the cities that you plan to do wholesale shows in row 6.
2. The sample shown has information from brochures from the trade shows.
3. Row 21 contains data from dividing your display cost by 4.
4. Row 30 shows the total expenses for each show.

☐ **Use Microsoft Word to print a sheet of return address labels**

Using the Label function in **Word**, you can print an entire sheet of the same label to create return address labels. Select Tools>Envelopes and Labels, then Labels, then Options. Select Avery standard and select 5160-Address for the Product number. Click OK, Type in your return address in the Address: Box. Click on New Document, and print as many pages as you need.

	A	B	C	D	E
1					
2			Trade Show Expenses		
3					
4			NATIONAL AND REGIONAL TRADE SHOWS		
5					
6			San Francisco	Los Angeles	New York
7		One booth....................	$2,200		$2,800
8		Two showcases...............	$200		$300
9		Two tables with draping..........	$150		$250
10		Four chairs...................	$80		$300
11		500 watts power.................	$65		$130
12		Four flood lights..................			
13		Housing & transportation			
14		for two staff and merchandise			
15		from Los Angeles................	$1,300		$1,900
16		Expenses for 2 staff..........	$600		$500
17		Totals:	$4,595	$0	$6,180
18					
19		Custom display			
20		(amortized over 4 years			
21		per show)...................			
22		Storage & shipping			
23		of custom display			
24		per show....................			$800
25		Set up & disassembly			
26		charges for custom			
27		display per show................			$300
28		Totals:	$0	$0	$1,100
29					
30		Amount to sell to break even:	$4,595	$0	$7,280
31					

Sales Representative Agreement (repagreement.doc)

Using a sales representative is another way to get your craft creations into stores. A good rep will not only take your samples to stores and take orders, but he or she will often have a booth at several major trade shows as well. They can also get your work into areas of the country that you can't reach.

The sales representative agreement example shown here has a 15% commission. That is 15% of the wholesale price, not the retail price. 15% is the craft industry average. High-priced items may call for a 5% or 10% commission, while very low-priced items may require a 20% - 30% commission. You can easily change the commission in this agreement with your computer.

Step-by-step instructions:
1. Read this agreement closely before using it. Change any time periods and percentages that you wish.
2. Fill in the territory that you want the rep to cover exclusively.

You may want the rep to pay for the samples or put a deposit before taking them.

☐ <u>Putting shortcuts on your desktop</u>

If you use a file very often, you can place it on your desktop. Open Explorer, and select the file. Hold down CTRL and Shift, and drag the file to the desktop. You now have a shortcut that when clicked on, will first load the file and the program that uses it. An even easier way is to right click on the file while in Explorer, select Send <u>T</u>o, and chose Desktop as Shortcut. Now look for the icon on your desktop. Right click on it and select Rename to give the shortcut icon a shorter name.

Sales Representative Agreement

This agreement is made on _____ (date) between _____ (name of sales representative), herein referred to as "sales rep", of _____ (address of sales representative)

and _____ (name of artist or craftsperson), herein referred to

as "we" or "artist", of _____ (address of artist or craftsperson).

This agreement shall be in force for the period of one year and shall continue thereafter for one-year periods unless either party gives notice to the other in writing three months in advance of the renewal date or on that date for a date three months hence.

The above sales rep shall be our exclusive representative to the gift shops and craft stores and galleries, in the following territory or states:

_____

We expect the sales rep to give this territory complete and thorough coverage for which a commission of 15% will be paid on all invoices of sales made by the sales rep.

Commission payments will be sent to the sales rep on the 15th of each month, accompanied by copies of invoices for all the billing to trade accounts in the above territory. All expenses of travel and maintenance will be paid by the sales representative. The sales rep will call on major accounts at least once a month.

We grant the sales rep the right of access at all times to our copies of all invoices to enable him (or her) to ascertain the correctness of our commission payments to him.

We agree that the sales rep's services to this company are not exclusive (meaning that the sales representative will continue to represent other companies).

We will provide product samples as needed for "selling tools". These samples will be replaced by us when damaged. These samples will remain our property and will be returned at the end of this agreement. These samples have a value of _____ (dollars), and the sales rep shall post a deposit with us for that amount, which will be refunded upon return of the samples in good condition.

The sales rep will only be paid commissions for sales made directly by him to accounts in this territory during the time of this agreement.

Date: _____

Sales representative's signature: _____
Artist's or craftsperson's signature: _____

Gallery Database (gallery list.xls)

You can use this database to keep track of gift shops and craft galleries you currently do business with (or plan to). You can also use it with the galleries list on the CD-Rom. You can note when you contacted them, or mailed them a brochure, and whether or not they have ordered.

Step-by-step instructions:
1. Select Data>Form to get to form view.
2. Use the tab key to go from field to field.
3. The keep and drop fields are used for sorting active from inactive galleries.
4. Save your mailing list as an Excel worksheet.

▢ Spreadsheet Tips

Sorting your mail list in an Excel database
To sort data, click Data>Sort. A dialog box will pop up, letting you specify how you want the data sorted. You can sort up to three levels. Select the first field you want to sort by and select Ascending order. Make sure the Header Row button is selected. To perform a more complex sort, select the criteria to sort by for the second and third levels. For example, if first and last names are different fields in your database, you may want to first sort by last name and then by first name in case some records have the same last name.

Filtering your database
If you want all of the names from a specific ZIP code or city, use AutoFilter to filter out unwanted records, leaving a list of those you want. The rest of the records are hidden from view. You can save the filtered database under a new name, without altering the first database. Choose Data>AutoFilter and an arrow appears at the top of each column in your database. Click on the arrow and a drop-down list displays all of the values that appear in that field. Chose Custom to specify values equal to what you want.

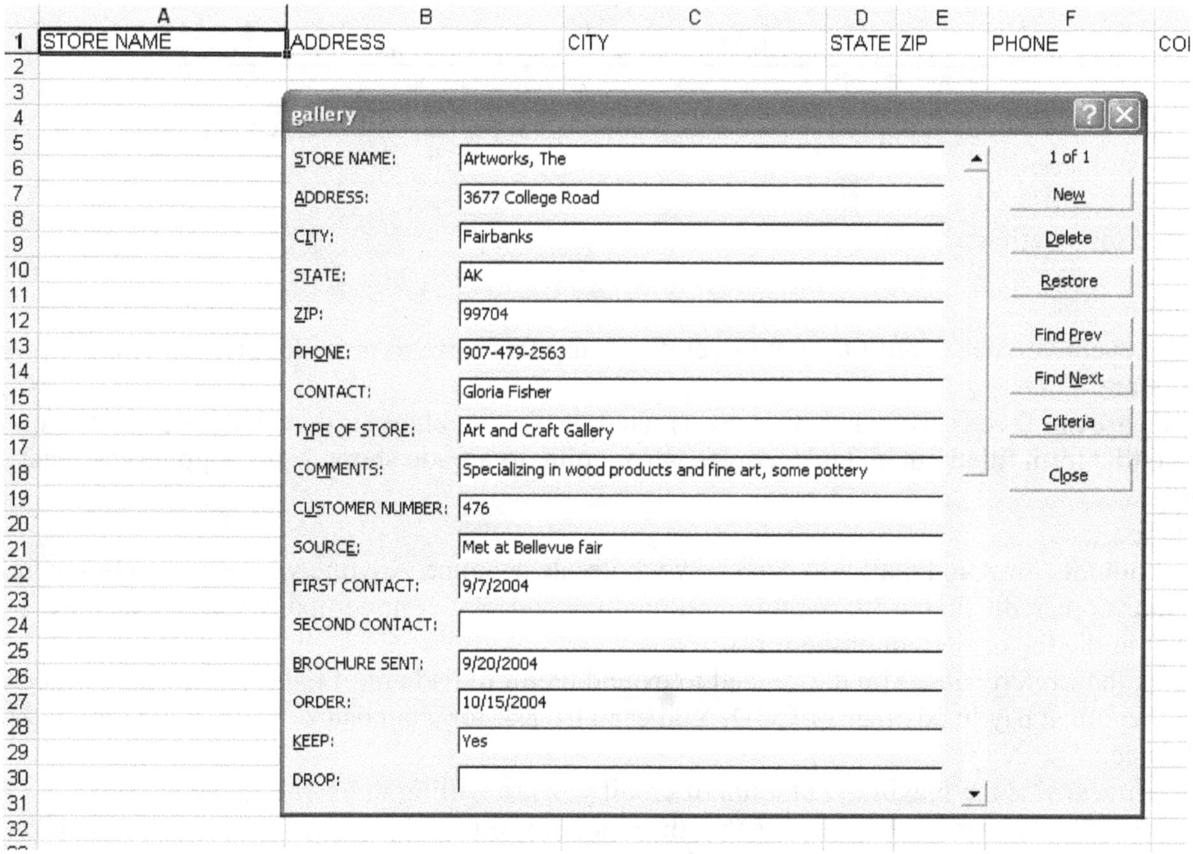

Spreadsheets

	A	B	C	D	E	F	
1	STORE NAME	ADDRESS	CITY	STATE	ZIP	PHONE	CO

gallery — 1 of 1

- STORE NAME: Artworks, The
- ADDRESS: 3677 College Road
- CITY: Fairbanks
- STATE: AK
- ZIP: 99704
- PHONE: 907-479-2563
- CONTACT: Gloria Fisher
- TYPE OF STORE: Art and Craft Gallery
- COMMENTS: Specializing in wood products and fine art, some pottery
- CUSTOMER NUMBER: 476
- SOURCE: Met at Bellevue fair
- FIRST CONTACT: 9/7/2004
- SECOND CONTACT:
- BROCHURE SENT: 9/20/2004
- ORDER: 10/15/2004
- KEEP: Yes
- DROP:

Buttons: New, Delete, Restore, Find Prev, Find Next, Criteria, Close

California Gift Show (setting up), Los Angeles, California

Credit Application (credit application.doc)

This form can be used both to apply for credit for your craft supplies, and to extend credit to your wholesale customers.

Step-by-step instructions:

To apply for credit:
1. In the event you need credit for your operations, use this form to provide references to your supplier.
2. If you are not D & B (Dun and Bradstreet) rated, leave that blank or delete it from your form.
3. Have this form filled out and take copies when going to a trade show. Most suppliers will ask for it.

To extend credit:
1. Print out this form and mail it to each new wholesale account. Anyone who wants to buy your products on credit should fill out this credit application. Put your company name and address either at the top or bottom of the form.
2. Check their references. You don't need to extend credit to bad credit risks. If they don't check out they must pay in advance or COD. You can also ask for a deposit or partial payment in advance.

Credit line requested is the maximum amount of credit you are willing to extend to the gallery.
Usual terms are 2% 10, net 30. That means that the amount is due and payable in 30 days, with a 2% discount (reward) if payment is received in 10 days.

More Spreadsheet Tips

Resizing Excel columns or rows
You can quickly and easily resize columns and rows in **Excel**. All you have to is point your mouse over the right side of a column letter or the bottom of a row number, click, and drag the edge of the row over until you are happy with its size.

Finding information about items in Excel
You can quickly find out information about any button, icon, cell and so on, by simply pressing Shift + F1, and clicking on the item in question.

Credit Application and References

Company Name_____Date_____

Address_____City_____State_____Zip_____

Owner/Manager_____Tel.No._____

How long in business?_____D & B Rated_____

Business Type __Sole Proprietorship ___Partnership ___Corporation in State of _____

Person to contact regarding purchase orders and invoice payments:

Name:_____Title_____Phone_____

Trade References:

Company_____Address_____

Contact _____Phone_____

Company_____Address_____

Contact_____Phone_____

Company_____Address_____

Contact_____Phone_____

Bank References:

Name_____Address_____

_____Account. #_____

Name_____Address_____

_____Account. #_____

Credit line requested:

$_____

The undersigned authorizes inquiry as to credit information and certifies the above information to be true. We further acknowledge that credit privileges, if granted, may be withdrawn at any time.

Signed:_____

Position: _____Date:____

Consignment Agreement (consignment.doc)

This is an agreement made between a gallery and a craftsperson, when the craftsperson elects to place his or her craft products in a store without advance payment, in order to receive a larger amount (60%) payable when the craft is sold.

I won't go into the pros and cons of consignment here. Most craftspeople don't like it, but for some it is the only way to sell their crafts. However you feel about it, if you place your product in a store without payment, a written agreement is necessary to protect your rights.

Step-by-step instructions:
1. In this form, the consignee is the gallery, and you are the seller. Change the percentage of the proceeds that is to be deducted by the gallery if necessary. Forty percent is the usual amount.
2. Describe the crafts you are placing in the store. If there is not enough room you can create a separate list.
3. Fill in the number of days you want to keep your merchandise in the store.
4. Read this form carefully. Check the insurance provisions, when the proceeds are paid, advertising materials, and termination notification.
5. The agreement is not valid unless signed by both parties.

☐ Keyboard shortcuts

You don't need a chart with all the keyboard shortcuts, nor do you have to remember them. Notice that File, Edit, and the other menus at the top of the page have a letter underlined. If you hold down the Alt key and press the letter, the menu drops down. Then simply type the underlined letter in the menu to select it. For example, to see a print preview, press the Alt key and F (for File menu, and the f does not have to be capitalized), then V (the "V" is underlined in Print Preview). To return to normal, press the Alt key and V (for View menu), then N (for Normal). Other useful commands using the keyboard are Control key and P for print, control and X for copy, and control and Y for paste.

Spreadsheets

Consignment Agreement

This agreement is made on _____ (date) between _____(store, herein referred to as "Consignee") and _____(artist, herein referred to as "Seller") as follows:

Seller hereby consigns to Consignee the following described merchandise, to be displayed at a prominent place at Consignee's premises and offered for sale at the price set forth, of which the designated percentage of 40% shall be deducted out of proceeds by Consignee for its compensation.

Quantity	Merchandise Description	Price
_____	_____	_____
_____	_____	_____
_____	_____	_____
_____	_____	_____
_____	_____	_____

Said merchandise shall be displayed until the earlier of sale or when ____days have elapsed.

Sales tax shall be collected and paid by consignee and shall not be considered part of the price nor subject to percentage allocation.

Merchandise is to be delivered by Seller in good and salable condition and free of defects.

Consignee shall maintain the merchandise with care, shall keep it insured for theft and damage, and shall make all reasonable efforts to comply with seller's instructions for the care of the merchandise. In the event Consignee fails to do so, Consignee shall be liable for the price for said merchandise set forth above, less the percentage thereof allocated to Consignee.

Consignee shall sell only at the price listed herein, unless authorized by Seller to sell at a different price. At the end of each month, Consignee shall account for and pay to Seller all proceeds of sales of the merchandise consigned by Seller.

Should the merchandise remain unsold at the end of the consignment period and an election made by the Consignee or Seller to remove said merchandise, any costs incurred by the delivery of same to Seller shall be borne by Seller and deducted from any proceeds then due the Seller.

Any advertising or other promotional materials provided by the Seller shall be returned in good condition after all merchandise is sold, or this agreement is terminated, or upon request of Seller.

This agreement may be terminated by either party upon sixty (60) days written notice.

This agreement is made under and shall be construed under the laws of the State of _____.

Consignee's signature_____

Seller's Signature_____

Monthly Accounting System (bookkeeping.xls)

There are two primary reasons to keep records of a business operation: they are required by law, and they are useful to you as the manager of your craft business.

This 12-month spreadsheet will satisfy all requirements by the IRS for record keeping (you must save your receipts and wholesale invoices, of course). All you have to do is enter your income and your expenses as they occur. The spreadsheet does the rest.

Step-by-step instructions:
1. Load **Excel**, then open the template accounts.xls from your Forms and Spreadsheets folder.
2. Enter the year in J2. Green boxes are for entering data.
3. Enter your company name in D3. Words typed in green are meant to be typed over. They will show up on your printout.
4. Enter the amount of tax (or tax included) in A3. If you have only one retail location this will be the sales tax you charge. If you have several retail locations or fairs in different states that have different tax rates, use an average here. This will show you approximately how much you need to set aside for sales tax. If you don't enter anything in these two boxes, it won't affect the rest of the template.
5. Enter the percentage in A4 of the amount of Social Security tax (FICA) you will be required to pay at the end of the year. This was 15.3% for 2006. This will give you a report each month for the total you will need to set aside for the year.
6. Enter income from direct sales in Column D and wholesale income in Column D.
7. Enter merchandise (products you resell) in Column I and supplies (fair fees, office supplies, etc., which you use) in Column J.
8. Rows 41-47 have formulas in them that show the results for the month. They have red borders to show you not to enter data in them.
9. Rows 591-597 will show you totals for the whole year.

This is a 12 page, 12-month template. If you only want to print one page and not the entire 12 months, select File, Print, then click on Page(s) from 1 to 1 (or 4 to 4, etc.) To print a specific area of a page, highlight the area by dragging the cursor from the upper left to the lower right of the area (or range), then select File, Print.

Spreadsheets

	A	B	C	D	E	F	G	H	I	J
1			**Monthly Accounting System**							
2								Montl	January	2006
3		0.06103	(Sales Tax)			Your Company Name				
4		0.153	(F.I.C.A.)							
5								EXPENSES		
6			INCOME				To Whom	Check		
7	Descript.	Date	Retail	Wholesale		Date	Paid	No.	Merch.	Supplies
8										
9		1				2	Pittsbgh App	631		350.00
10		2				2	Post Office	632		37.00
11		3				6	Columbus	633		20.00
12	Tucson	4	1342.00			6	Columbus	634		400.00
13		5	879.00							
14		6	983.00							
15		7								
16		8								
17		9								
18		10								
19		11								
20		12								
21		13								
22		14								
23		15								
24	Sunshine Gall	16		450.00						
25		17								
26		18								
27		19								
28		20								
29		21								
30		22								
31		23								
32		24								
33		25								
34		26								
35		27								
36		28								
37		29								
38		30								
39		31								
40										
41		Month total:	3204.00	450.00			Total Expenses:		0.00	807.00
42		Previous total:	0.00	0.00			Previous total:		0.00	0.00
43		Year total:	3204.00	450.00			Total for year:		0.00	807.00
44		Sales tax:	195.54				Monthly net income:		2847.00	
45		Prev. tax:	0.00				F.I.C.A. tax:		435.59	
46		Gross income YTD:		3654.00			Net income YTD:			2847.00
47		Sales tax YTD:	195.54				F.I.C.A. YTD:			435.59

Invoice (invoice.xls)

This form is sent to the customer as a request for payment. It can be mailed before the product is shipped, or with the product. It is only sent once. (Additional requests for payments are called statements. A statement consists of a list of all unpaid invoices.)

You keep a copy of this for yourself and mark it "paid" when you receive payment.

Step-by-step instructions:
1. Fill in your company name and address as shown. You can save a copy with just your name and address as a template and use it when starting a new invoice.
2. Enter Sold To, Ship To, and Price information. If there is nothing in Column A, Column G won't calculate.
3. If this is a taxable retail sale, enter 1 in G10, if wholesale enter 0 (zero, not the letter O).
4. If the order is prepaid, enter a 1 in G11. This will calculate a 2% discount in G33. If you want to change the discount rate, change the formula in G33 from 0.02 to 0.01 for example. A 2% discount may encourage prepayment.
5. The tax charge (for a retail order if 1 is entered in G12) in G34 is based on the rate in your state that you enter in C32. To enter 7%, enter .07, not 7.
6. Enter shipping charges that you pay in G35.
7. Enter any prepaid amount in G37. G38 shows the amount due.
8. Totals are calculated automatically.

You can add the following additional statements under the Invoice heading, depending on what you would like the customer to do:
"Please pay from this invoice; no statement will be issued."
"Payment due on receipt of this invoice. Items will be shipped on payment."

Spreadsheets

	A	B	C	D	E	F	G
1				**Invoice**			
2							
3						Date:	
4		From:	Your Company Name			Invoice Number:	4201
5					Customer Order # or Account #:		
6						Terms:	Net 30
7						Salesperson:	Tom
8						Shipped Via:	
9		SEND PAYMENT & INQUIRIES TO				Shipper Number:	
10		ABOVE ADDRESS. REFER TO INVOICE			Taxable? (1=yes,0=no):		0
11		NUMBER IN ALL CORRESPONDENCE.			Prepaid? (1=yes,0=no):		0
12							
13		Sold To:	Company Name		Ship to:	Same	
14							
15							
16							
17							
18					Zone:		Cust. #:
19	Quantity	Quantity	Stock			Unit	
20	Ordered	Shipped	Number	Description		Price	Total
21	7	7		Barettes		$12.00	$84.00
22	3	3		Goblets		$22.00	$66.00
23							
24							
25							
26							
27							$0.00
28							
29							
30							
31							
32	State Sales Tax:		7.00%			Subtotal:	$150.00
33	Pulled by:				(If pre-paid: 2% Discount):		$0.00
34	Checked by:					State Sales Tax:	$0.00
35						Shipping and handling:	
36						Total:	$150.00
37		THANK YOU FOR YOUR ORDER!				Amount Paid:	
38						TOTAL DUE:	$150.00
39		Make checks payable to:					
40	Note: A service charge of 1 1/2% will be added to all						
41	invoices unpaid in 30 days and every month thereafter.						

Business Plan (business plan.doc)

This one-page business plan is a "personal success" business plan, as opposed to a "formal" business plan used to obtain financing from banks. Making a business plan will force you to think about what choices you must make to have a more successful business.

Review and modify this plan every 6 months. Notice how well (or how poorly) you have estimated your costs, goals, etc.

Guidelines:

1. Structure—Sole proprietorship, partnership, corporation
2. Background—List the skills required to make and market your products.
3. Qualifications—Why are you especially qualified to make these products?
4. Products—List all of the products you make.
5. Short description of product—Describe product in one sentence. If you cannot describe your product concisely, the user will not recognize their need for it.
6. Long description—Describe products and their purpose.
7. Features—List up to 5 features that benefit or interest customers.
8. Cost—How much do your materials cost and can costs be reduced?
9. Pricing strategy—Are your prices high, medium, or low relative to the market?
10. Uniqueness—List at least one unique feature of your product.
11. Competition—How do their costs, pricing, and quality compare to yours?
12. Customers—List their average age, education, and profession.
13. Interests—What motivates your customers to buy? Status, quality, price?
14. Customer benefits—How does your product improve the customers' quality of life?
15. Marketing plan—Advertising, trade shows, promotional activities, yearly sales objectives, price, packaging, support, etc.
16. New products—What products are you planning in addition to the ones you have now?
17. One-year goal—Where will your business be in one year in terms of monthly income, net assets (money in the bank), name recognition, number of customers, etc.?
18. Five-year goal—Same as above, except for five years.
19. Ten-year goal—What would you like to be doing in ten years, in terms of your craft?

Spreadsheets

One Page Business Plan

Company Name: _____

Structure: _____

Owner's Name: _____

Background: _____

Qualifications: _____

Products: _____

Short Description of Products: _____

Long Description: _____

_____

Features:

1. _____

2. _____

3. _____

Cost: _____

_____

Pricing Strategy: _____

Uniqueness: _____

Competition: _____

Customers: _____

Interests: _____

Customer Benefits: _____

Marketing Plan: _____

New Products: _____

One year goal: _____

Five year goal: _____

Ten year goal: _____

Inventory (inventory.xls)

Many small craft business owners overlook the importance of inventory management. Running out of stock (products) causes you to lose customers and sales. Too much stock reduces your cash, limiting your growth and creating a risk that your stock will become obsolete before you can sell it. A close watch on your inventory is very important. If you use this form on a regular basis you will know at a glance what you have in stock and what you need to make.

This form calculates both the parts value and finished value, and tells you when to order parts (as your inventory drops below a certain level). The parts inventory column will work well when there is only one or a single group of parts in your product. Fill in the number of parts on hand and the cost per unit.

If there are too many component parts in your craft, just use this form for finished products. Fill in the required inventory level that you feel comfortable with (five shows worth, for example). You might want more for an approaching Christmas season.

Step-by-step instructions:
1. Fill in as shown in sample. Columns E, I, and J have formulas in them.
2. Required Inventory Level is the minimum number of items you want to have on hand at any time. The last column shows how many more products you have to make or parts to order.
3. The number in C33 is the number of parts on hand that need to be made. The other numbers in row 33 indicate the inventory value of unfinished parts and finished products.
4. This example shows parts and finished value of barrettes. These barrettes each have a metal clip. To help the craftsperson decide what to order, this spreadsheet adds the number of clips on hand to the number of finished barrettes. It then compares it to the minimum number of total barrettes (required inventory level, column H) you would like to have on hand, and shows the number of parts to order in column J. Even though it says 17 in the To Order column, you would go ahead and order a batch of 50. If you waited until it indicated 50 in the To Order column, you would have none left and probably not enough time to order and make them before you needed them. So, if any amount is shown in the To Order column J, order the usual quantity.

Spreadsheets

	A	B	C	D	E	F	G	H	I	J
1					Inventory					
2										
3	**Department:**							**Date:**		
4			Present	Parts Cost	Present	Present	Finished	Required	Finished	
5			Parts	per	Parts	Finished	Value	Inventory	Inventory	To
6	**Description**	#	Inventory	Unit	Value	Inventory	per unit	Level	Value	Order
7	Barette		211	$0.80	$169	19	$33	15	$627	
8										
...										
32										
33		To make:	211		$169				$627	0
34										

Marketing Plan (marketing plan.xls)

A marketing plan will be nearly as useful to you as your business plan. This plan will indicate if you are using your marketing tools in the best way, and will focus your attention on those marketing activities that are most likely to work, as well as those that are most affordable. It will also give you a total anticipated marketing budget.

Step-by-step instructions:
1. Decide which customers you are targeting with each marketing tool.
2. Enter dates when you plan to use the tool. Enter the time allowed or actually spent on each specific marketing technique.
3. Enter the projected total cost in column F until or unless the actual cost is known.

Learn as much as possible about the market which you'll be targeting.

Who are your potential customers?
How many?
Where are they located?
Where do they now buy the crafts you want to sell them?
Can you offer them anything they are not getting now?
How can you persuade them to do business with you?

The marketing process involves three steps:
1. Budgeting, calculated by what you can afford.
2. Determining the best way to reach customers and prospects without wasting your money.
3. Gathering facts on the advertising media and their market to justify the dollars to be spent.

Spreadsheets

	A	B	C	D	E	F
1		**Marketing Plan**				
2						
3		Target	Date	Date	Hours	
4		Customers	Started	Compl.	Spent	Cost
5	Mailing List	Galleries	Apr. 19	Apr. 30	40	$300
6	Letterheads	All			2	$35
7	Business Cards	All			2	$50
8	Logo					
9	Color Photography for Brochure	Galleries			5	$700
10	Press Release	Fairs			4	$50
11	B & W Photos for Press Release					
12	Brochures					
13	Color Postcards	All			9	$190
14	Signs					
15	Portfolio					
16	Newspaper Advertising					
17	Magazine Advertising	All			15	$1,200
18	Radio Advertising					
19	Internet Website	All			20	$300
20	Catalog Company					
21				Total:	97	$2,825
22						
23	Projections (Goals)					
24	Gross Sales First Year	$110,000				
25	Gross Sales Second Year	$130,000				

Press Release (press release.doc)

Send a press release to all of the local media at a craft fair that you are going to be doing to generate public awareness of you, your unique product, and the fair as well. A press release is also useful in promoting your craft at a local store, and the store will appreciate the free advertising. You can also send it to magazines those gallery owners read.

Not every press release will be accepted by the media, but whatever is accepted will be a form of free advertising for you. An interesting angle could be the environmental aspects or safety issues involved with the creation or use of your product. A new product, a contest promotion, something charitable or anything unusual about your business is a newsworthy event and worth letting the media know about.

A press release has more credibility than an ad, because it will appear only if it meets the standards of the editor.

You can reach more periodicals with it than you could afford to reach through paid advertising. A news story or magazine article takes more time to read than an ad. The more time a reader spends with your story, the more likely he or she is to remember you.

Step-by-step Instructions:
1. Fill in the name, address and contact information. Use a headline that will grab the reader's attention.
2. Fill in the date and place of the event. Editors want to be able to use your press release without changes. In the body of the press release, tell whom, what, when, where, and why. Put the important information at the beginning. Don't forget to include a brief background of the artist.
3. Use 10 point type to get this press release all on one page if possible. Notice the text is always double-spaced. Use the number -30- to show the end of the press release, followed by directions to the editor, if needed.
4. After you have written your announcement, call up the newspaper, ask for the name of the city editor, and be sure you have the correct spelling of his or her name and the exact address. This is common courtesy and is extremely important to some media people.
5. Take a picture of yourself holding your craft or working in your shop. Have the picture blown up to an 8 x 10 or 5 x 7 glossy black-and-white print. Send this along with your press release. Don't expect photos back unless you include a SASE.

Press Release

For Immediate Release

Rocklin Jewelry
7865 Thomson St.
Clayton, CA 95447
707-987-5843
Contact: Randy Rocklin

Local Jeweler Introduces New Tru-Stone Product For a Safer Environment.

Feb. 27, 2007, Clayton, CA--Alan Hardy, a professional jeweler living in Clayton, California, announces his use of a new stone product for his handcrafted inlay rings. The product is called Tru-Stone, a professionally recognized substitute for Turquoise.

Mr. Hardy began using this product after realizing that his customers were concerned about the open pit mining of copper and its by-product Turquoise and were boycotting the gemstone.

Tru-Stone consists of lower grades of Turquoise mixed with epoxy under very high pressure. The result is a totally homogenous stone product with a wide range of characteristics superior to conventional Turquoise. It is stable and not affected by extremes in temperature or moisture. When ground and polished, sanded and buffed to a satin or gloss finish, Tru-Stone produces a beautiful and long lasting stone product.

Mr. Hardy's rings made from Tru-Stone are available in many unique shapes. A selection of his rings will be on display and available for purchase at the Peach Blossom Festival in Beck's Park in Atlanta on April 26 and 27.

-30-

Letterheads (letterheads.doc)

These are samples of letterheads you can create with only your word processor. To use one of these, select one you like, then type over with your own name, address and phone number. You can change the fonts to any fancy font you like. Use Insert Picture to add a logo.

Step-by-step instructions:
1. Delete the letterheads you don't need and move yours to the top of the page
2. Save it with a file new name. Instant letterhead! No trip to the offset printer necessary.
3. You can print this out, make copies, and then use them in your printer for future letters.
4. Or you can load this letterhead into your word processor, and start typing directly on it.

Fourth Avenue Street Fair, Tucson, Arizona

Letterheads

Richard Adam   Jeweler

42 HUTCHINSON STREET   SANTA ROSA, CA 97654   PH. 707-545-4400

RICHARD'S JEWELRY
42 Hutchinson Street, Santa Rosa, Ca. 97654
Telephone 707-545-4400

Richard's Jewelry   RICHARD ADAMS, OWNER
_____
42 HUTCHINSON ST.   SANTA ROSA, CA 97654   707-545-4400

RICHARD'S JEWELRY
42 HUTCHINSON STREET SANTA ROSA, CALIFORNIA 97654   TELEPHONE (707) 545-4400

 RICHARD ADAMS, JEWELER
                                                                              42 HUTCHINSON ST.
SANTA ROSA, CA 97654   707) 545-4400 FAX (707) 542-7138

Resume (resume.doc)

Occasionally a show will ask for a resume.

Here's one to use as an example. Now you won't have to go out and get a book about resumes just to remember what they look like or pay someone $50 or more to create one for you.

Using the format shown, delete and type over with your own information.

Employment directors and art shows expect only a one page, concise resume. If they need more information, they will request it.

Your abilities, experiences, education, and goals must be presented clearly and sequentially. A resume can be a very important document. It shows you at your best.

Contemporary Crafts Market, Ft. Mason, San Francisco, CA

Resume

Richard Adams
42 Hutchinson Street
Santa Rosa, CA 97654
(707)-545-4400

EXPERIENCE RELATED TO ARTS AND CRAFTS

Freelance Jeweler
    1991-Present Self-employed jewelry products manufacturing, making rings and selling them wholesale and at craft fairs and art shows throughout the U.S.

Jewelry Designer
1988-1990 Whitewind Jewelers, 298 West Street, Santa Rosa, KS 19884
    Mrs. Sharon Rock, Supervisor

Industrial Arts Instructor
    1983-1986 Santa Rosa High School, 12 Marks Road, Santa Rosa, KS 19885
        Mr. Mel Rosenbloom, Principle

EDUCATION
Associate of Arts
    1976   Merrit College, Oakland, CA
Bachelor of Arts Creative Arts Interdisciplinary
    1978   California College of Arts and Crafts, Oakland, CA

OTHER ACTIVITIES
Member: MJSA, Midwest Handcrafts Collective, Santa Rosa Art Trails
Guest Lecturer, Art Department, California College of Arts and Crafts
Articles on design published in *Metalsmith*, 1984, 1987
First Place, American Craft Competition, Madison, Wisconsin, 1986

REFERENCES
Personal:
    Mrs. Sharon Rock, 5 Martin Rd, Topeka, CA 96566
    Robert Smith, 2783 Fisk Lane, Santa Rosa, CA 97544
Professional:
    Dr. Pressnel Gibbs, 232 Grant Rd, Santa Rosa, CA 97534
    Mr. Frank Hudley, 26 Hessel St., Santa Rosa, CA 97543

How to Use Microsoft Publisher

This is a short lesson about how to use **Publisher**. If you purchased Microsoft **Office, Small Business Edition**, you received **Publisher** at no extra charge. If you want to purchase it separately, it is available for under $100. It is a very useful program for creating brochures, order forms, business cards, hang tags, signs, price tags, and much more.

1. Start **Publisher** by clicking on the Start button, select Programs, then Applications, and select **MS Publisher.**
2. Click on Blank Page, then Full Page, then Okay.
3. Click on the box with the A in it on the left side of the page. Then draw a box by holding down the left mouse button and dragging the mouse to the lower right 2".
4. Start typing. Click on the Plus (+) sign at the bottom to zoom in on your text.
5. Highlight the text by holding down the left mouse button and dragging the cursor over it. Then change the font type and size by clicking on the drop down arrows at the top of the page.
6. Click on the small black square at the lower right of the box, hold down the button, and make the square smaller to fit your text.
7. Hold the cursor at the bottom of the box until a truck appears with the word "Move." Then hold down the button and move the box around.
8. Now, click on the picture of a cactus on the left side of the page. Make a box as you did earlier. This will be an image Box. You can manipulate it the same as the text box.
9. Double click on the center of the image box. An "Insert Picture File" window will appear with a list of images. Make sure "All Picture Formats" is selected next to Files of type. It might take a few minutes for all the images to appear. Use the yellow directory button with the arrow to search other folders on your hard drive for clip art.
10. Select an image. If the "Preview File" box to the right of the window is checked, then images in the left window will appear in the box to the right of the window to be previewed. Click on Okay, then Okay again to place the image in your document.
11. Select any of the small black squares on the image box to change the shape of the image. Try making it bigger or smaller, wider or taller. To make the image keep its proportion as you change its size, select a corner square and hold down the shift key as you change the size of the image box.
12. Finally, to move a box on top of another, just move it as shown earlier. If you want the hidden box to be on top, select it, then select Arrange, Bring to Front from the menu.

How to Make an Artist's Statement

An Artist's Statement is written by the craftsperson to describe the work that he or she has created. Art shows and craft fairs often request that the craftsperson display an artist's statement in their booth for the public to read. The statement tells the customer (and sometimes the show promoters) a little more about the craft than is obvious in the presentation. Sometimes the craftsperson will learn more about his motives by writing the statement.

Writing your own statement is not that hard. Just answer the following questions in one page, and you will have your own artist's statement.

1. Why do you work with the medium or process you have chosen.
2. How many people help you create your work?
3. Is there a central theme or interest from which you generate your work?
4. Is there symbolism in your work?
5. Are there contemporary or historical images or crafts that you are influenced by?
6. Are you trying to invoke an emotion or stimulate the intellect of the user/viewer?
7. What associations do you hope viewers make when viewing your work?
8. What formal aspects interest you? Color? Line? Value? Shape? Form? Movement? Function?

The statement should be 8 ½" by 11." It should have your photo and your name and address at the top, along with your email and website. There are some sample artist statements at http://www.naia-artists.org/work/statement2.htm

Shipping Labels (labels.doc)

You can use Microsoft **Word** to print your own shipping labels. You will need Avery Laser Labels #5164 (or compatible), which are 3 1/3" by 4".

Step-by-step instructions:
1. Open labels.doc.
2. Change printed information as needed for the first label by deleting, backspacing, and typing in your return address.
3. Insert graphic at beginning of address if desired.
4. Highlight and copy the first label and paste on the rest of the labels.
5. Save under your own file name and print as needed on 5164 laser label paper. Print as many sheets as you need. You might want to print the first one on plain paper, in case you have to make any changes.

Top 900 Craft Fairs and Art Shows

The following list consist of the best shows around the country. Exact show dates and deadline dates are not shown, because these change yearly. When you write one of these shows and ask for information, they will send you an application with the correct dates at no charge. Then you will have the exact dates of the show every year, and much more information than any guide can give you.

☐ **How to get your craft fair applications and organize them.**

1. Get 12 file folders. Write the name of a month on each one. 12 folders, 12 months.
2. Get 50 stamps at the post office.
3. Get a box of 50 envelopes. A return address label or stamp is handy but not essential.
4. Write a letter by hand or with your word processor (see next page) asking for an application. Make sure your name and address is on the letter in big, clear letters. Make 50 copies of this letter.
5. Put the letters in the envelopes and put stamps on them.
6. Address the envelopes with shows on this list you might want to do.
7. Mail them.
8. When you get each application, write down the show name, show date, and deadline date on the craft fair organizer on page 82.
9. File the applications in the file folder for the month the show is held.

This is all you need to get up-dated, accurate information about the best shows every year in your mailbox. Once you are on their mailing list, shows will send you applications every year without you having to write them again.

You may do better or worse at any of the shows listed here then we do. We do not guarantee any of them, but after you do a few of them you will find that they are better than most. It seems that at nearly every show we do, whether it is a well-known show or not, the craftsperson or artist on one side will take in much more money than we do, and the person on the other side will not do nearly as well as we do. The inclusion of specific shows is based on word of mouth, magazine articles, attendance, years show has been in business, and personal experience.

We recommend writing the shows instead of calling them. Many shows do not have a full time staff member to answer phones. In addition, they might get your address wrong over the phone.

Letter to craft fair promoter for application (fairletter.doc)

When sending for craft fair applications, first select the desirable fairs from your craft fair list or guides. Write the addresses on #10 business envelopes. Add or delete questions from this letter as desired, then date and sign it. Make as many copies as you have address labels or addressed envelopes for.

Craft Fair Application Request

Date_____

Dear Craft Fair Organizer:

Please forward an application and any other information about your upcoming show. I would also like to be placed on your mailing list for future shows.

If the following information is not included with your application, please write the answers on this letter and return it with the application.

- Do you provide or assist in canopy and table rental for this show?

- Are there nearby areas for self-contained RV parking?

- Do you allow amplified music in close proximity to the artists to the extent that they cannot converse with their customers without raising their voice?

- Do you give artists who demonstrate their craft preference in the jurying process?

- How many people attended the show last year?

Sincerely,

_____

Send information to:

Top Craft Fairs

The names and addresses listed here were accurate at the time this book went to print. Addresses and phone numbers do change. If you get your letter back, google the fair to get the new address.

ST	CRAFT FAIR	ATT	DATE	ADDRESS	CITY	ST	ZIP	PHONE	
AL	Magic City Art Connection	20,000	April	1128 Glen View Rd.	Birmingham	AL	35222	205-595-6306	B+
AL	The Bluff Park Art Show	20,000	Oct.	P. O. Box 26012	Birmingham	AL	35226	205-408-4312	B+
AL	Christmas Village Festival	45,000	Nov.	P. O. Box 101441	Birmingham	AL	35210	205-836-7178	A
AL	Alabama Blueberry Festival	25,000	June	1010-B Douglas Avenue	Brewton	AL	36426	251-867-3224	B
AL	Fairhope Arts and Crafts Festival	180,000	March	P. O. Drawer 10	Daphne	AL	36526	334-621-8222	B
AL	Foley Heritage Harbor Days	40,000	November	P. O. Box 448	Foley	AL	35636	251-943-1200	nr
AL	Foley Art in the Park	35,000	May	119 West Laurel Avenue	Foley	AL	36535	251-943-4381	B
AL	National Shrimp Festival	200,000	Oct.	P. O. Box 3869	Gulf Shores	AL	36547	251-968-6904	A
AL	Hartselle Depot Days	15,000	September	P. O. Box 817	Hartselle	AL	35640	256-773-4370	B
AL	NEACA Fall Show	30,000	Sept.	P. O. Box 1113 West Station	Huntsville	AL	35805	205-274-7918	A
AL	NEACA Spring Craft Show	25,000	March	3206 Holmes Ave	Huntsville	AL	35816	256-533-3283	B+
AL	NEACA Christmas Craft Show	25,000	December	13011 Percivale Drive	Huntsville	AL	35805	256-883-2199	B+
AL	Delta Zone Market Place	15,000	November	P. O. Box 18696	Huntsville	AL	35804	256-894-0117	B
AL	Panoply	85,000	April	700 Monroe St., Ste 2	Huntsville	AL	35802	256-519-2787	B
AL	Azalea Arts and Crafts Festival	25,000	October	4850 Museum Drive	Mobile	AL	36608	251-208-5200	B+
AL	Mobile Bay Fest	200,000	October	P. O. Box 1827	Mobile	AL	36633	251-470-7730	A-
AL	Montgomery Festival in the Park	13,000	October	1010 Forest Avenue	Montgomery	AL	36106	334-241-2300	B
AL	Festival in the Park	19,000	Oct.	1010 Forest Avenue	Montgomery	AL	36106	334-241-2300	B
AL	Kentuck Fest of Arts	32,000	Oct.	503 Main Ave	Northport	AL	35476	205-758-1257	A-
AL	Oxfordfest	17,000	October	P. O. Box 3159	Oxford	AL	36203	256-831-2934	B-
AL	Cityfest Arts and Crafts Show	12,000	May	1002 East Main Street	Prattville	AL	36066	334-365-7392	nr
AL	Selma Riverfront Market	35,000	October	P. O. Box 565	Selma	AL	36702	334-874-8044	B+
AL	Homestead Hollow Christmas	13,000	November	P. O. Box 190	Springville	AL	35146	205-836-8483	B
AL	Homestead Hollow Harvest	18,000	October	P. O. Box 190	Springville	AL	35146	205-836-8483	B
AL	Christmas on Coosa	20,000	December	P. O. Box 936	Wetumpka	AL	36092	334-567-1313	B
AR	Arts & Carafts Festival	35,000	Oct.	P. O. Box 5009	Bella Vista	AR	72714	479-855-2064	A-
AR	Applegate Place Autumn A&C Fest.	200,000	Oct.	P. O. Box 1041	Bentonville	AR	72712	479-273-7478	A
AR	New Sugar Creek A and C Fair	300,000	October	201 N. W. J Street	Bentonville	AR	72712	479-273-3270	B+
AR	Clarion Spring Arts and Crafts Show	10,000	May	P. O. Box 1041	Bentonville	AR	72712	479-273-7478	B-

Top Craft Fairs

AR	Ole Applegate Arts and Crafts	30,000	September	P. O. Box 1041	Bentonville	AR	72712	479-273-7478	B+
AR	Ole Applegate Spring Arts and Crafts	100,000	May	P. O. Box 1041	Bentonville	AR	72712	479-273-7478	B+
AR	Mountain View Folkfest	60,000	April	2926 Highway 150	Blytheville	AR	72560	870-763-5512	B
AR	Beanfest	60,000	October	2926 Highway 150	Blytheville	AR	72560	888-679-2859	B
AR	BPW Barn Sale A and C	14,000	September	692 Jenkins	Camden	AR	71701	870-231-6244	nr
AR	Toad Suck Daze	155,000	April	900 Oak Street	Conway	AZ	72032	501-327-7788	B
AR	Old Fort River Festival	12,000	July	P. O. Box 3025	Fort Smith	AR	72913	479-783-6363	nr
AR	Old Hardy Spring A & C	12,000	April	P. O. Box 668	Hardy	AR	72542	870-856-3571	nr
AR	Harvest Homecoming	12,000	October	P. O. Box 2049	Harrison	AR	72601	870-741-4889	nr
AR	Springfest	10,000	April	1001 West Main St.	Heber Springs	AR	72530	501-362-2444	nr
AR	Hillbilly Corner Arts, Craft	25,000	May	22530 Deer Run Road	Hindsville	AR	72738	479-789-5685	B
AR	War Eagle Fair	195,000	Oct.	11036 High Sky	Hindsville	AR	72738	479-789-5398	A+
AR	Hope Watermelon Festival	40,000	August	P. O. Box 250	Hope	AR	71801	870-777-3640	B+
AR	Hot Springs Arts and Crafts Fair	50,000	October	121 Ellis Court	Hot Springs	AR	71902	501-767-0254	B+
AR	Arkansas Apple Festival	45,000	October	P. O. Box 382	Lincoln	AR	72744	479-267-3916	B
AR	Springdale Fall Craft Fest	20,000	October	5557 Walden Street	Lowell	AR	72745	479-756-2979	B
AR	Old Timer's Days	40,000	May	P. O. Box 245	Van Buren	OR	72957	501-474-8322	B
AR	Jonquil Festival	15,000	March	P. O. Box 98	Washington	AR	71862	870-983-2684	B
AR	Autumn Arts and Crafts Show	15,000	October	P. O. Box 1041	Bentonville	AR	72712	479-273-7478	B
AZ	Peoria Stadium Fall Fest. Of A and C	10,000	November	P. O. Box 1803	Cave Creek	AZ	85327	480-488-2014	B
AZ	Fair of Life Festival	10,000	July	P. O. Box 997	Flagstaff	AZ	86004	928-779-1227	nr
AZ	Fine Arts and Wine Festival		March	15648 North Eagles Nest Dr.	Fountain Hills	AZ	85268	480-837-5637	A
AZ	Fine Arts and Chocolate Festival	40,000	Feb.	15648 North Eagles Nest Dr.	Fountain Hills	AZ	85268	480-837-5637	B+
AZ	Carefree Fine Art & Wine Festival	40,000	November	15648 N. Eagles Nest Dr	Fountain Hills	AZ	85268	480-837-5637	A-
AZ	Fountain Hills Great Fair	150,000	Nov.	P O Box 17598	Fountain Hills	AZ	85269	602-837-1654	A
AZ	Desert Festival of Fine Arts	40,000	Aug.	15648 North Eagles Nest	Fountain Hills	AZ	85268	480-837-5637	A
AZ	Glendale Chocolate Affaire	75,000	February	5850 West Glendale Ave.	Glendale	AZ	85301	623-930-2959	B
AZ	Litchfield Park Festival of the Arts	60,000	November	101 Wigwam Blvd.	Litchfield Park	AZ	85326	623-393-5338	B+
AZ	Patagonia Fall Festival	15,000	October	P. O. Box 241	Patagonia	AZ	85624	520-394-0060	B
AZ	Sonoran Festival of the Arts	12,000	April	9862 South 44th Street	Phoenix	AZ	85044	480-598-9090	nr
AZ	Prescott Courthouse Plaza A and C	15,000	July	4196 Coburn	Prescott	AZ	86392	928-771-1498	B
AZ	Scottsdale Arts Festival	50,000	March	7380 E 2nd St.	Scottsdale	AZ	85251	602-994-2787	A
AZ	Sedona Arts Festival	5,000	Oct.	P. O. Box 2729	Sedona	AZ	86339	928-204-9456	A-

Top Craft Fairs

AZ	Sierra Vista Art in the Park	20,000	October	P. O. Box 247	Sierra Vista	AZ	85636	520-378-1763	B
AZ	Fall Festival of the Arts	230,000	Dec.	520 South Mill Avenue #201	Tempe	AZ	85281	480-967-4877	A
AZ	Artfest of Fifth Avenue	22,000	October	P. O. Box 328	Tempe	AZ	85280	480-968-5353	B
AZ	Fagstaff Festival in the Pines	45,000	July	P. O. Box 328	Tempe	AZ	85280	480-968-5353	B+
AZ	Tempe Spring Festival of the Arts	300,000	March	520 S. Mill Ave., Suite 201	Tempe	AZ	85281	602-967-4877	A-
AZ	Festival of the Arts	250,000	Feb.	P O Box 1866	Tubac	AZ	85646	520-398-9296	B+
AZ	4th Avenue Street Fair (Spring)	300,000	March	329 East 7th	Tucson	AZ	85705	520-624-5004	A
AZ	4th Avenue Street Fair (Fall)	325,000	December	329 East 7th	Tucson	AZ	85705	520-624-5004	A-
AZ	Yuma Christmas Craft Festival	20,000	December	180 First Street Ste C	Yuma	AZ	85364	928-782-5712	B
CA	Cupertino Rotary Octoberfest	30,000	October	P. O. Box 1343	Alameda	CA	94501	510-865-3636	B
CA	Art Affaira	9,000	Oct.	3051 Via Maderas	Altadena	CA	91001	818-797-6803	A
CA	North Country Fair and Harvest Celebration	10,000	September	P. O. Box 664	Arcata	CA	95518	707-822-5320	B
CA	Catalina Festival	15,000	Sept.	P O Box 235	Avalon	CA	90704	310-510-0808	B+
CA	KPFA Holiday Crafts Fair	10,000	December	1919 Mlk Jr. Way	Berkeley	CA	94704	510-848-6767	A
CA	Live Oak Park Fair	5,000	June	P O Box 9188	Berkeley	CA	94709	510-526-7363	A-
CA	Affaire in the Gardens (Fall)	60,000	Oct.	8400 Gregory Way	Beverly Hills	CA	90211	310-550-4628	A-
CA	Big Bear Lake Octoberfest	15,000	September	P. O. Box 7186	Big Bear Lake	CA	92315	909-585-3000	nr
CA	Boulder Creek Art and Wine Fest.		May	12805 Highway 9	Boulder	CA	95006	831-338-2578	B
CA	Burlingame Art in the Park	35,000	June	P. O. Box 1963	Burlingame	CA	94011	650-348-7699	B
CA	Los Gatos Fiesta De Artes	30,000	August	P. O. Box 1963	Burlingame	CA	94011	650-348-7699	B
CA	Avocado Festival	110,000	October	P. O. Box 146	Carpenteria	CA	93014	805-684-0038	A-
CA	Downtown Burbank Fine Arts Fest	15,000	November	P. O. Box 4389	Chatsworth	CA	91311	818-709-2907	B
CA	Warner Park Fine Arts and Crafts	15,000	November	P. O. Box 4389	Chatsworth	CA	91311	818-709-2907	B
CA	Desert Arts Festival, Palm Springs	15,000	December	P. O. Box 4389	Chatsworth	CA	91311	818-709-2907	B
CA	Village Arts Festival	30,000	Nov.	P. O. Box 4389	Chatsworth	CA	91311	818-709-2907	B
CA	4th of July Arts and Craft Show	10,000	July	P. O. Box 977	Chester	CA	96020	530-258-2677	nr
CA	Village Venture A and C Faire	20,000	October	205 Yale Avenue	Claremont	CA	91711	909-624-1681	B
CA	Riverside Dickens Festval	25,000	February	P. O. Box 1959	Corona	CA	92879	909-735-0101	B
CA	Courtland Pear Fair	15,000	July	P. O. Box 492	Courtland	CA	95615	916-775-2000	B
CA	Whole Earth Festival	20,000	May	260 S. Silo	Davis	CA	95616	916-752-2569	B
CA	Fairfield Tomato Festival	45,000	August	1000 Texas Street #D	Fairfield	CA	94533	707-422-0103	B
CA	International Gourd Art Festival	10,000	June	40635-D De Luz Road	Fallbrook	CA	92928	760-728-4271	nr
CA	Folsom Christmas Art	20,000	December	724-26 Sutter	Folsom	CA	95630	916-941-6714	B

Top Craft Fairs

State	Fair	Attendance	Month	Address	City	State	Zip	Phone	Grade
CA	Peddlers Fair	30,000	September	724-26 Sutter Street	Folsom	CA	95630	530-241-4063	B
CA	Fine Art Show at River Park	40,000	October	1756 West Bullard	Fresno	CA	93650	559-449-9818	B
CA	Gilroy Garlic Festival	125,000	July	P O Box 2311	Gilroy	CA	95021	408-842-1625	A
CA	Pumpkin Festival	200,000	Oct.	P O Box 274	Half Moon Bay	CA	94019	415-726-9652	A
CA	Hayward Zucchini Festival	26,000	August	P. O. Box 247	Hayward	CA	94543	510-264-9466	B-
CA	Contemporary Craft Market	11,000	June	575 Cooke St. A2820	Honolulu	HI	96813	808-422-7362	A
CA	Contemporary Crafts Market	12,000	Nov.	575 Cooke St A2820	Honolulu	HI	96813	808-422-7362	A
CA	Indio Tamale Festival	120,000	December	100 Civic Center Mall	Indio	CA	92201	760-342-6532	B
CA	Festival of the Arts	17,000	Sept.	4130 La Jolla Vil. Dr.7	La Jolla	CA	92037	619-456-1268	A+
CA	La Quinta Arts Festival	25,000	March	P O Box 777	La Quinta	CA	92253	760-564-1244	A-
CA	Winter Fantasy Laguna Beach	20,000	November	935 Laguna Canyon Road	Laguna Beach	CA	92651	949-494-3030	A-
CA	Sawdust Festival	200,000	July/Aug.	935 Laguna Canyon Road	Laguna Beach	CA	92651	949-494-3030	A
CA	Art-A-Fair Festival	50,000	June	P. O. Box 547	Laguna Beach	CA	92652	714-494-4514	B+
CA	Museum of Art Artists Market	4,000	June	2300 East Ocean	Long Beach	CA	90803	310-439-2119	A-
CA	Hist. Society Craft Fair	15,000	August	P. O. Box 286	Long Beach	CA	11561	516-432-1192	B-
CA	Fiesta Broadway	55,000	April	2130 San Telle Blvd 304	Los Angeles	CA	90025	310-914-1933	B
CA	Spring May Day Fair	55,000	April	P. O. Box 71	Los Banos	CA	93635	209-826-5166	B
CA	Los Altos Rotary Art Show	9,000	May	132 Belvue Dr.	Los Gatos	CA	95032	408-358-3373	B+
CA	Labor Day Festival	15,000	Aug.	P. O. Box 56	Mammoth Lakes	CA	93546	760-873-7042	A-
CA	California Peach Fest.	62,000	July	P. O. Box 3231	Marysville	CA	95993	530-671-9599	B
CA	Mill Falley Fall Arts Festival	15,000	Sept.	P O Box 300	Mill Valley	CA	94942	415-381-0525	A
CA	Millbrae Art and Wine Festival	80,000	Aug.	50 Victoria Ave. Ste. 103	Millbrae	CA	94030	415-697-8737	B
CA	Montrose Arts and Crafts Festival	55,000	June	P. O. Box 187	Montrose	CA	91021	818-248-3829	B+
CA	Morro Bay Harbor Festival	25,000	October	P. O. Box 18696	Morro Bay	CA	93443	805-772-1155	B
CA	Four Seasons Arts and Crafts Fest	12,000	July	P. O. Box 5672	Norco	CA	92860	909-735-4751	B
CA	Great Dickens Christmas Fair	20,000	November	P. O. Box 1768	Novato	CA	94948	800-510-1558	B
CA	Festival at the Lake	45,000	June	1630 Webster	Oakland	CA	94612	510-286-1061	B+
CA	Oceanside Harbor Days	75,000	September	928 North Coast Highway	Oceanside	CA	92054	760-722-1534	B+
CA	Southwest Arts Festival		Feb.	P. O. Box 62	Palm Desert	CA	92261	760-346-0042	A
CA	Harvest Festival	30,000	Nov.	601 N. McDowell	Petaluma	CA	94954	707-778-6300	A-
CA	Strawberry Festival	65,000	May	P O Box 280	Pine Grove	CA	95665	209-296-1195	A
CA	Wildlife Art Festival	5,000	Nov.	2024 Orange Tree Ln.	Redlands	CA	92374	909-798-8570	B+
CA	Fiesta Hermosa Arts and Crafts	150,000	May	1926 S. Pc Hwy #109-B	Redondo Beach	CA	90501	310-316-0951	A-
CA	Route 66 Rendezvous	550,000	Sept.	201 North 3. Street Ste 103	San Bernadino	CA	92401	800-867-8366	B
CA	San Carlos Art & Wine	70,000	October	P. O. Box 1086	San Carlos	CA	94070	209-296-1195	B

Top Craft Fairs

CA	CityFest 2005	170,000	August	P. O. Box 3655	San Diego	CA	92163	619-299-3330	B+
CA	Castro Street Fair	150,000	October	P. O. Box 14405	San Francisco	CA	94114	415-841-1824	B
CA	San Francisco State A and C Fair	26,000	April	Sc T-115, 1650 Holloway	San Francisco	CA	94132	415-338-2444	B
CA	Almaden Valley Art and Wine Fest	23,000	September	P. O. Box 20084	San Jose	CA	95160		B
CA	Tapestry in Talent	75,000	Aug.	255 N. Market St #124	San Jose	CA	95110	408-494-3490	A-
CA	Berryessa Art and Wine Festival	7,000	May	1127 Summergarden Ct.	San Jose	CA	95132	408-272-1578	B
CA	Artwalk Festival of Art	5,000	Oct.	2559 Puesta Del Sol	Santa Barbara	CA	93105	805-682-4711	B
CA	Rotary Art Show	30,000	May	P. O. Box 2215	Saratoga	CA	95070	408-725-2434	A
CA	Sausalito Arts Festival	50,000	Aug.	P O Box 10	Sausalito	CA	94966	415-332-3555	A+
CA	Connoisseur's Market Place	80,000	July	1384 Weston Road	Scotts Valley	CA	95066	831-438-4751	A-
CA	Palo Alto Festival of the Arts	25,000	Aug.	1384 Weston Road	Scotts Valley	CA	95066	831-438-4751	A
CA	Sherman Oaks Street Fair	80,000	October	14827 Ventura Blvd. Ste 207	Sherman Oaks	CA	91403	818-906-1951	B
CA	University Holiday Craft Faire	15,000	Dec.	P O Box 6508	Stanford	CA	94309	415-723-3542	B+
CA	Asparagus Festival	100,000	April	425 N. El Dorado St.	Stockton	CA	95202	209-937-7488	B
CA	Tehachapi Mountain Festival	40,000	August	P. O. Box 401	Tehachapi	CA	93561	661-822-4180	B
CA	Artwalk	18,000	June	P O Box 1616	Thousand Oaks	CA	91358	805-492-8778	B+
CA	Redwood Empire Fair	25,000	August	1055 North State Street	Ukiah	CA	95482	707-462-3884	B
CA	Nuts for Art	15,000	October	15954 Woods Valley Road	Valley Center	CA	92082	760-749-3388	nr
CA	Kings Mountain Art Fair	20,000	Sept.	13106 Skyline Boulevard	Woodside	CA	94062	650-851-2710	A+
CA	Beaumont Cherry Festival	60,000	June	P. O. Box 307	Beaumont	CA	92223	909-845-9541	B+
CA	Corte Madera 4th of July Fair	10,000	July	129 Town Center	Corte Madera	CA	94925	415-924-0441	B-
CA	Fairfield Candy Festival	50,000	October	1000 Texas Street #D	Fairfield	CA	94533	707-422-0103	B
CA	Country Folk Art Craft Show	20,000	Nov.	15045 Dixie Highway	Holly	MI	48442	248-634-4151	B
CA	Celebration Of Craftswomen	10,000	November	3453 18th Street	San Francisco	CA	94110	415-431-1180	A
CA	Topanga Country Fair	12,000	May	P. O. Box 1611	Topanga	CA	90290	310-455-1890	B
CO	Halloween With Horses	12,000	October	46100 Cr 65	Bennet	CO	80102	303-621-8081	nr
CO	Downtown Boulder Fall Festival	55,000	September	1942 Broadway 301	Boulder	CO	80302	303-484-0820	B
CO	Artfair	50,000	July	P. O. Box 1634	Boulder	CO	80306	303-499-0199	B
CO	Breckenridge July Art Festival	30,000	July	P. O. Box 2938	Breckenridge	CO	80424	970-547-9326	B
CO	Mountain Fair	15,000	July	P O Box 175	Carbondale	CO	81623	970-963-1680	B
CO	Colorado Springs Territory Days	140,000	May	211 Farragut	Colorado Springs	CO	80909	719-475-0955	A-
CO	Crested Butte Festival Of The Arts	10,000	Aug.	Box 324	Crested Butte	CO	81224	970-349-1184	B+
CO	A Taste Of Colorado	500,000	Sept.	511 16th St. Ste 200	Denver	CO	80202	303-295-6330	A-

Top Craft Fairs

State	Fair	Attendance	Month	Address	City	State	Zip	Phone	Rating
CO	Littleton Pumpkin Festival	13,000	October	909 York Street	Denver	CO	80206	720-865-3554	nr
CO	Colorado Arts Festival	170,000	May	P. O. Box 101870	Denver	CO	80250	303-388-2137	B+
CO	Cherry Creek Arts Festival	350,000	July	2 Steele Street B100	Denver	CO	80206	303-355-2787	A+
CO	Capitol Hill Peoples Fair	275,000	June	1490 Lafayette #104	Denver	CO	80218	303-830-1651	B
CO	Evergreen Arts Festival	10,000	Aug.	P. O. Box 1511	Evergreen	CO	80439	303-838-3948	B+
CO	Greely Arts Picnic	33,000	July	651 Tenth Avenue	Greeley	CO	80631	970-350-9451	B
CO	Jones Quality Arts And Craft Show	20,000	October	844 S. 291 Hwy, #323	Liberty	MO	64068	816-781-8110	B-
CO	Friends Of The Museum Craft Fair	20,000	October	6028 South Gallup	Littleton	CO	80120	303-795-3950	B+
CO	Manitou Springs A and C Festival	30,000	September	P. O. Box 42	Manitou Springs	CO	80829	719-577-7700	B
CO	Beaver Creek Arts Festival	25,000	Aug.	9695 West Broward Blvd.	Plantation	FL	33324	954-472-3755	B
CO	Denver's Holiday Gift Festival	33,000	July	P. O. Box 91369	Portland	OR	97291	503-526-1080	B
CO	Snowmass Arts And Crafts Fair	10,000	July	P. O. Box 5566	Snowmass Village	CO	81615	970-923-2000	A-
CO	Steamboat Springs Art In The Park	10,000	July	P. O. Box 774284	Steamboat Springs	CO	80477	970-879-9008	B
CO	Vail Arts Festival	20,000	July	P O Box 1153	Vail	CO	81658	970-476-4255	A
CT	Craft Village Arts And Crafts Festival	10,000	Oct.	779 East Main St.	Branford	CT	06405	203-488-4689	B
CT	On The Green Art And Craft Show	10,000	Sept.	P. O. Box 304	Glastonbury	CT	06033	203-659-1196	B
CT	Crafts Fest of The Brice Museum	15,000	May	1 Museum Dr.	Greenwich	CT	06830	203-869-0376	B+
CT	Guilford Handcraft Exh.	20,000	July	P. O. Box 589	Gilford	CT	06437	203-453-5947	A+
CT	Mystic Seaport Outdoor Art Festival	60,000	Aug.	P. O. Box 300	Mystic	CT	06355	860-572-7844	B
CT	Christmas Crafts Expo	18,000	Dec.	P. O. Box 227	North Granby	CT	06060	860-653-6671	B
CT	Old Saybrook Art And Craft Show	250,000	July	P. O. Box 625	Old Saybrook	CT	06475	860-388-3266	B
CT	Oyster Festival	90,000	Sept.	132 Water St.	South Norwalk	CT	06854	203-838-9444	A-
CT	Sono Arts Celebration	60,000	Aug.	P O Box 500	South Norwalk	CT	06856	203-866-7916	B
CT	Westport Handcrafts Show	10,000	May	10 Lyons Plains Road	Weston	CT	06883	203-227-7844	A
CT	Creative Arts Festival	8,000	Nov.	144 Imperial Ave.	Westport	CT	06880	203-222-1388	A-
CT	Dtn Merchants Outdoor Art Show	30,000	July	P O Box 5132	Westport	CT	06880	203-454-8688	B
CT	Celebrate West Hardford A & C Show	30,000	May	50 South Main Street	West Hartford	CT	06107	860-570-3705	B
DC	Washington Craft Show	10,000	Nov.	P. O. Box 603	Greens Farms	CT	06436	203-254-0486	A+
DC	Smithsonian Craft Show	20,000	April	A & I Bldg, Rm 1465	Washington	DC	20560	202-357-4000	A+
DC	National Christmas Show	38,000	Nov.	P. O. Box 11565	Winston Salem	NC	27116	910-924-8337	A+
DE	Delaware Fine Art And Craft Show	10,000	July	P. O. Box 347	Ardmore	PA	19003	877-244-9768	B
DE	Boardwalk Arts Festival	8,000	Sept.	P O Box 881	Bethany Beach	DE	19930	800-962-7873	B+
DE	Dover Officer Spouses Club Craft Show	10,000	November	P. O. Box 02069	Dover	DE	19901	302-677-6032	B

Top Craft Fairs

State	Name	Attendance	Month	Address	City	State	Zip	Phone	Rating
DE	Sea Witch Halloween And Fiddlers	150,000	October	P. O. Box 216	Rehoboth Beach	DE	19971	302-227-2233	B
DE	Brandywine Arts Festival	35,000	Sept.	2903 B Philadelphia Pike	Wilmington	DE	19703	302-529-0761	A-
FL	Fall Country Jamboree	18,000	November	P. O. Box 5	Barberville	FL	32105	386-749-2959	B
FL	Arts Festival	150,000	March	1800 N. Dixie Hwy.	Boca Raton	FL	33432	407-395-4433	B
FL	Boca Museum Art Festival	50,000	Feb.	801 W. Palmetto Park	Boca Raton	FL	33486	561-392-2500	A+
FL	Fiesta Of Arts	30,000	Feb.	150 Nw Crawford Blvd	Boca Raton	FL	33432	407-393-7827	B
FL	The Riverview Art Fest.	10,000	Jan.	P. O. Box 1346	Cape Coral	FL	33910	941-945-1988	B
FL	Celebration Fall Art Festival	50,000	October	671 Front Street Ste 210	Celebration	FL	34747	407-566-1200	B
FL	Art Harvest in the Park	60,000	Nov.	1265 Bayshore Blvd.	Clearwater	FL	34698	727-738-5523	B
FL	Space Coast Art Festival	100,000	Nov.	P. O. Box 320135	Cocoa Beach	FL	32932	407-784-3322	B
FL	Coconut Grove Arts Festival	800,000	Feb.	3427 Main Highway	Coconut Grove	FL	33233	305-447-0401	A+
FL	Banyan Arts & Crafts Festival	40,000	Nov.	2820 Mcfarlane Rd.	Coconut Grove	FL	33233	305-444-7270	B
FL	St Stephen's Arts & Crafts Show	750,000	Feb.	2750 Mcfarlane Rd	Coconut Grove	FL	33133	305-558-1758	B+
FL	Florida Manatee Fine Arts Show	40,000	Feb.	28 Nw Hwy 19	Crystal River	FL	34428	904-795-3149	B
FL	Deerfield Beach Fest. Of The Arts	25,000	Jan.	150 N.E. 2nd Ave	Deerfield Beach	FL	33441	454-421-6161	B
FL	Deland Fall Festival Of The Arts	54,000	November	P. O. Box 3194	Deland	FL	32721	386-738-5705	B
FL	Delray Affair	250,000	April	64 Se 5th Ave.	Delray Beach	FL	33483	561-279-1380	B
FL	Isle Of Eight Flags Shrimp Fest	175,000	May	P.O. Box 1251	Fernandina Beach	FL	32035	904-261-7020	A-
FL	Holiday Arts And Crafts Show	12,000	Nov.	16520 Tamiami Trail #18	Fort Meyers	FL	33908	508-737-0998	A-
FL	Fort Myers Arts And Crafts Show	12,000	January	16520 S. Tamiami Trail #18	Fort Myers	FL	33908	508-737-0998	nr
FL	Lido Keys Holiday A And C Show	12,000	December	16520 S. Tamaimi Trail	Fort Myers	FL	33908	508-737-0998	B
FL	Fishermen's Village Fall A And C	16,000	October	16520 S. Tamaima Trail #18	Fort Myers	FL	33908	508-737-0998	B
FL	Naples Art And Craft Show	12,000	March	16520 S. Tamaimi Trail #18	Fort Myers	FL	33908	508-737-0998	B
FL	Saint Simon's On The Sound Craft	25,000	November	28 Miracle Strip Parkway	Fort Walton Beach	FL	32548	850-244-8621	B
FL	Promenade In The Park	75,000	Nov.	P. O. Box 2307	Ft Lauderdale	FL	33303	954-764-5973	B
FL	Riverwalk Arts And Crafts Show	100,000	Jan.	301 N. Andrews Ave	Ft. Lauderdale	FL	33301	305-761-5359	A-
FL	Santa Fe C. College Spring Arts Fest	129,000	April	3000 Nw 83rd St.	Gainesville	FL	32606	352-392-5355	B
FL	Carols In The Park	28,000	December	P. O. Box 2237	Haines City	FL	33845	239-573-6764	B
FL	Anna Maria Island Winterfest	20,000	December	5312 Holmes Boulevard	Holms Beach	FL	34217	941-778-2099	B

Top Craft Fairs

State	Fair	Attendance	Month	Address	City	State	Zip	Phone	Grade
FL	Homosassa Art, Craft And Seafood	30,000	November	P. O. Box 709	Homosassa	FL	34447	352-628-2666	B
FL	Artworks	3,000	May	P O Box 41564	Jacksonville	FL	32203	904-387-7007	B
FL	Key Biscayne Arts Festival	25,000	January	P. O. Box 490174	Key Biscayne	FL	33149	305-361-0049	B-
FL	Old Island Days Art Festival	25,000	Feb.	3124 Riviera Dr.	Key West	FL	3040	305-294-0431	A+
FL	Osceola Art Festival	10,000	November	P. O. Box 451088	Kissimmee	FL	34745	407-846-6257	B-
FL	Festival Of The Masters	125,000	Nov.	Box 10150 (Walt Disney World)	Lake Buena Vista	FL	32830	407-934-6743	A
FL	Heathrow Festival Of The Arts	125,000	Oct.	P. O. Box 952125	Lake Mary	FL	32795	407-585-2086	B
FL	Lutz Arts And Crafts Festival	35,000	December	P. O. Box 656	Lutz	FL	33548	813-949-7060	B
FL	Grouper Fest And Art Market	24,000	October	150 John's Pass Boardwlk	Madeira Beach	FL	33706	813-645-4954	B
FL	Maitland Rotary Arts Fest	100,000	Oct.	P. O. Box 941234	Maitland	FL	32794	407-263-5218	B+
FL	Marco Art	8,000	Feb.	1010 Winterberry	Marco Island	FL	34145	239-394-4221	B+
FL	Christmas Made In The South	35,000	Nov.	P. O. Box 853	Matthews	NC	28106	704-847-9480	A+
FL	1890's Mcintosh Festival	35,000	October	P. O. Box 1890	Mcintosh	FL	32664	352-591-1890	B
FL	Melbourne Art Festival	50,000	April	P.O. Box 611	Melbourne	FL	32902	321-722-1964	B+
FL	Artworks Of Eau Gallie	12,000	November	1490 Highland Ave, Ste. A	Melbourne	FL	32935	321-242-1456	nr
FL	Historical Museum Of Southern FL	30,000	November	101 West Flagler Street	Miami	FL	33130	305-375-1492	nr
FL	Miami Beach Festival Of The Arts	50,000	March	1700 Civic Center Drive	Miami Beach	FL	33139	305-673-7577	B
FL	Mount Dora Craft Show	250,000	October	P. O. Box 378	Mount Dora	FL	32756	352-735-1191	A-
FL	Mount Dora Arts Festival	250,000	Feb.	138 E 5th Ave	Mount Dora	FL	32757	352-383-0880	B
FL	Invitational Art Fest	10,000	Jan.	P.O. Box 995	Naples	FL	34106	941-263-1667	B+
FL	Naples National Art Festival	60,000	Feb.	P O Box 839	Naples	FL	34106	239-513-2492	B+
FL	Images In Art Show	30,000	Oct.	P. O. Box 6229	Ocala	FL	34478	352-867-4788	B
FL	Fiesta In The Park	200,000	Nov.	P. O. Box 1883	Orlando	FL	32802	407-246-2827	A
FL	Halifax Art Festival	20,000	Oct.	P. O. Box 2038	Ormond Beach	FL	32175	904-673-2098	B
FL	Great Day In The Country	60,000	November	P. O. Box 621607	Oviedo	FL	32762	407-365-9420	B
FL	Florida Azalea Festival	25,000	March	623 Saint Johns Ave.	Palatka	FL	32177	386-328-4021	B
Fl	Palatka Blue Crab Fest.	200,000	May	P. O. Box 1351	Palatka	FL	32178	386-325-4406	B+
FL	Artigras Fine Arts Festival	150,000	Feb.	3970 RCA Boulevard Ste 7010	Palm Beach Gardens	FL	33410	561-691-8506	A-
FL	Palm Harbor Arts, Crafts And Music	15,000	December	1151 Nebraska Ave	Palm Harbor	FL	34683	727-784-4287	B
FL	Saint Andrews Fall Seafood Fest	22,000	September	1618 Isabella Avenue	Panama City	FL	32410	850-784-9542	B
FL	Panama City Beach Indian Summer	60,000	October	P. O. Box 9473	Panama City	FL	32417	850-233-5070	B-
FL	Great Gulfcoast Art Festival	150,000	Nov.	P. O. Box 10744	Pensacola	FL	32524	904-432-9906	A-

Top Craft Fairs

FL	Florida Strawberry Festival	600,000	Feb.	P. O. Drawer 1869	Plant City	FL	33564	813-752-9194	A+
FL	Downtown Delray Festival	125,000	Jan.	9695 West Broward Blvd	Plantation	FL	33324	954-472-3755	B
FL	Los Olas Art Fair	100,000	Jan.	1350 W. Broward Blvd.	Plantation	FL	33324	954-472-3755	B
FL	Downtown Festival Of The Arts	90,000	Feb.	9695 West Broward Blvd	Plantation	FL	33324	954-472-3755	B
FL	Old Hyde Park Village Art Festival	65,000	Oct.	9695 West Broward Blvd	Plantation	FL	33324	954-472-3755	A
FL	Plantation Art In The Park	50,000	October	P. O. Box 15473	Plantation	FL	33318	954-797-9762	B
FL	Baptist Hospital Artist's Showcase	30,000	April	P. O. Box 800035	Roswell	GA	30075	800-293-4983	A-
FL	Baptist Hospital Artists Showcase	40,000	Nov.	P. O. Box 800035	Roswell	GA	30075	800-293-4983	B+
FL	Safety Harbor Holiday A And C Show	30,000	December	125 5th Ave. North	Safety Harbor	FL	34695	727-725-1562	B
FL	Saint Cloud Craft Festival	18,000	December	P. O. Box 700522	Saint Cloud	FL	34770	407-892-1667	B
FL	Rotary Club Arts And Crafts Fair	10,000	Feb.	Box 736	Sanibel	FL	33957	239-489-4862	B
FL	Sarasota Arts Day	15,000	January	1226 N. Tamaimi Trail #300	Sarasota	FL	34236	941-365-5118	B+
FL	Museum Of Art Las Olas Art Festival	50,000	March	8 Seneca Road	Sea Ranch Lakes	FL	33308	954-942-9697	B
FL	Highlands Art Festival	20,000	November	351 West Center Ave	Sebring	FL	33870	863-385-5312	B
FL	South Miami Art Festival	50,000	November	6410 S. W. 80th Street	South Miami	FL	33141	305-661-1621	B+
FL	Artexp. O. South Miami	45,000	January	7800 Red Road, Ste 215d	South Miami	FL	33143	305-558-1758	B
FL	Beaux Arts Festival Of Art	100,000	Jan.	P O Box 431216	South Miami	FL	33143	305-789-9254	B
FL	South Miami Art Festival	60,000	Nov.	6410 Sw 80th	South Miami	FL	33143	305-661-1621	B
FL	St Augustine Art & Crafts Festival	25,000	March	22 Marine St	St. Augustine	FL	32084	904-824-0716	B
FL	Mainsail Arts Festival	90,000	April	P O Box 2842	St. Petersburg	FL	33731	727-892-5885	A-
FL	Market Days	16,000	Dec.	3491 11 Thomas Road	Tallahassee	FL	32308	850-576-9820	A
FL	Gasparilla Festival Of The Arts	300,000	March	P O Box 10591	Tampa	FL	33679	813-876-1747	A
FL	Tarpoon Springs Art Fest.	50,000	April	210 S. Pinellas Ave. Ste 120	Tarpon Springs	FL	34689	813-937-6109	B+
FL	Temple Terrace Community Arts Fest	15,000	November	P. O. Box 291266	Temple Terrace	FL	33687	813-989-7181	B
FL	Indian River Festival A And C Show	30,000	April	2000 S. Washington St.	Titusville	FL	32780	321-267-3036	B
FL	Under The Oaks Arts Festival	30,000	March	3001 Riverside Park Dr	Vero Beach	FL	32963	407-231-0707	B+
FL	Sunfest	325,000	May	525 Clematis St.	West Palm Beach	FL	33401	561-659-5980	A-
FL	Winter Park Autumn Art Festival	60,000	Oct.	P. O. Box 280	Winter Park	FL	32790	407-646-2284	A-
FL	Winter Park Sidewalk Art Festival	350,000	March	P. O. Box 597	Winter Park	FL	32789	407-672-6390	A+

Top Craft Fairs

GA	Dogwood Festival	300,000	April	20 Executive Park Dr # 2019	Atlanta	GA	30329	404-329-0501	A
GA	Arts Festival Of Atlanta	100,000	Sept.	140 First Union	Atlanta,	GA	30309	404-589-8777	A+
GA	Canton Riverfest	24,000	September	P. O. Box 1132	Canton	GA	30169	770-704-5991	B
GA	Paulding Meadows A And C Festival	25,000	September	P. O. Box 654	Dallas	GA	30132	770-505-1987	B
GA	Prater's Mill Country Fair	10,000	May	848 Sugart Rd	Dalton	GA	30720	706-275-6455	A
GA	Possum Hollow Arts And Crafts Fair	15,000	September	P. O. Box 584	Dexter	GA	31019	478-875-3200	B
GA	Duluth Fall Festival	95,000	September	P. O. Box 497	Duluth	GA	30096	770-476-0240	B
GA	Peachtree Art And Craft Show	13,000	Nov.	4664 North Peachtree Road	Dunwoody	GA	30338	404-451-4613	A+
GA	Georgia Apple Festival	50,000	October	P. O. Box 505	Ellijay	GA	30540	706-636-4500	B+
GA	Mule Camp Market	50,000	October	P. O. Box 36	Gainesville	GA	30503	770-714-9309	B
GA	Lazy Daze In Georgia, Georgia Mall	50,000	July	5010 Strickland Rd	Gainesville	GA	30507	770-967-4753	B
GA	Cotton Pickin' Country Fair	30,000	Oct.	P. O. Box 1	Gay	GA	30218	706-538-6814	A-
GA	Georgia Mountain Fair	100,000	Aug.	P. O. Box 444 Us 76 West	Hiawassee	GA	30546	706-896-4191	A+
GA	Christmas Made In The South	20,000	Nov.	P. O. Box 853	Matthews	NC	28106	704-847-9480	B+
GA	Spring Made In The South Augusta	18,000	March	P. O. Box 853	Matthews	NC	28106	704-847-9480	B+
GA	Brown's Crossing Festival	12,000	Oct.	400 Brown's Crossing	Milledgeville	GA	31061	912-452-9327	A-
GA	Calico Holiday Arts And Crafts Fair	15,000	November	290-G Harper Boulevard	Moultrie	GA	31788	229-985-1968	B
GA	Powers' Crossroads Art Fest	50,000	Aug.	4766 W. Hwy. 34	Newnan	GA	30263	770-253-2011	A+
GA	Norcross Artfest	15,000	October	P. O. Box 331	Norcross	GA	30091	770-729-0200	B
GA	Telfair Museum Of Art Art Fair	10,000	November	P. O. Box 10081	Savannah	GA	31412	912-232-1177	nr
GA	Peachtree Crossings County Fair	30,000	Sept.	3869 Redbud Court	Smyrna	GA	30082	404-434-3661	A-
GA	Million Pines A And C Festival	15,000	November	P. O. Box 135	Soperton	GA		912-529-6611	B
GA	Yellow Daisy Festival	200,000	Sept.	P. O. Box 778	Stone Mountain	GA	30086	770-498-5633	B+
GA	Mossy Creek Barnyard A And C	20,000	Oct.	106 Anne Drive	Warner Robins	GA	31093	912-922-8265	A
IA	Autumn Fest Arts & Crafts Affair	20,000	Oct.	Box 184	Boys Town	NE	68010	402-331-2889	A
IA	Art In The Park	5,000	June	P. O. Box 2164	Clinton,	IA	52733	815-772-8856	B
IA	Quad Cty Riversance Fine Arts Fest	15,000	Sept.	P. O. Box 2183	Davenport	IA	52809	319-386-7013	B
IA	Beaux Art Invitational Spring Art Fair	27,000	May	3 North Garfield Ct.	Davenport	IA	52801	563-323-9042	B
IA	Two Rivers Art Expo.	8,000	Nov.	4055 Sw 30th St.	Des Moines	IA	50321	515-285-6765	B
IA	Art In The Park	20,000	June	4700 Grand Ave.	Des Moines	IA	50312	515-277-4405	B+
IA	Iowa Arts Festival	40,000	June	P. O. Box 3128	Iowa City	IA	52244	319-337-7944	B
IA	McGregor Spring A And C Festival	10,000	May	P. O. Box 105	Mcgregor	IA	52157	800-896-0910	nr
IA	Antiques, Craft, And Collectables	10,000	September	124 S. Main	Mount Pleasant	IA	52641	319-385-3101	nr

Top Craft Fairs

IA	Storm Lake Spect.	30,000	July	P. O. Box 584	Storm Lake	IA	50588	712-732-3787	B
ID	Boise River Festival	500,000	June	404 S. 8th St. Ste 404	Boise	ID	83702	208-338-8887	B
ID	Art In The Park	175,000	Sept.	670 S Julia Davis Dr.	Boise	ID	83702	208-345-8330	B
ID	Art On The Green	50,000	Aug.	P O Box 901	Coeur D'arlene	ID	83816	208-667-9346	B+
ID	Sun Valley Arts & Crafts Festival	20,000	Aug.	P. O. Box 656	Ketchum	ID	83353	208-726-9491	A+
ID	Mccall Winter Carnival	75,000	January	P. O. Box 350	Mccall	ID	83638	208-634-7631	B
IL	Baac Art Fair	2,500	June	207 Park Ave	Barrington	IL	60010	847-382-5626	B+
IL	Art In The Barn	8,000	Sept.	450 W. Hwy 22	Barrington	IL	60010	847-842-4496	B+
IL	Art On The Square	42,000	May	P. O. Box 23561	Belleville	IL	62223	618-257-0747	A-
IL	Autumn Festival	30,000	Nov.	P. O. Box 184	Boys Town	NE	68010	402-331-2889	A+
IL	Celebrate On State Street	600,000	June	16w129 83rd Street	Burr Ridge	IL	60521	708-325-8080	A+
IL	Arlington Racecourse Art, Craft And Folk	15,000	November	16W129 83rd Street	Burr Ridge	IL	60521	630-325-8080	B
IL	Lambs Farm Holiday Art And Craft	20,000	December	16W129 83rd Street	Burr Ridge	IL	60521	630-325-8080	B
IL	Orland Square Art And Craft Show	50,000	February	16W129 83rd Street	Burr Ridge	IL	60521	630-325-8080	B
IL	Carlinville Christmas Market	15,000	December	126 Main Street	Carlinville	IL	62626	217-854-2141	B
IL	Urbana Arts And Crafts Festival	50,000	June	301 North Randolph	Champaign	IL	61820	217-398-2376	B
IL	Chicago's New East Side Artworks	70,000	Aug.	857 West Webster Ave	Chicago	IL	60614	773-404-0763	B
IL	One Of A Kind Show And Sale	25,000	Dec.	Merchandise Mart, Ste 470	Chicago	IL	60654	312-527-7642	nr
IL	North Halstead Market Days	200,000	September	1960 N. Clybourn, R Bldg.	Chicago	IL	60614	773-868-3010	A-
IL	Brookfest Summer Festival	20,000	July	1960 N. Clybourn, R Bldg.	Chicago	IL	60614	773-868-3010	B
IL	Old Town Art Fair	40,000	June	1763 North Park Ave	Chicago	IL	60614	312-337-1938	A+
IL	57th Street Art Fair	100,000	June	1763 North Park Ave	Chicago	IL	60614	312-337-1938	A+
IL	Wells Street Art Festival	50,000	June	1545 N. Wells St.	Chicago	IL	60610	312-951-6106	B+
IL	American Craft Exposition	13,000	Aug.	Henry Crown Sports Pavilion	Evanston	IL	60201	708-570-5099	A+
IL	Evanston Lakeshore Arts Festival	20,000	Aug.	927 Noyes	Evanston	IL	60201	847-448-8260	B
IL	Evanston Ethnic Arts	20,000	July	927 Noyes St	Evanston	IL	60201	847-448-8260	B
IL	Fountain Square Arts Festival	20,000	June	1560 Sherman Ave. #860	Evanston	IL	60201	708-328-1500	B+
IL	Midwest Salute To The Masters	40,000	Aug.	P. O. Box 2032	Fairview Heights	IL	62208	618-394-0022	B
IL	Frankfort Fall Festival	200,000	Sept.	123 Kansas Street	Frankfort	IL	60423	815-469-3356	B+
IL	Galena Arts Festival	6,000	July	P. O. Box 23	Galena	IL	61036	815-777-9341	B
IL	Acc Craft Fair	8,000	April	21 South Eltings Corner	Highland	NY	12528	800-836-3470	B+
IL	Hinsdale Fine Arts Festival	5,000	June	22 E First St	Hinsdale	IL	60521	708-323-3952	B

Top Craft Fairs

IL	Lagrange West End Art Festival	30,000	September	106 Calendar Ave. Lgba	Lagrange	IL	60525	630-536-8416	B
IL	Deer Path Art League Fall Festival	200,000	September	1 Market Square Court	Lake Forest	IL	60045	847-234-3743	B+
IL	Lexington Taste Of Country Festival	11,000	September	205 North Center Street	Lexington	IL	61753	309-365-7200	B-
IL	Gold Coast Art Fair	750,000	Aug.	90 Oakwood St Ste 101	Lincolnshire	IL	60069	847-444-9600	B+
IL	Port Clinton Art Festival	275,000	Aug.	90 Oakwood, Ste 101	Lincolnshire	IL	60069	847-444-9600	A+
IL	Cedarhurst Craft Fair	20,000	Sept.	P. O. Box 923 / Richview Rd	Mt Vernon	IL	62864	618-242-1236	B
IL	Naperville Sizzlin Summer	75,000	July	1310 Frederick Lane	Naperville	IL	60565	630-355-1708	nr
IL	Eyes To The Sky Craft Show	250,000	July	1310 Frederick Lane	Naperville	IL	60565	630-355-1708	B+
IL	Riverwalk Art Fair	20,000	Sept.	508 N Center	Naperville	IL	60563	708-355-2530	B
IL	Invitational Crafts Exhibit	100,000	July	P O Box 1350	Oak Brook	IL	60522	630-573-0700	A+
IL	Palatine Street Fest And Art Show	35,000	August	200 E. Wood Street	Palatine	IL	60067	847-359-9050	nr
IL	Water Tower Arts & Craft Festival	25,000	June	P. O. Box 1326	Palatine,	IL	60078	312-751-2500	B
IL	Park Forest Art Fair	15,000	Sept.	Box 776	Park Forest	IL	60466	708-748-5016	B+
IL	Fine Art Fair	40,000	Sept.	203 Harrison	Peoria	IL	61602	309-637-2787	B
IL	Greenwich Village Art Fair	15,000	Sept.	711 N. Main St.	Rockford	IL	61103	815-968-2787	A
IL	Holiday Folk Craft And Art	25,000	Nov.	P. O. Box 228	Rockton	IL	61072	815-629-2060	A
IL	Autumn On The Fox Art And Craft Show	75,000	October	43w987 Empire Road	Saint Charles	IL	60175	630-365-2753	B+
IL	Springfield Old Capitol Art Fair	25,000	May	1508 Daylilly Pl	Springfield	IL	62707	217-585-8000	B
IL	Midwest Craft Festival	40,000	May	620 Lincoln Avenue	Winnetka	IL	60093	708-446-2870	A+
IL	Old Orchard Craft Festival	100,000	May	620 Lincoln Avenue	Winnetka	IL	60093	708-446-2870	A+
IL	Spring Festival Arts & Crafts Affair	16,000	April	Box 184	Boys Town	NE	68010	402-331-2889	B+
IN	4th St. Festival Of The Arts & Crafts	25,000	Aug.	P O Box 1257	Bloomington	IN	47402	812-334-4447	A-
IN	Chesterton Arts & Crafts Fair	10,000	Aug.	P. O. Box 783	Chesterton	IN	46304	219-926-4711	A-
IN	Chautauqua Of The Arts	25,000	Sept.	P. O. Box 2624	Columbus	IN	47202	812-265-5080	B
IN	Talbot Street Art Fair	60,000	June	P. O. Box 44166	Danville	IN	46244	317-745-6479	B
IN	Leeper Park Art Fair	10,000	June	16200 Continental Dr	Granger	IN	46530	574-272-8598	A-
IN	Broad Ripple Art Fair	20,000	May	820 E 67th St.	Indianapolis	IN	46220	317-255-2464	B
IN	The Penrod Arts Fair	35,000	Sept.	P. O. Box 40817	Indianapolis	IN	46240	317-252-9895	B+
IN	Round The Fountain Art Fair	5,000	May	P O Box 1134	Lafayette	IN	47902	317-477-4230	B
IN	Chautauqua Festival Of Art	75,000	Sept.	601 West First Street	Madison	IN	47250	812-265-6100	B
IN	Amish Acres Arts And Crafts Fest	80,000	Aug.	1600 W. Market Street	Nappanee	IN	46550	574-773-4188	A+

Top Craft Fairs

State	Fair	Attendance	Month	Address	City	State	Zip	Phone	Grade
IN	Covered Bridge Festival	1,000,000	October	7975 E. Chandler Ave.	Terre Haute	IN	47803	812-877-9550	A-
KS	River Valley Arts	8,000	June	P O Box 147	Arkansas City	KS	67005	620-442-5895	B+
KS	Arts And Crafts Fair	40,000	Sept.	109 South Main	Hillsboro	KS	67063	620-947-3506	A-
KS	Hutchinson Art Association Art Fair	10,000	April	405 N. Washington	Hutchinson	KS	67501	620-663-2461	nr
KS	Overland Park Arts And Crafts Fair	15,000	September	6300 West 87th Street	Overland Park	KS	66212	913-895-6357	B
KS	Smoky Hill River Festival	100,000	June	P. O. Box 2181	Salina	KS	67402	913-823-1900	B
KS	Christmas In July	10,000	July	Box 12707	Wichita	KS	67212	316-773-9300	B
KS	Wichita Art And Book Fair	40,000	May	P. O. Box 20885	Wichita	KS	67208	316-683-3144	B
KS	Pioneer Christmas Arts And Crafts	12,000	November	P. O. Box 9024	Wichita	KS	67277	316-729-9443	B
KY	Bardstown Arts, Crafts, And Antiques	12,000	October	P. O. Box 867	Bardstown	KY	40004	502-348-4877	B
KY	Berea Craft Festival	11,000	July	P. O. Box 128	Berea	KY	40403	859-986-2818	B+
KY	Holiday Fine Art And Craft Fair	8,000	Nov.	P. O. Box 21882	Columbus	OH	43221	614-486-3537	B
KY	Cincinnati Winterfair	13,000	November	1665 West Fifth Avenue	Columbus	KY	43212	614-486-7119	B
KY	Newport Arts And Music Festival	20,000	July	915 Lincoln Road	Dayton	KY	41074	859-441-3139	B
KY	St. James Ct. Art Fair - 1300 3rd St.	900,000	Oct.	1362 S 3rd St	Louisville	KY	40208	502-635-2844	A
KY	St. James Ct Art Show/S. 4th Street	300,000	Oct.	P. O. Box 186	Louisville	KY	40201	502-634-8587	B
KY	Cherokee Triangle Art Fair	25,000	April	P. O. Box 4306	Louisville	KY	40204	502-458-3905	B
KY	St. James Court Art Sh.	300,000	Oct.	P. O. Box 3804	Louisville	KY	40201	502-635-1842	A
KY	St. James Ct. Art Fair/Belgravia Sect.	300,000	Oct.	511 Belgravia Ct.	Louisville	KY	40201	502-634-8950	A-
KY	Louisville Christmas	13,000	Nov.	P. O. Box 66	Madison	IN	47250	812-265-6100	A
LA	Covington Three Rivers Art Festival	35,000	November	P. O. Box 633	Covington	LA	70434	985-705-7968	B
LA	Christmas In New Orleans	17,000	Nov.	16471 Highway 40	Folsom	LA	70437	504-796-5853	A
LA	Cottontails Trail Arts And Crafts Show	10,000	April	16741 Highway 40	Folsom	LA	70437	985-796-5853	nr
LA	Kenner Christmas In July A And C	15,000	July	16741 Highway 40	Folsom	LA	70437	985-796-5853	B
LA	Christmas Extravaganza	25,000	December	16741 Highway 40	Folsom	LA	70437	985-796-5853	B+
LA	New Orleans Jazz & Heritage Fest	500,000	April	1205 North Rampart St.	New Orleans	LA	70116	504-522-4786	A
LA	Red River Revel Arts Festival	200,000	Sept.	101 Milam	Shreveport	LA	71101	318-424-4000	B
MA	Apple Harvest And Crafts Festival	10,000	October	Umass Commuter Svs	Amherst	MA	01003	413-545-4466	nr
MA	Christmas Festival	37,000	Nov.	83 Mt. Vernon Street	Boston	MA	02108	617-742-3973	A
MA	Crafts At The Castle	10,000	Dec.	34 1/2 Beacon St.	Boston	MA	02108	617-523-6400	A
MA	Cranberry Professional A And C	30,000	Nov.	220 Rte 6h	Brewster	MA	02631	508-385-8689	B+
MA	Festival Of The Arts	10,000	Aug.	154 Crowell Rd	Chatham	MA	02633	508-945-3583	B

Top Craft Fairs

MA	Old Deerfield Christmas Sampler	17,000	Nov.	P. O. Box 323	Deerfield	MA	1342	413-774-7476	A-
MA	Danforth Craft Festival	5,000	June	123 Union Ave.	Framingham	MA	01701	508-620-0050	A+
MA	The Berkshire Crafts Fair	5,000	Aug.	Monument Mt. Reg. H.S/Rt. 7	Great Barrington	MA	01230	413-528-3346	B+
MA	Gloucester Waterfront Fest.	25,000	Aug.	4 Greenleaf Woods Dr, #302	Portsmouth	NH	03801	207-439-2021	B+
MA	Original Castleberry	25,000	November	38 Charles St	Rochester	NH	03867	603-332-2616	B
MD	Fell's Point Fun Festival	700,000	October	812 South Ann Street	Baltimore	MD	21231	410-675-6756	A-
MD	Fells Point Art & Craft Show	6,000	Aug.	1606 Portugul St.	Baltimore	MD	21231	410-563-2606	B
MD	Fell's Point Fun Festival	700,000	Oct.	812 South Ann Street	Baltimore	MD	21231	410-675-6750	A-
MD	Artscape	750,000	July	7 E. Redwood St. Ste 500	Baltimore	MD	21202	410-752-8632	B
MD	BelAir Festival For The Arts	30,000	September	1909 Wheel Road	Bel Air	MD	21015	410-836-2395	B
MD	National Craft Fair	25,000	Oct.	4845 Rumler Rd	Chambersburg	PA	17201	717-369-4810	A
MD	Waterfowl Festival	15,000	November	P. O. Box 929	Easton	MD	21601	410-822-4567	B
MD	Frederick Festival Of The Arts	25,000	June	P O Box 3080	Frederick	MD	21705	301-694-9632	B
MD	Sugarloaf Crafts Festival	24,000	April	200 Orchard Ridge Dr.#215	Gaithersburg	MD	20878	800-210-9900	B
MD	Christmas Wonderland	20,000	November	P. O. Box 1921	Hagerstown	MD	21742	301-791-2346	B
MD	Havre De Grace Arts And Crafts Show	10,000	August	P. O. Box 150	Havre De Grace	MD	21078	410-939-9342	B
MD	ACC Craft Fair	35,000	March	72 Spring Street	New York	NY	10012	212-274-0630	A+
MD	Shaker Forest Festival	37,000	Sept.	275 Pleasantview Drive	Midland	PA	15059	724-643-6627	B
MD	North Beach Bayfest	18,000	August	P. O. Box 99	North Beach	MD	20714	301-855-6681	B
MD	Ocean City Holiday Shoppers Fair	15,000	November	4001 Coastal Highway	Ocean City	MD	21842	410-289-8311	B
MD	Christmas Craft Expo.	10,000	November	10549 Sussex Rd.	Ocean City	MD	21842	410-524-9177	B
MD	Sunfest	200,000	Sept.	200 125th St	Ocean City	MD	21842	410-250-0125	A
MD	Catoctin Colorfest	100,000	October	P. O. Box 33	Thurmont	MD	21788	301-271-4432	B+
MD	Kennedy Krieger Festival Of Trees	25,000	November	200 E. Joppa Road #403	Towson	MD	21204	410-769-8223	B
MD	Townstown Spring Fest	250,000	May	P O Box 10115	Towson	MD	21285	410-825-1144	B
MD	Brandywine Lions Craft Fair Festival	20,000	October	13200 Old Marlboro Pike	Upper Marlboro	MD	20772	301-627-7575	B
MD	Maryland Christmas Show	40,000	Nov.	P. O. Box 187	Walkersville	MD	21793	301-898-5466	B+
MD	Cabin Fever Festival		Feb.	P. O. Box 187	Walkersville	MD	21793	301-898-5466	B
MD	Ocean City Labor Day A And C Fest.	15,000	September	9005 Whaleyville Rd	Whaleyville	MD	21872	410-524-9177	B
MD	Sugarloaf Crafts Festival	26,000	Oct.	200 Orchard Ridge Dr. #215	Gaithersburg	MD	20878	800-210-9900	A
ME	Bath Heritage Days	50,000	July	60 Pleasant Point Road	Topsham	ME	04086	207-373-1325	B
MI	Algonac Rotary Art Fair	30,000	September	P. O. Box 1959	Algonac	MI	48001	810-794-5937	B
MI	Allen Park Arts And Crafts	50,000	Aug.	16850 Southfield Rd.	Allen Park	MI	48101	313-928-1400	A

Top Craft Fairs

State	Fair Name	Attendance	Month	Address	City	State	Zip	Phone	Rating
MI	South Univ. Art Fair	100,000	July	P. O. Box 4525	Ann Arbor	MI	48106	734-663-5300	A
MI	Southfield City Art Fair	30,000	August	118 N. Fourth Ave	Ann Arbor	MI	48104	734-662-3382	B
MI	The Ann Arbor Street Art Fair	500,000	July	P O Box 1352	Ann Arbor	MI	48106	734-994-5260	A+
MI	State Street Area Art Fair	500,000	July	P. O. Box 4128	Ann Arbor	MI	48106	313-663-6511	A+
MI	The Summer Art Fair	500,000	July	118 N. Fourth Ave.	Ann Arbor	MI	48104	313-662-3382	A+
MI	Birmingham Art Fair (At Shain Park)	80,000	May	1516 S. Cranbrook Rd.	Birmingham,	MI	48009	248-644-0866	B+
MI	Summit Place Mall Christmas Show	80,000	December	40750 Woodward Ave, 32	Bloomfield Hills	MI	48304	248-302-1610	B
MI	Brighton Art Festival	20,000	August	131 Hyne Street	Brighton	MI	48116	810-227-5086	B
MI	Cadillac Festival Of The Arts	25,000	July	P. O. Box 841	Cadillac	MI	49601	231-775-7853	B
MI	Charlevoix Waterfront Art	30,000	Aug.	Box 57	Charlevoix	MI	49720	616-547-5759	B
MI	Clarkston Art In The Village	15,000	September	P. O. Box 261	Clarkston	MI	48347	248-922-0270	B
MI	Clinton Fall Festival	60,000	September	P. O. Box 205	Clinton	MI	49236	517-456-7396	B
MI	Art On The Avenue	15,000	June	15801 Michigan Ave	Dearborn	MI	48126	313-943-3095	B
MI	Detroit Festival Of The Arts	250,000	Sept.	4735 Cass St	Detroit	MI	48202	313-577-5088	B+
MI	East Lansing Art Festival	50,000	May	410 Abbott Rd	East Lansing	MI	48823	517-319-6804	B
MI	MSU Crafts Fair	60,000	May	322 MSU Student Union	East Lansing	MI	48824	517-355-3354	B
MI	MSU Holiday Arts And Crafts Show	15,000	December	322 MSU Union	East Lansing	MI	48824	517-355-3354	B
MI	Shipshewana On The Road/Battle Cr.	10,000	November	10740 Three Mile Road	East Leroy	MI	49051	269-979-8888	B
MI	Farmington Founders Festival	65,000	July	P. O. Box 291	Farmington	MI	48332	248-932-3378	B
MI	Flint Art Fair	20,000	June	1120 E Kearsley St.	Flint	MI	48503	810-234-1695	A
MI	Americana Folk Art Show	100,000	September	613 S. Main Street	Frankenmuth	MI	48734	989-652-9701	B
MI	Festival Of The Arts	500,000	June	P. O. Box 2265	Grand Rapids	MI	49503	616-459-2787	B+
MI	Reeds Lake Arts Fest	10,000	June	P O Box 1287	Grand Rapids	MI	49503	616-458-0315	B+
MI	Hasting Summerfest Arts And Crafts	20,000	August	221 West State Street	Hastings	MI	49058		nr
MI	Holland Art In The Park	12,000	August	150 West 8th Street	Holland	MI	49423	616-395-3278	B-
MI	Jackson Civil War Muster Craft Show	25,000	August	3117 Earl Drive	Jackson	MI	49283	517-206-8489	B-
MI	Hot Air Jubilee Arts And Crafts Show	60,000	July	3606 Wildwood Avenue	Jackson	MI	49204	517-782-1515	B
MI	Christmas At Wings	60,000	December	P. O. Box 516	Kalamazoo	MI	49004	269-349-1185	B+
MI	Kia/Bronson Park Art Fair	50,000	June	314 S. Park	Kalamazoo	MI	49007	616-349-7775	B+
MI	Lake Odessa Art In The Park	10,000	July	839 Fourth Avenue	Lake Odessa	MI	48849	616-374-4325	B-

Top Craft Fairs

MI	Lexington's Fine Art And Craft Street	20,000	August	7276 Huron Avenue	Lexington	MI	48450	810-359-5151	B
MI	Art On The Rocks	12,000	July	P. O. Box 9	Marquette	MI	49855	906-942-7865	B
MI	Cornwell's Sept. Arts And Crafts Show	22,000	September	18935 15 1/2 Mile Road	Marshall	MI	49068	239-781-4293	B
MI	Milford Memories Summer Festival	100,000	August	317 Union Street	Milford	MI	48381	248-685-7129	B+
MI	New Boston Applefest	100,000	October	P. O. Box 58	New Boston	MI	48164	734-783-5524	B+
MI	Petoskey Art In The Park	20,000	July	401 E. Mitchell St.	Petoskey	MI	49770	616-347-4150	B
MI	Art In The Park	75,000	July	51220 Northview	Plymouth	MI	48170	734-454-1314	B
MI	Birmingham Art In The Park	60,000	Sept.	7 South Perry St	Pontiac	MI	48342	810-456-8150	A-
MI	Chrysler Arts, Beats And Eats	800,000	Sept	17 Water St.	Pontiac	MI	48342	248-975-8812	A
MI	Art & Apples Festival	150,000	Sept.	407 Pine St.	Rochester	MI	48307	810-651-7418	A+
MI	Roscommon Arts And Crafts Show	15,000	July	P. O. Box 486	Roscommmon	MI	48653	989-275-8760	B-
MI	Royal Oak Outdoor Art Fair	30,000	July	P. O. Box 64	Royal Oak,	MI	48068	810-585-4736	A+
MI	Saint Joseph Venetian Festival	120,000	July	P. O. Box 510	Saint Joseph	MI	49085	269-983-7917	B
MI	South Haven Art Fair	10,000	July	P. O. Box 505	South Haven	MI	49090	616-637-1041	B
MI	South Haven Summer Art Fair	20,000	July	P. O. Box 505	South Haven	MI	49090	269-637-1041	B
MI	St Clair Art Fair	60,000	June	201 Riverside	St. Clair	MI	48079	810-329-9576	B
MI	Krasl Art Fair On Bluff	75,000	July	707 Lake Blvd	St. Joseph	MI	49085	616-983-0271	A+
MI	Traverse Bay Fair	9,000	July	720 S. Elmwood	Traverse City	MI	49684	517-268-5656	B
MI	Saint Nick's Warehouse	11,000	November	P. O. Box 180359	Utica	MI	48318	586-566-1353	B
MI	West Branch Victorian Art Fair	20,000	August	124 N. 4th Street	West Branch	MI	48661	989-345-3856	B-
MI	Westland Summer Festival	225,000	July	7910 Nankin Mill Street	Westland	MI	48185	734-261-5955	B
MI	Wyandotte Heritage Days	40,000	September	2630 Biddle Avenue	Wyandotte	MI	48192	734-324-7297	B
MI	Wyandotte Street Art Fair	250,000	July	3131 Biddle Avenue	Wyandotte	MI	48192	734-324-4506	B+
MI	Clay And Glass Show	28,000	June	268 Taft	Ypsilanti	MI	48197	734-216-3958	B+
MI	Art In The Park	230,000	July	587 West Western	Muskegon	MI	49440	231-722-6520	B
MN	Old Fashioned 4th Of July Fine Arts	30,000	July	P. O. Box 805	Blooming Prarie	MN	55917	507-583-4472	B-
MN	Autumn Festival, An Arts & Crafts Affair	350,000	Nov.	Box 184	Boys Town	NE	68010	402-331-2889	A+
MN	Spring Festival An Arts & Crafts Affair	12,000	April	Box 184	Boys Town	NE	68010	402-331-2889	B
MN	Edina Art Fair	35,000	June	P. O. Box 24122	Edina,	MN	55424	612-922-1524	A-
MN	Little Falls Sidewalk Arts And Crafts	65,000	Sept.	200 Nw 1st Street	Little Falls	MN	56345	320-630-5155	A
MN	Little Falls Indoor Show	10,000	September	73 East Broadway	Little Falls	MN	56345	218-330-6141	nr
MN	Maple Grove Days Art Fair	30,000	July	P. O. Box 2009	Maple Grove	MN	55311	612-494-5984	B
MN	Marine Art Fair	20,000	Sept.	1313 Bdway	Marine/ St Croi	MN	55047	612-433-3636	B+
MN	Powderhorn Festival	60,000	Aug.	P. O. Box 7372	Minneapolis	MN	55047	612-724-8179	A-

Top Craft Fairs

MN	Metris Uptown Art Fair	300,000	Aug.	1406 W. Lake St Ste 2002	Minneapolis	MN	55408	612-823-4581	A+
MN	Minnesota Crafts Festival	15,000	June	528 Hennepin Ave. Ste 216	Minneapolis	MN	55403	612-333-7789	A
MN	Red Wing Fall Festival Of Arts	10,000	October	418 Levee Street	Red Wing	MN	55066	651-388-7569	nr
MN	River City Days	25,000	August	439 Main Street	Red Wing	MN	55066	651-388-4719	B
MN	Old Creamery Arts And Crafts Show	15,000	September	40 S. Main St. E Box 176	Rice	MN	56367	320-393-4100	B
MN	Highland Fest	65,000	August	790 Cleveland Ave S. #219	Saint Paul	MN	55116	651-699-9042	B
MN	Art At Ramsey Junior High School	30,000	December	1015 South Snelling	Saint Paul	MN	55116	651-222-2483	B
MN	Minnesota Renaissance Festival	312,000	Aug.	3525 West 145 Th Street	Shakopee	MN	55379	612-445-7361	A
MO	Autumn Daze Craft Show	800,000	Sept.	P. O. Box 1034	Branson	MO	65615	417-334-1548	A-
MO	Plumb Nellie Festival And Craft Show	800,000	May	P. O. Box 1034	Branson	MO	65615	417-334-1548	A
MO	Christmas Arts And Crafts Extrav.	10,000	November	P. O. Box 901	Cape Girardeau	MO	63702	573-334-9233	B
MO	Plaza Arts Fair	270,000	Sept.	310 Ward Pky	Kansas City	MO	64112	816-753-0100	A+
MO	Brookside Art Annual	50,000	May	3920 W. 69th	Prarie Village	KS	66208	913-362-9668	A+
MO	Festival Of The Little Hills	250,000	August	P. O. Box 1323	Saint Charles	MO	63302	636-940-0095	B+
MO	Central West End Art Fair And Taste	50,000	June	304-A North Euclid Ave.	Saint Louis	MO	63108	314-361-2850	B
MO	Festival Of The Little Hills	300,000	Aug.	P. O. Box 7	St Charles	MO	63302	636-940-0095	B+
MO	Saint Louis Art Fair	100,000	Sept.	7818 Forsyth Ste 210	St Louis	MO	63105	314-863-0278	A+
MO	Historic Shaw Art Fair	15,000	Oct.	2211 S. 39th	St Louis	MO	63110	314-771-3101	B
MO	Laumeier Cont. Arts & Crafts Fair	20,000	May	12580 Rott	St. Louis	MO	63127	314-821-1209	A
MO	Washington Art Fair And Wine fest	30,000	May	P. O. Box 144	Washington	MO	63090	636-583-3270	B-
MS	Mississippi Fine Arts And Crafts Fest.	20,000	October	P. O. Box 347	Ardmore	PA	19003	877-244-9768	B
MS	Flea Market Arts & Crafts Show	30,000	Oct.	P. O. Box 382	Canton	MS	39046	601-859-8055	B+
MS	Meridian Arts In The Park Festival	17,000	April	P. O. Box 1405	Meridian	MS	39302	601-693-2787	B
MS	Peter Anderson Festival	50,000	November	1000 Washington Ave.	Ocean Springs	MS	39564	228-875-4424	B+
MS	Oxford Double Decker Arts Festival	50,000	April	107 Courthouse Sq. Ste 1	Oxford	MS	38655	800-758-9177	B
MS	Picayune Fall Street Fair	55,000	November	P. O. Box 1656	Picayune	MS	39466	601-799-3070	B
MT	Art In Washoe Park	12,000	July	401 East Commercial	Anaconda	MT	59711	406-563-2422	nr
MT	Bigfork Festival Of The Arts	14,000	August	P. O. Box 1892	Bigfork	MT	59911	406-881-4636	B
MT	Summerfair	20,000	July	401 N. 27th St.	Billings	MT	59101	406-245-8688	A
MT	Billings Strawberry Festival	15,000	June	2906 Third Avenue North	Billings	MT	59101	406-259-5454	B
MT	Arts In The Park	10,000	July	P. O. Box 83	Kalispell	MT	59901	406-755-5268	B

Top Craft Fairs

MT	Kalispell Arts In The Park	11,000	July	302 Second Avenue East	Kalispell	MT	59901	406-755-5268	nr
MT	Huckleberry Days A And C Fair	10,000	August	P. O. Box 1120	Whitefish	MT	59937	406-862-3501	nr
NC	Bele Chere	350,000	July	P. O. Box 7148	Asheville	NC	28802	828-259-5821	A
NC	Village Art And Craft Fair	20,000	Aug.	7 Boston Way	Asheville	NC	28803	828-274-2831	B
NC	Sourwood Festival	30,000	August	201 East State Street	Black Mountain	NC	28711	828-669-2300	B
NC	Fine Arts And Crafts Showcase	15,000	July	P. O. Box 1229	Brevard	NC	28712	828-884-2787	B
NC	Mountain Heritage Day	35,000	Sept.	Wcu	Cullowhee	NC	28723	828-227-2169	A-
NC	Cityfest Live	110,000	April	518 N. Hwy 16	Denver	NC	28037	704-483-6266	A+
NC	Centerfest	20,000	October	120 Morris Street	Durham	NC	27701	919-560-2722	B
NC	Holly Day Fair	20,000	November	2605 Fort Bragg Road	Fayetteville	NC	28303	910-323-5509	B
NC	Craftsmens Christmas Classic	35,000	Nov.	1240 Oakland Ave	Greensboro	NC	27403	336-274-5550	A-
NC	Craftsmen's Classic	20,000	April	1240 Oakland Ave	Greensboro	NC	27403	336-274-1084	B
NC	A Christmas Carousel Hol. Fest	15,000	November	P. O. Box 7282	Greensboro	NC	24717	336-855-0208	B+
NC	Craftscene And Marketplace Fun 4th	100,000	July	P. O. Box 29212	Greensboro	NC	27429	336-274-4595	B
NC	Seaboard Festival Day	25,000	October	P. O. Box 132	Hamlet	NC	28345	910-582-3505	B
NC	North Carolina Apple Festival	100,000	September	P. O. Box 886	Henderson	NC	28793	828-891-3939	B+
NC	Hickory Octoberfest	95,000	October	P. O. Box 9086	Hickory	NC	28603	828-322-3125	B+
NC	Mountain Makings	10,000	July	Box 1776	Highlands	NC	28741	828-526-3181	nr
NC	Matthews Alive!	125,000	September	716 Meadow Lake Drive	Matthews	NC	28106	704-668-9681	B+
NC	Carolina Designer Craftsmen Fair	10,000	Nov.	P. O. Box 33791	Raleigh	NC	27636	919-571-4217	B
NC	Fourth Of July Festival	40,000	July	4841 Long Beach Rd Se	Southport	NC	28461	910-457-6964	B
NC	Church Street Art And Craft Show	20,000	October	P. O. Box 1409	Waynesville	NC	28786	828-456-3517	B
NC	Ashe County Christmas In July	33,000	July	P. O. Box 1107	West Jefferson	NC	28694	336-246-5855	B
NC	Merlefest	800,000	April	P.O. Box 120	Wilkelsboro	NC	28697	336-838-6292	B+
NC	Azalea Festival	375,000	April	P. O. Box 3275	Wilmington	NC	28406	910-790-9564	B+
NC	Piedmont Crafts Fair		Nov.	1204 Reynolds Avenue	Winston-Salem	NC	27104	336-72651516	B+
ND	Island Park Show	15,000	August	701 Main Aven	Fargo	ND	58103	701-476-6771	B
ND	Downtown Red River Street Fair	75,000	July	203 4th Ave North	Fargo	ND	58107	701-241-1570	B+
NE	Autumn Fest, An Arts &	30,000	Nov.	Box 184	Boys Town	NE	68010	402-331-2889	A
NE	Art In The Park	16,000	July	Box 1368	Kearney	NE	68848	308-234-2662	B
NE	Omaha Summer Arts Festival	80,000	June	P. O. Box 31036	Omaha	NE	68131	402-963-9020	A
NE	Countryside Village Art Fair	15,000	June	2336 S 138th	Omaha	NE	68144	402-333-9629	A-
NE	Rockbrook Village Art Fair	30,000	Sept.	2800 S. 110 Court Ste 1	Omaha	NE	68144	402-390-0890	B
NH	Craftsmen's Fair	50,000	Aug.	205 North Main St.	Concord	NH	03301	603-224-3375	A+
NH	Lincoln Fall Craft Festival	35,000	October	38 Charles Street	Rochester	NH	03867	603-332-2616	B+

Top Craft Fairs

NH	Mills Falls Autumn Craft Festival	10,000	October	38 Charles Street	Rochester	NH	03867	603-332-2616	B
NH	New England Craft And Food Fair	22,000	November	38 Charles Street	Rochester	NH	03867	603-332-2616	B
NH	Christmas Craft Show	9,000	December	38 Charles Street	Rochester	NH	03867	603-332-2616	B
NJ	Atlantic City Arts Alive	140,000	August	47 N. Tallahassee Ave	Atlantic City	NJ	08401	609-345-0899	A
NJ	Bordentown Cranberry Fest	40,000	October	P. O. Box 686	Bordentown	NJ	08505	609-499-4410	B
NJ	Chester Fall Craft Show	12,000	September	P. O. Box 330	Chester	NJ	07930	973-377-3260	B
NJ	Montclair Craft Show	5,000	Dec.	P. O. Box 8252	Glen Ridge	NJ	7028	973-743-4110	A+
NJ	Haddenfield Art And Craft Show	130,000	July	114 Kings Highway E	Haddonfield	NJ	08033	856-216-7253	B
NJ	Fine Art And Crafts Show	16,000	Oct.	12 Galaxy Court	Hillsborough	NJ	08844	908-874-5247	B
NJ	Country Folk Art Craft Show	25,000	Oct.	15045 Dixie Highway	Holly	MI	48442	248-634-4151	B
NJ	Peters Valley Craft Fair	10,000	Sept.	19 Kuhn Rd	Layton	NJ	07851	973-948-5200	B
NJ	Spring Chester Craft Show	12,000	June	P. O. Box 613	Madison	NJ	07940	973-377-3260	B
NJ	Flemington Crafts Festival	30,000	April	Box 326	Masonville	NY	13804	607-265-3230	B
NJ	Flemington Crafts Festival	30,000	October	Box 326	Masonville	NY	13804	607-265-3230	B+
NJ	Little Falls Street Fair	15,000	September	5 Jeanette Lane	Milford	NJ	08848	908-996-3866	B
NJ	Maywood Street Fair	10,000	May	5 Jeanette Lane	Milford	NJ	08848	908-996-3866	nr
NJ	Morristown Craft Mkt.	5,000	Oct.	P. O. Box 2305	Morristown	NJ	07062	201-263-8332	A+
NJ	Nutley Festival In The Park	15,000	September	51 Enclosure	Nutley	NJ	07110	973-667-3013	nr
NJ	Westfield Craft Market	10,000	Nov.	P. O. Box 480	Slate Hill	NY	10973	914-355-2400	A
NJ	Art And Craft Show	30,000	Aug.	P. O. Box 274	Stone Harbor	NJ	08247	609-368-4112	A-
NJ	Midsummer Craft Show	10,000	July	6101 Pacific Avenue	Wildwood Crest	NJ	08260	609-522-1669	nr
NM	New Mexico Arts And Crafts Fair	15,000	June	5500 San Mateo N. E. #106	Albuquerque	NM	87109	505-884-9043	B+
NM	Int. Balloon Fiesta	850,000	October	4401 Alameda N. E.	Albuquerque	NM	87113	505-821-1000	B
NM	Wine Festival At Bernalillo	18,000	September	P. O. Box 57060	Albuquerque	NM	87187	505-867-3311	B
NM	Southwest Arts Festival	30,000	Nov.	525 San Pedro NE., #107	Albuquerque	NM	87108	505-262-2448	A
NM	Weems Artfest	50,000	Nov.	2801-M Eubank Ne	Albuquerque	NM	87112	505-293-6133	A
NM	Cloudcroft Oct.Fest	3,000	July	P O Box 1290	Cloudcroft	NM	88317	505-682-2733	B
NM	Farmington Riverfest Fine Arts Fair	13,000	May	901 Fairgrounds Rd.	Farmington	NM	87401	505-599-1140	B
NM	Santa Fe Fiesta Arts & Crafts Fair	30,000	Sept.	P. O. Box 22303	Santa Fe	NM	87502	505-988-2889	B
NM	Girls, Inc. Arts And Crafts Show	35,000	August	301 Hillside Avenue	Santa Fe	NM	87501	505-982-2042	B+
NV	Las Vegas Fine Art And Craft Fest	25,000	October	P. O. Box 347	Ardmore	PA	19003	610-896-9839	B+
NV	Art In The Park	100,000	Oct.	P O Box 61512	Boulder City	NV	89006	702-294-1611	B+

Top Craft Fairs

NV	Candy Dance Arts & Crafts Festival	80,000	Sept.	P O Box 155	Genoa	NV	89411	702-782-3696	B+
NV	Reno Street Vibrations	40,000	September	4790 Caughlin Parkway 507	Reno	NV	89509	775-324-6435	B
NV	Best In The West Cook-Off	350,000	September	4790 Caughlin Parkway 507	Reno	NV	89509	775-324-6435	A-
NV	The Big Easy	45,000	July	814 Victorian Avenue	Sparks	NV	89432	775-353-1513	B+
NY	Armonk Outdoor Art Show	14,000	Oct.	One Boulder Trail	Armonk,	NY	10504	914-273-5986	B
NY	Eagle Mills Arts And C	30,000	September	P. O. Box 788	Broadalbin	NY	12025	518-883-5479	B+
NY	Elmwood Ave. Fest. Of The Arts	100,000	August	P. O. Box 786	Buffalo	NY	14213	716-830-2484	B+
NY	Adirondack Mountain Craft Fair	12,000	Sept.	P. O. Box 300	Charlotte	VT	05445	802-425-3399	A-
NY	International Festival A And C Show	18,000	September	166 Little Robin Hood	Darien	NY	14228	716-689-1100	nr
NY	Albany Holiday A And C Showcase	14,000	December	P. O. Box 404	Delmar	NY	12054	518-439-8379	B
NY	Ellicottville Fall Festival	40,000	October	P. O. Box 456	Ellicottville	NY	14731	716-699-5046	B
NY	Fairport Canal Days	200,000	July	6 N. Main St	Fairport	NY	14450	585-234-4323	A
NY	Larac June Arts Festival	20,000	June	7 Lapham Place	Glens Falls	NY	12801	518-798-1144	B+
NY	Elms Christmas Craft Show	18,000	November	341 Spier Falls Road	Greenfield Center	NY	12833	518-893-7488	B
NY	Haverstraw Street Festival	20,000	September	P. O. Box 159	Haverstraw	NY	10927	845-947-5646	B
NY	Hilton Apple Fest	65,000	October	P. O. Box 1	Hilton	NY	14468	585-234-3378	B+
NY	Lafayette Apple Festival	75,000	October	P. O. Box 456	Lafayette	NY	13084	315-677-3644	B+
NY	100 American Craftsmen	15,000	May	433 Locust St	Lockport	NY	14094	716-433-2617	B+
NY	Long Beach A And C Festival	100,000	July	Mag. Blvd And W. Bay Dr.	Long Beach	NY	11561	516-431-3890	B+
NY	Maple Festival	40,000	April	2861 Clarks Corners Road	Marathon	NY	13803	607-849-3518	B
NY	Holiday Art And Craft Spectacular	20,000	Dec.	Box 326	Masonville	NY	13804	607-265-3230	B
NY	Craft Festivals	5,000	July	P O Box 89	Mayville	NY	14757	716-753-0240	B
NY	Amer. Crafts Fest. / Lincoln Center	100,000	June	P. O. Box 650	Montclair	NJ	07042	973-746-0091	A+
NY	Naples Grape Festival	100,000	September	P. O. Box 70	Naples	NY	14512	585-374-2240	A-
NY	Autumn Crafts On Columbus	50,000	Oct.	461 Central Park West #1	New York	NY	10025	212-866-2239	A-
NY	Washington Sq Outdoor Art Exhibit	200,000	Aug.	115 E 9th St. #7c	New York	NY	10003	212-982-6255	B
NY	Quaker Arts Fest	90,000	Sept.	P. O. Box 202	Orchard Park	NY	14127	716-655-4147	A
NY	Letchworth A And C Show And Sale	100,000	October	P. O. Box 249	Perry	NY	14530	585-237-3517	A-
NY	Waterfront Art Festival	15,000	July	50 State Street	Pittsford	NY	14534	585-383-1472	B
NY	Remsen Barn Festival Of The Arts	75,000	Sept.	P. O. Box 218	Remsen	NY	13438	315-831-4257	B+
NY	Crafts At Rhinebeck	15,000	Oct.	P. O. Box 389	Rhinebeck	NY	12572	914-876-4001	B
NY	Park Avenue Arts Festival	25,000	May	171 Reservoir Ave	Rochester	NY	14620	585-256-4960	B
NY	Clothesline Festival		Sept.	500 University Avenue	Rochester	NY	14607	585-473-7720	B
NY	Corn Hill Arts Fest.	250,000	July	133 S. Fitzhugh	Rochester	NY	14608	585-262-3142	A-

Top Craft Fairs

NY	Masapequa Park Street	50,000	August	P. O. Box 477	Smithtown	NY	11787	631-724-5966	B
NY	West Hempstead Street Fair	20,000	October	P. O. Box 477	Smithtown	NY	11787	631-724-5966	B
NY	Market Street: A Festival Of Art	40,000	July	320 Montgomery St	Syracuse	NY	13202	315-472-4245	B
NY	The Syracuse Arts & Crafts Festival	60,000	June	109 S. Warren St. Ste !900	Syracuse	NY	13202	315-422-8284	A-
NY	Harvest Crafts Festival	20,000	Nov.	P O Box 1688	Westhampton Bch	NY	11978	516-288-2004	B+
NY	Westhampton Outdoor Art Show	10,000	Aug.	P. O. Box 1228	Westhampton Bch	NY	11978	516-288-3337	A
NY	Handmade In The Usa	12,000	Jan.	10 Bank Street #1200	White Plains	NY	10606	914-421-3287	A
NY	Christmas In The Country	53,000	Nov.	4310 Tilson Road	Wilmington	NC	28412	910-799-9424	A+
NY	Woodstock-New Paltz A & C Fair	25,000	Sept.	P. O. Box 825	Woodstock	NY	12498	845-679-8087	B
NY	Fall Crafts At Lyndhurst	20,000	September	P. O. Box 286	Woodstock	NY	12498	845-331-7900	B+
NY	Woodstock New Paltz Crafts Fest	20,000	May	P. O. Box 825	Woodstock	NY	12498	845-679-8087	B+
NY	Crafts Park Avenue	10,000	April	4 Deming St	Woodstock	NY	12498	914-679-7277	A+
NY	Allentown Art Festival	500,000	June	Ellicott Station Box 1566	Buffalo	NY	14205	716-881-4269	A
OH	Wonderful World Of Ohio Mart	20,000	Oct.	714 Portage Path	Akron	OH	44303	216-836-5535	A
OH	Christmas In The Colonies	12,000	November	P. O. Box 40298	Bay Village	OH	44140	440-835-1765	B
OH	Fine Craft Festival	7,000	April	26001 S Woodland	Beachwood	OH	44122	216-831-0700	A+
OH	Salt Fork Arts & Crafts Festival	50,000	Aug.	7570 Marysville Rd	Byesville	OH	43723	740-685-1350	B
OH	Christkindl Market	10,000	Nov.	1001 Market Ave. N.	Canton	OH	44702	216-453-7666	A
OH	Art By The Falls	25,000	June	155 Bell St	Chagrin Falls	OH	44022	216-247-7507	A-
OH	Summerfair	79,000	May	P. O. Box 8277	Cincinnati	OH	45208	513-531-0050	A
OH	Clifton Arts And Musicfest	40,000	June	11650 Detroit Avenue	Cleveland	OH	44102	216-228-4383	B
OH	Cain Park Arts Festival	60,000	July	40 Severance Circle	Cleveland Heights	OH	44118	216-2913669	A+
OH	Firestone Park Festival Of The Arts	12,000	August	28 West Friend Street	Columbiana	OH	44408	330-482-6183	nr
OH	Craftfair At Hathaway Brown	11,000	June	1665 West 5th Avenue	Columbus	OH	43212	614-486-7119	B
OH	Winterfair	19,000	Dec.	1665 W. 5th	Columbus	OH	43212	614-486-7119	A
OH	Columbus Arts Festival	500,000	June	100 E. Broad Street # 2250	Columbus	OH	43215	614-224-2606	A
OH	Kettering Holiday And Home	25,000	September	2511 Revere Avenue	Dayton	OH	45420	937-258-1104	B
OH	Oktoberfest	32,000	Oct.	456 Belmonte Park N.	Dayton	OH	45405	513-223-5277	B
OH	Groveport Festival Of The Arts	5,000	Sept.	655 Blacklick St	Groveport	OH	43125	614-836-5301	B
OH	Nutcracker Sweets	5,000	Oct.	7743 Salem Dr	Hudson	OH	44236	216-650-4327	A-
OH	Kent Art In The Park	21,000	September	497 Middlebury Rd.	Kent	OH	44240	330-673-8897	B
OH	Art On The Commons	15,000	Aug.	2655 Olson Drive	Kettering	OH	45420	513-296-O294	A
OH	Lakewood Arts Festival	15,000	Aug.	P O Box 771288	Lakewood	OH	44107	216-521-7063	B

Top Craft Fairs

State	Name	Attendance	Month	Address	City	State	Zip	Phone	Rating
OH	Yankee Peddler Festival	100,000	Sept.	171 Granger Rd. #159	Medina	OH	44256	330-665-3669	A+
OH	Shaker Woods Festival	100,000	Aug.	46000 New England Sq.	New Waterford	OH	44445	216-457-7615	A+
OH	Butler Prairie Peddler Old West Fest.	32,000	October	P. O. Box 287	Norwalk	OH	44857	419-663-1818	B
OH	Boston Mills Artfest	25,000	June	P O Box 175	Peninsula	OH	44264	216-657-2334	A
OH	Visions Of Sugarplums	10,000	Nov.	P. O. Box 21093	S. Euclid	OH	44121	216-932-2603	A-
OH	Crosby Festival Of Arts	15,000	June	5403 Elmer Dr.	Toledo	OH	43615	419-936-2986	B+
OH	Troy Strawberry Festival	175,000	June	405 S. W. Public Sq. 330	Troy	OH	45373	937-339-7714	A-
OH	Upper Arlington Labor Day Arts	30,000	Sept.	3600 Tremont Rd.	Upper Arlington	OH	43221	614-583-5310	A-
OH	Art In The Park	15,000	July	791 Broad St.	Wadsworth	OH	44281	216-334-4484	B+
OH	Sauerkraut Fest	300,000	Oct.	P. O. Box 281	Waynesville	OH	45068	513-897-8855	B
OH	Westerville Music And Arts Fest	40,000	July	99 Commerce Park Drive	Westerville	OH	43082	614-882-8917	A-
OH	The Christmas Show	60,000	Nov.	P. O. Box 45395	Westlake	OH	44145	440-835-9627	A-
OH	Xenia Old Fashioned Days Fest.	80,000	September	334 West Market Street	Xenia	OH	45385	937-372-3591	B+
OK	Beavers Bend Folk Fest. And Craft	14,000	November	P. O. Box 157	Broken Bow	OK	74728	580-494-6497	nr
OK	Downtown Edmond Art Festival	50,000	April	P. O. Box 3653	Edmond	OK	73083	405-249-9391	B
OK	Grovefest	20,000	June	9630 Highway 59 N, Ste A	Grove	OK	74344	918-786-9070	nr
OK	Pumpkin Patch Benefit A And C Show	10,000	November	213 S. Oklahoma	Guymon	OK	73942	580-338-4576	nr
OK	Arts For All Festival	23,000	May	P. O. Box 592	Lawton	OK	73502	580-248-5384	B
OK	An Affair Of The Heart		Oct.	P. O. Box 890778	Oklahoma City	OK	73189	405-632-2652	A-
OK	Paseo Arts Festival	40,000	May	3000 North Lee	Oklahoma City	OK	73103	405-525-2688	B
OK	Arts Festival Oklahoma	30,000	September	7777 South May Avenue	Oklahoma City	OK	73159	405-682-7576	B+
OK	Spring Festival Of The Arts	700,000	April	400 W. California	Oklahoma City	OK	73102	405-270-4848	A+
OK	Tulsa International Mayfest	300,000	May	201 W. 5th Ste. 460	Tulsa	OK	74103	918-582-6435	B+
OK	Children's Medical Center Arts Fest	10,000	Feb.	5839 E 63rd St	Tulsa	OK	74136	918-494-7985	B+
OK	Tulsa Arts & Crafts Fall Festival	15,000	Nov.	P. O. Box 54424	Tulsa	OK	74155	918-743-4311	B+
OR	Wah Change Northwest Art And Air	30,000	August	P. O. Box 490	Albany	OR	97321	541-917-7777	B
OR	Fall Festival	25,000	Sept.	420 NW Second	Corvalis	OR	97330	503-757-1505	A-
OR	Oregon Country Fair	50,000	July	P. O. Box 2972	Eugene	OR	97402	541-343-4298	A-
OR	Lake Oswego Festival Of The Arts	25,000	June	P. O. Box 385	Lake Oswego	OR	97034	503-636-1060	B
OR	Artquake-Art Street	200,000	Aug.	P O Box 9100	Portland	OR	97207	503-227-2787	A
OR	Salem Art Fair & Festival	110,000	July	600 Mission Street SE	Salem	OR	97302	503-581-2228	A-
OR	Crafts On The Coast Spring Fest.	23,000	May	P. O. Box 1023	Yachats	OR	97498	541-547-4738	B-
PA	Mayfair Festival Of The Arts	400,000	May	2020 Hamilton St	Allentown	PA	18104	610-437-6900	B

Top Craft Fairs

State	Fair	Attendance	Month	Address	City	State	Zip	Phone	Rating
PA	Penn's Colony Festival	50,000	September	P. O. Box 247	Allison Park	PA	15101	724-352-9922	A-
PA	Philadelphia Fine Art And Craft	10,000	July	P. O. Box 347	Ardmore	PA	19003	877-244-9768	nr
PA	Buyers Markets Of American Craft	10,000	Feb.	3000 Chestnut Avenue, #300	Baltimore	MD	21211	410-889-2933	A+
PA	Bedford Fall Foliage Festival	35,000	October	P. O. Box 234	Bedford	PA	15522	814-624-3111	B+
PA	Bellefonte Arts And Crafts Fair	12,000	August	P. O. Box 472	Bellefonte	PA	16823	814-353-1115	nr
PA	Christkindl Market Bethlehem	54,000	November	25 West Third St. Ste 300	Bethlehem	PA	18015	610-332-1327	B+
PA	National Apple Harvest Festival	100,000	October	P. O. Box 38	Biglerville	PA	17307	717-677-9413	A-
PA	Fall Pumpkin Fest	24,000	October	P. O. Box 646	Conneaut Lake	PA	16316	800-332-2338	B
PA	Celebrate Erie	75,000	August	626 Sate Street Rm 500	Erie	PA	16501	814-870-1269	B
PA	Ford City Area Heritage Days	100,000	July	P. O. Box 205	Ford City	PA	16226	724-783-1617	B
PA	Patriot News Art Fest	150,000	May	444 S 2nd St.	Harrisburg	PA	17104	877-826-8614	B+
PA	Arts And Crafts Colonial Festival	40,000	Sept.	P. O. Box 166	Irwin	PA	15642	724-863-4577	A-
PA	North Park's Colonial Arts/Crafts Fair	22,000	Sept.	P. O. Box 166	Irwin	PA	15642	724-863-4577	B+
PA	Pymatuning Pioneer And Art Festival	20,000	July	P. O. Box 146	Jamestown	PA	16134	724-927-9473	B
PA	Fort Armstrong Folk Fest.	100,000	Aug.	138 North Water St.	Kittanning	PA	16201	724-545-9622	B+
PA	Kutztown Festival	110,000	June	P. O. Box 306	Kutztown	PA	19530	610-285-0368	A-
PA	Peddler's Village Apple Festival	21,000	November	P. O. Box 218	Lahaska	PA	18931	215-794-4059	B-
PA	Long's Park Art And Craft Festival	17,000	Aug.	P. O. Box 1553	Lancaster	PA	17608	717-295-7054	A-
PA	Westmoreland Arts And Heritage Fest.	250,000	July	Rr2, Box 355a	Latrobe	PA	15650	724-834-7474	A-
PA	Fort Ligonier Days	100,000	Oct.	120 East Main	Ligonier	PA	15658	724-238-4200	A-
PA	Heart Of Lancaster County A And C	20,000	September	P. O. Box 257	Lititz	PA	17543	717-626-7369	B
PA	Mt Gretna Outdoor Art Sh.	20,000	Aug.	P. O. Box 561	Mt Gretna	PA	17064	717-964-2340	A-
PA	Pennsylvania Nat. Arts & Crafts Show	20,000	March	P O Box 449	New Cumberland	PA	17070	717-796-0531	B+
PA	New Hope Arts And Crafts Festival	20,000	October	P. O. Box 633	New Hope	PA	18938	215-598-3301	B
PA	Dutch Folk Festival	50,000	June	3760 Layfield Road	Pennsburg	PA	18073	215-679-9610	A+
PA	Germantown Friends Craft Show	5,000	March	31 W Coulter St	Philadelphia	PA	19144	215-951-2340	A
PA	Manayunk Arts Festival	250,000	June	111 Grape Street	Philadelphia	PA	19127	215-482-9565	A
PA	Philadelphia Mus. Of Art Craft Show	30,000	Nov.	P. O. Box 7646	Philadelphia	PA	19101	215-684-7931	A+
PA	Shadyside Summer Arts Festival	150,000	Aug.	P. O. Box 4866	Pittsburgh	PA	15206	412-621-8481	A+
PA	Three Rivers Art Festival	600,000	June	707 Penn Ave.	Pittsburgh	PA	15222	412-281-8723	A+
PA	A Fair In The Park (Mellon Park)	25,000	Sept.	340 Bigbee St, #2	Pittsburgh	PA	15211	412-431-6270	A-
PA	Annual State Craft Fair	18,000	July	10 Stable Mill Trail	Richboro	PA	18954	215-579-5997	B

Top Craft Fairs

PA	Tall Oaks Autumn Fest In The Woods	50,000	September	154 Star Rte	Sheffield	PA	16347	814-968-5558	B
PA	Mountain Craft Days	14,000	September	10649 Somerset Pike	Somerset	PA	15501	814-445-6077	B
PA	Central Penn.Festival	150,000	July	P O Box 1023	State College	PA	16804	814-237-3682	A
PA	Yorkfest	20,000	August	1 West Market Street	York	PA	17401	717-848-9339	B
PA	Greater Pittsburgh Holiday Spect.	19,000	Nov.	P. O. Box 166	Irwin	PA	15642	724-863-4577	A-
PA	Arts And Crafts Christmas Festival	22,000	Oct.	P. O. Box 166	Irwin	PA	15642	724-863-4577	B+
RI	Scituate Art Festival	100,000	Oct.	P. O. Box 126	North Scituate	RI	02857	401-647-0057	A+
RI	Virtu Art Festival	20,000	May	1 Chamber Way	Westerly	RI	02891	401-596-7761	B
RI	Wickford Fine Art Fest	60,000	July	36 Beach St.	Wickford	RI	02852	401-295-4075	A-
SC	Aiken's Makin's	30,000	September	P. O. Box 892	Aiken	SC	29801	803-641-1111	B
SC	Columbia Fine Art And Craft Show	25,000	September	P. O. Box 347	Ardmore	PA	19003	877-244-9768	B
SC	Craft Show At Piccolo Spoleto	10,000	May	P. O. Box 22152	Charleston	SC	29413	843-723-2938	B
SC	Southeastern Arts & Crafts Expo	70,000	Sept.	1112 Bull St	Columbia	SC	29201	803-343-2155	B
SC	Atalaya Arts & Crafts Festival	10,000	Sept.	1205 Pendleton St	Columbia	SC	29201	803-734-0517	B
SC	Craftsmen's Classic	30,000	Oct.	1240 Oakland Ave	Greensboro	NC	27403	336-274-5550	B
SC	Craftsmens Classic A and C	20,000	Aug.	1240 Oakland Ave	Greensboro	NC	27403	336-274-5550	B
SC	Hill Skills	15,000	Oct.	627 Pelham Rd	Greenville	SC	29615	803-288-4088	B+
SC	Taste Of Town Food Festival	75,000	April	5157 Thoroughbred Way	Grovetown	GA	30813	706-840-1877	B-
SC	Coastal Carolina Fair, Ladson	250,000	October	P. O. Box 762	Ladson	SC	29456	843-572-3161	B
SC	Charleston Made In The South	15,000	December	P. O. Box 853	Matthews	NC	28106	704-847-9480	B+
SC	Myrtle Beach Arts And Fall Festival	90,000	October	1325 Celebrity Circle	Myrtle Beach	SC	29577	706-840-1877	B
SC	Flowertown Festival	250,000	March	140 South Cedar Street	Summerville	SC	29483	843-871-9622	A
SC	Ware Shoals Catfish Festival	25,000	May	P. O. Box 510	Ware Shoals	SC	29692	864-456-7664	B
SD	Aberdeen Arts In The Park	20,000	June	P. O. Box 126	Aberdeen	SD	57402	605-226-1557	B
SD	Sioux Falls Autmn Fest.	20,000	October	P. O. Box 184	Boys Town	NE	68010	402-331-2889	B+
SD	Summer Arts Festival	50,000	July	P O Box 555	Brookings	SD	57006	605-693-4595	A
SD	Sioux Falls Sidewalk Arts Festival	50,000	September	301 South Main Street	Sioux Falls	SD	57104	605-367-7397	B
TN	Memphis Fine Art Show	25,000	June	P. O. Box 347	Ardmore	PA	19003	877-244-9768	B
TN	Webb School Arts And Crafts Fest	85,000	October	P. O. Box 222	Bell Buckle	TN	37020	931-389-6784	B
TN	Ketner's Mill Cntry Fair	25,000	Oct.	P. O. Box 1447	Chattanooga	TN	37401	615-821-3238	A+
TN	Meriwether Lewis Arts And Crafts	30,000	October	P. O. Box 676	Columbia	Tn	38401	931-381-9494	B
TN	Holiday Market A And C Memphis	12,000	November	P. O. Box 1327	Cordova	TN	38088	901-854-6589	B
TN	Unicoi County Apple Festival	90,000	October	P. O. Box 713	Erwin	TX	37650	423-743-3000	B

Top Craft Fairs

State	Name	Attendance	Month	Address	City	State	Zip	Phone	Rating
TN	Lenoir City Arts And Crafts Festival	15,000	June	P. O. Box 183	Lenoir City	TN	37771	865-986-7757	B
TN	Pink Palace Crafts Fair	40,000	Oct.	3050 Central Ave.	Memphis	TN	38111	901-320-6408	A+
TN	Art In The Park	45,000	Oct.	3100 Walnut Grove # 402	Memphis	TN	38111	901-761-1278	A-
TN	American Artisan Festival	50,000	June	4231 Harding	Nashville	TN	37205	615-298-4691	A+
TN	Taca Fall Crafts	40,000	Sept.	P O Box 120066	Nashville	TN	37212	615-385-1904	A
TN	Christmas Village	30,000	Nov.	P O Box 158826	Nashville	TN	37215	615-320-5353	B
TN	Harvest Crafts Festival	35,000	Oct.	2354 Chapman Hy	Sevierville	TN	37876	423-453-3497	A-
TX	Shrimporee Of Texas	55,000	June	P. O. Box 1949	Aransas Pass	TX	78335	361-758-2750	B
TX	Laguna Gloria Festival	30,000	May	P. O. Box 5705	Austin	TX	78763	512-458-6073	A
TX	Armadillo Christmas Bazaar	35,000	Dec.	4428 Gillis St.	Austin	TX	78745	512-447-1605	A+
TX	The Peddler Show/Arlington	20,000	November	5508 Hwy 290 West #208	Austin	TX	78735	512-358-1000	B
TX	Bryan College Station Arts And Music	25,000	September	3160 Bee Caves Road #201	Austin	TX	78704	512-441-9015	B
TX	The Peddler Show/Fredericksburg	20,000	November	5508 Hwy 290 West #208	Austin	TX	78735	512-358-1000	B
TX	Scarecrow Festival	20,000	October	9220 Poplar Street	Chappel Hill	TX	77426	979-836-6033	B
TX	Deep Ellum Arts Festival	80,000	April	2626 Cole Ave. Ste. 400	Dallas	TX	75204	214-855-1881	B-
TX	Artfest / The 500, Inc.	80,000	May	11300 N Central, #415	Dallas	TX	75243	214-565-0200	A
TX	Main Street Fort Worth Arts Festival	40,000	April	306 W 7th St, #400	Fort Worth	TX	76102	817-336-ARTS	A+
TX	Fulton Oysterfest	30,000	March	P. O. Box 393	Fulton	TX	78358	361-729-2388	B
TX	Dickens On The Strand	42,000	November	502 20th Street	Galveston	TX	77550	409-765-7834	B
TX	Georgetown Red Poppy Festival	25,000	April	P.O. Box 409	Georgetown	TX	78627	512-930-3545	B
TX	Granbury Arts And Crafts Festival	45,000	July	3408 East Highway 377	Granbury	TX	76049	817-573-1622	B
TX	Bayou City Art Festival	27,000	Oct.	P. O. Box 66650	Houston	TX	77266	713-521-0133	B+
TX	Bayou City Art Fest. Memorial Park	35,000	March	P. O. Box 66650	Houston	TX	77266	713-521-0133	B+
TX	Conroe Cajun Catfish Festival	35,000	October	P. O. Box 541992	Houston	TX	77254	713-863-9994	B
TX	Nutcracker Market	63,000	November	P. O. Box 130487	Houston	TX	77219	713-523-6300	B+
TX	The Houston International Fest.	500,000	April	1221 Lamar, #715	Houston	TX	77010	714-654-8808	B
TX	Keller Festival	20,000	May	P. O. Box 761	Keller	TX	76244	817-498-1292	B
TX	Texas State Arts And Crafts Fair	20,000	May	P. O. Box 1527	Kerrville	TX	78029	210-896-5711	B
TX	Lubbock Arts Festival	30,000	April	2109 Bdwy	Lubbock	TX	79401	806-744-2787	B
TX	Poteet Strawberry Fest	75,000	April	P. O. Box 227	Poteet	TX	78065	830-276-8436	B
TX	Cottonwood Arts Festival	20,000	Oct.	711 West Arapaho	Richardson	TX	75080	214-231-4624	A
TX	Christmas At Old Fort Concho	20,000	December	630 South Oakes	San Angelo	TX	76903	325-657-4441	B

Top Craft Fairs

TX	San Antonio Memorial Day A And C	45,000	May	110 Broadway, Ste 60	San Antonio	TX	78205	210-227-4286	B
TX	Fiesta Arts Fair	20,000	April	300 Augusta	San Antonio	TX	78205	210-224-1848	B
TX	Art On The Square		April	P. O. Box 92611	Southlake	TX	76092	817-421-6792	B
TX	Texarkana Quadrangle Art And Music	35,000	September	P. O. Box 2343	Texarkana	TX	75504	903-793-4831	B
TX	Parker County Peach Festival	35,000	July	P. O. Box 310	Weatherford	TX	76086	888-594-3801	B
TX	Spring Fling	20,000	April	2 Eureka Circl.	Wichita Falls	TX	76308	940-692-0923	A-
UT	Salt Lake Family Christmas Gift Show	25,000	November	P. O. Box 2815	Kirkland	WA	98083	800-521-7469	B
UT	Orem Summerfest	100,000	June	859 E. 1810 North	Orem	UT	84097	801-229-7027	B+
UT	Park City Art Festival	70,000	Aug.	P O Box 1478	Park City	UT	84060	801-649-8882	A+
UT	America's Freedom Festival/Provo	100,000	July	P. O. Box F	Provo	UT	84603	801-431-0027	B
UT	The Utah Arts Festival	69,000	June	331 W. Pierpoint Ave	Salt Lake City	UT	84101	801-322-2428	A
UT	St George Art Festival	15,000	April	86 S Main St.	St George	UT	84770	801-634-5850	B
VA	Richmond Fine Art And Craft Show	25,000	August	P. O. Box 347	Ardmore	PA	19003	877-244-9768	B
VA	Bedford Centerfest Art Show	20,000	September	P. O. Box 405	Bedford	VA	24523	540-586-2148	nr
VA	Virginia Craft And Folk	6,000	Oct.	P. O. Box 310	Cashtown	PA	17310	717-337-3060	A-
VA	Craftsmen's Christmas Classic	35,000	Nov.	P. O. Box 305	Chase City	VA	23924	434-372-3996	A+
VA	Crozet Arts And Crafts Festival	10,000	October	P. O. Box 699	Crozet	VA	22932	434-823-2211	nr
VA	Crozet Arts & Crafts Festival	10,000	May	P O Box 699	Crozet	VA	22932	804-977-0406	A
VA	City Of Fairfax Fall Festival	40,000	Oct.	3730 Old Lee Highway	Fairfax	VA	22030	703-385-7949	B
VA	Arts And Crafts Augusta Expo Land	14,000	November	P. O. Box 83	Fishersville	CA	22939	540-337-2552	nr
VA	Craftsmens Classic Arts And Crafts	20,000	Oct.	1240 Oakland Ave	Greensboro	NC	27403	336-274-5550	A
VA	Virginia Carolina Craftsmen	30,000	Nov.	1240 Oakland Ave	Greensboro	NC	27403	910-274-5550	A+
VA	Taste Of The Mountains Main Street	20,000	September	P. O. Box 373	Madison	VA	22727	540-948-4455	B
VA	Manassas Fall Jubilee	20,000	October	9431 West St.	Manassas	VA	20110	703-361-6599	B
VA	Fall Festival Of Folklife	375,000	Oct.	700 Town Center Drive	New Port News	VA	23606	757-926-1400	B+
VA	Gosport Arts Festival	60,000	May	1211 Colley Avenue #1	Norfolk	VA	23517	757-446-2250	B
VA	Ghent Art Show	45,000	May	2308 Granby	Norfolk,	VA	23517	804-446-2250	A-
VA	Stockley Gardens Spring Arts Fest	25,000	May	801 Boush St. Ste 302	Norfolk,	VA	23510	757-625-6161	B
VA	Occoquan Fall Arts And Crafts	200,000	Sept.	P. O. Box 258	Occoquan	VA	22125	703-491-2168	A
VA	Northern Va Fine Arts Festival	50,000	May	11911 Freedom Drive Ste 110	Reston	VA	20190	703-471-9242	A+
VA	Bazaar Christmas Col.	25,000	December	P. O. Box 8330	Richmond	VA	23226	804-673-7015	B-
VA	Hand Workshop Craft & Design Show	10,000	Nov.	1812 West Main St.	Richmond	VA	23220	804-353-009	A-
VA	Arts In The Park	100,000	May	1112 Sunset Ave	Richmond	VA	23221	804-353-8198	B+

Top Craft Fairs

VA	Festival In The Park-Craft Show	375,000	May	P. O. Box 8276	Roanoke	VA	24014	703-342-2640	A-
VA	Roanoke Sidewalk Art Show	10,000	June	One Market Square	Roanoke	FL	24011	540-342-5760	B-
VA	Christmas Market	23,000	Nov.	P. O. Box 909	Virginia Beach	VA	23451	757-417-7771	A
VA	Neptune Fest Art And Craft Show	250,000	Sept.	2200 Parks Ave	Virginia Beach	VA	23451	757-425-0000	A-
VA	Boardwalk Art Show	300,000	June	2200 Parks Av	Virginia Beach	VA	23451	757-425-0000	B
VA	Waterford Fair	30,000	October	P. O. Box 142	Waterford	VA	20197	540-882-3018	B
VA	An Occasion For The Arts	15,000	Oct.	P O Box 1520	Williamsburg	VA	23187	804-229-5450	A-
VA	Apple Harvest Arts And Crafts Fest.	15,000	September	P. O. Box 412	Winchester	VA	22604	540-868-7160	nr
VA	Richmond Holiday Arts And Crafts	15,000	October	P. O. Box 11565	Winston-Salem	NC	27116	336-924-4539	B
VT	Hildene Folage Art And Craft Fest.	14,000	Oct.	P. O. Box 538	Putney	VT	05346	802-387-5772	B
VT	Art In The Park	7,000	Aug.	16 S. Main St.	Rutland	VT	05701	802-775-0356	A-
WA	Anacortes Arts & Crafts Festival	50,000	Aug.	819 Commercial, E	Anacortes	WA	98221	360-293-6211	B
WA	Battle Ground Harvest Days	35,000	July	912 East Main Street	Battle Ground	WA	98604	360-687-1510	B
WA	Art Museum Fair	280,000	July	510 Bellevue Way NE	Bellevue	WA	98004	425-519-0742	A+
WA	Sixth Street Fair & Taste Of Bellevue	50,000	July	500 108th Ave, NE Ste 210	Bellevue	WA	98004	206-453-1223	A-
WA	Holiday Festival Of Arts	20,000	December	P. O. Box 2584	Bellingham	WA	98227	360-676-8548	nr
WA	Camas Days	20,000	July	P. O. Box 919	Camas	WA	98607	206-834-2472	B
WA	Chataqua	45,000	July	P. O. Box 501	Chewelah	WA	99109	509-935-8891	B+
WA	Best Of The Northwest	10,000	Nov.	P O Box 1057	Clinton	WA	98236	360-221-6191	B+
WA	Coupeville Arts And Crafts Festival	20,000	August	P. O. Box 611	Coupeville	WA	98239	360-678-5116	B
WA	Federal Way Festival	20,000	August	P. O. Box 4724	Federal Way	WA	98063	253-568-7351	B-
WA	Tidefest	5,000	Dec.	5101 Rosedale St, Nw	Gig Harbor	WA	98335	206-851-6131	B
WA	Issaquah Salmon Days Festival	150,000	Oct.	155 Nw Gilman Blvd	Issaquah	WA	98027	206-270-2532	B
WA	Summerfest: Art And Wine Waterfront	35,000	July	620 Market Street	Kirkland	WA	98033	425-822-7161	B
WA	Tacoma Holiday Food And Gift Fest.	45,000	October	P. O. Box 2815	Kirkland	WA	98083	800-521-7469	B
WA	Skagit Valley Tulip Festival Fair	20,000	April	P O Box 1801	Mount Vernon	WA	98273	360-336-9277	B
WA	Edmonds Arts Festival	90,000	June	P O Box 125, 10924 Mukilteo	Mukilteo	WA	98275	206-745-0799	B+
WA	Super Saturday	20,000	June	College Activities Bldg. 301	Olympia	WA	98501	360-705-2556	B+
WA	Celebrate Lavender Festival	30,000	July	105 1/2 East First Street	Pprt Angeles	WA	98362	877-681-3035	B
WA	North Kitsap Arts And Crafts Fest.	30,000	July	P. O. Box 2043	Poulsbo	WA	98370	360-297-2490	B
WA	Meeker Days	100,000	June	P. O. Box 476	Puyallop	WA	98371	253-840-2631	B+
WA	A Victorian Country Christmas	45,000	November	P. O. Box 73129	Puyallup	WA	98373	253-770-0777	B
WA	Allied Artists Sidewalk Show	45,000	July	89 Lee Boulevard	Richland	WA	99362	509-375-1345	A-
WA	Christmas Memories	17,000	November	619 Meadows Drive East	Richland	WA	99352	509-627-1854	B

Top Craft Fairs

State	Name	Attendance	Month	Address	City	ST	Zip	Phone	Rating
WA	Fremont Fair	115,000	June	P. O. Box 31151	Seattle	GA	98103	206-694-6706	B+
WA	Pike Place Street Festival	200,000	May	85 Pike Street #506	Seattle	WA	98101	206-682-7453	B+
WA	Festival Of The Arts	250,000	July	1916 Pike Place, #146	Seattle	WA	98101	206-363-2048	A+
WA	Northwest Folklife Festival-Crafts	220,000	May	305 Harrison Street	Seattle	WA	98109	206-684-7327	A
WA	University District Street Fair	200,000	May	4714 University Way N E, #516	Seattle	WA	98105	206-523-4272	B
WA	Bumbershoot Art Market	185,000	Aug.	P O Box 9750	Seattle	WA	98109	206-281-7788	B+
WA	Spokane Christmas Arts And Crafts	15,000	November	P. O. Box 14987	Spokane	WA	99214	509-924-0588	B
WA	Artfest: Spokane	20,000	May	West 2316 First Ave.	Spokane	WA	99204	509-456-3932	B+
WI	Art In The Park	25,000	Aug.	130 N Morrison St	Appleton	WI	54911	414-733-4089	B
WI	Madison Autumn A And C Affair	15,000	December	P. O. Box 184	Boys Town	NE	68010	402-331-2889	B
WI	Mt. Mary Starving Artist Fair	15,000	Sept.	17160 Deer Park Dr.	Brookfield	WI	53005	(NO) PHONE	A+
WI	Franciscan Harvest Festival	15,000	August	503 S. Browns Lake Dr.	Burlington	WI	53105	262-763-3600	B-
WI	Ozaukee Center Harvest Festival	30,000	September	W62 N718 Riveredge Dr.	Cedarburg	WI	53012	262-377-8230	B
WI	Wine And Harvest Festival Fine Arts	30,000	September	P. O. Box 348	Grafton	WI	53024	262-276-0549	B-
WI	Artstreet	600,000	Aug.	P O Box 704	Green Bay	WI	54305	414-435-2787	B
WI	Holy Hill Arts And Crafts Fair	15,000	September	1525 Carmel Road	Hubertus	WI	53033	262-966-7172	B
WI	Art Fair On The Square	200,000	July	211 State St	Madison,	WI	53703	608-257-0158	A+
WI	Lakefront Festival Of Arts	50,000	June	750 N. Art Museum Dr	Milwaukee	WI	53202	414-224-3200	A+
WI	The Mile Of Art	5,000	Aug.	6801 N Yates Rd.	Milwaukee	WI	53217	414-351-7516	B
WI	Morning Glory Crafts Fair	10,000	Aug.	1630 E Royall Pl.	Milwaukee	WI	53202	414-278-8295	B
WI	Mount Horeb Art Fair	15,000	July	P. O. Box 84	Mount Horeb	WI	53572	608-437-5914	B
WI	Oconomowoc Festival Of The Arts	25,000	Aug.	P O Box 651	Oconomowoc	WI	53066	414-567-1243	A
WI	Sauk Prarie Today's Women A And C	40,000	September	P. O. Box 143a	Prarie Du Sac	WI	53578		nr
WI	Outdoor Arts Fest	25,000	July	608 New York Ave	Sheboygan	WI	53081	920-458-6144	B
WI	Townline Art Fair	5,000	Oct.	10376 Hwy 42	Sister Bay	WI	54234	414-854-4343	B
WI	Cranberry Festival Art/Craft Show	100,000	Sept.	P. O. Box 146	Warrens	WI	54666	608-378-4250	B-
WI	Wausau Festival Of The Arts	30,000	Sept.	P O Box 1763	Wausau	WI	54402	715-842-1676	A
WI	Watermelon Days Craft Fest	15,000	July	705 Bugbee Avenue	Wausau	WI	54401	715-675-6201	B
WI	Apple Harvest Craft Fair	13,000	September	705 Bugbee Avenue	Wausau	WI	54401	715-675-6201	B
WI	Art World	30,000	September	705 Bugbee Avenue	Wausau	WI	54401	715-675-6201	B
WI	Craft Fair Usa	18,000	Oct.	9312 West National Ave	West Allis	WI	53227	414-321-2100	A

Top Craft Fairs

WV	West Virginia Strawberry Festival	65,000	May	P. O. Box 117	Buchannon	WV	26201	304-473-8122	B
WV	Mountain Heritage Art & Craft Fest.	25,000	Sept.	P O Box 426	Charles Town	WV	25414	800-624-0577	A+
WV	New River Gorge Bridge Day	70,000	October	310 Oyler Avenue	Oak Hill	WV	25901	304-658-5574	B
WV	Firemen's Art And Craft Festival	25,000	September	R.R. 3, Box 35	Phillippi	WV	26416		B
WV	Mountain State Arts & Craft Fair	30,000	July	P. O. Box 389	Ripley	WV	25271	304-372-8159	A
WV	Stonewall Jackson Heritage A And C	45,000	September	P. O. Box 956	Weston	WV	26452	304-369-1863	B+
WV	Oglebayfest Artists' Market	50,000	Oct.	1330 National Rd.	Wheeling	WV	26003	304-242-7700	B
WY	Mountain Artists Rendezvous	7,000	July	P. O. Box 1248	Jackson Hole	WY	83001	307-733-8792	B

Top 1,100 Galleries in the United States

This is a list of the best art and craft galleries in the U. S. It is correct as of January, 2009. Galleries on this list seem to go out of business at the rate of about 50 per year.

You can get postcards from www.printing4less.com (800) 930-6040. They have a very good web site for estimating price, and you can upload files made with Microsoft Publisher.

The 4" x 6" postcard size will usually be adequate, or you can get 6" by 8" for a bigger impression. The smaller size takes a 23 cent stamp, while the next size requires a 42 cent stamp (these prices will probably change, of course, by the time you read this).

NAME	ADDRESS	CITY	ST	ZIP
Alaska Gift Gallery	Box 322	Sitka	AK	99385
Annie Kaill's	244 Front Street	Juneau	AK	99801
Artique, Ltd.	314 G. St.	Anchorage	AK	99501
Artworks, The	3677 College Road	Fairbanks	AK	99709
Blue Heron Gallery	123 Steadman Street Ste. B	Ketchikan	AK	99901
Color Creek-Fiber Art	3901 Mountain View Drive	Anchorage	AK	99508
Decker/Morris Gallery	P. O. Box 101403	Anchorage	AK	99510
Dockside Gallery and Bead Shoppe	5 Salmon Landing, Ste. 212	Ketchikan	AK	99901
Echos Of Alaska	4th and Broadway	Skagway	AK	99840
Lynch & Kennedy	350 Broadway	Skagway	AK	99840
Scanlon Gallery	318 Mission St.	Ketchikan	AK	99901
Anton Haardt Gallery	1226 South Hull St.	Montgomery	AL	36104
Gallery Alegria	600 Olde English Lane #128	Birmingham	AL	95223
Gallery at Kentuck	503 Main Ave.	Nortport	AL	35476
Marcia Weber Art Studio	1050 Woodley Rd.	Montgomery	AL	36106
Rattling Gourd Gallery	P. O. Box 69	Loachapoka	AL	36865
Space One Eleven	2409 Second Ave. North	Birmingham	AL	35203
The Villager	824 East Glenn Ave	Auburn	AL	36830
Big Muddy	P. O. Box 118	Bentonville	AR	72712
Blue Moon Gallery	718 Central Ave.	Hot Springs	AR	71901
Cliff Cottage Gallery	42 Armstrong St.	Eureka Springs	AR	72632
Enigma American Craft Gallery	15 N. Block AVe	Fayetteville	AR	72071
Gryphon's Roost Gallery/Day Spa	137 Spring St.	Eureka Springs	AR	72632
Heights Gallery	5801 Kavanaugh Blvd.	Little Rock	AR	72207
Iris at the Basin Park	8 Spring St.	Eureka Springs	AR	72632
Muse Gallery	509 W. Spring St. Ste 450	Fayetteville	AR	72701
Quickslver Gallery	73 Spring Street	Eureka Springs	AR	72632
River Market Artspace	301 E. Markham St.	Little Rock	AR	72201
Stanhope's	1302 State Line Avenue	Texarkana	AR	71854
Zarks ? A Fine Design Gallery	67 Spring Street	Eureka Springs	AR	72632
Arkansas Craft Gallery	Box 800	Mountain View	AR	72560

Top Craft Galleries

Name	Address	City	State	Zip
A'Loft Gallery of Fine Art	130 W.Gurley St., Ste. 302	Prescott	AZ	86301
Details & Green Shoe Laces	2990 North Swan Road, #147	Tucson	AZ	85712
Ertco	336 HWY 179	Sedona	AZ	86336
Gallery Materia	4222 N. Marshall Way	Scottsdale	AZ	85251
Genesis Gift Gallery	6501 E. Cave Creek Rd.	Cave Creek	AZ	85331
Gifted Hands Gallery	P. O. Box 1388	Sedona	AZ	86336
LeKAE Gallery	7175 E. Main St.	Scottsdale	AZ	85251
Mariah James Gallery	P. O. BOX 3121	TUBAC	AZ	85646
Obsidian Gallery	4340 N. Campbell	Tucson	AZ	85718
Philabaum Glass Gallery	4280 N. Cambell Ave Ste 105	Tucson	AZ	85718
Pinnacle Gallery	23417 North Pima Road, #161	Scottsdale	AZ	85255
Scherer Gallery	671 Hwy 179	Sedona	AZ	86336
Seasons of Tucson	7121 N. Oracle Road	Tucson	AZ	85704
The Bead Museum	5754 W. Glenn Dr.	Glendale	AZ	85301
Vision Gallery	80 South San Marcos Pl.	Chandler,	AZ	85224
A Gallery of Fine Art	73-956 El Paseo	Palm Desert	CA	92260
ACCI	1652 Shattuck	Berkeley	CA	94709
Acropolis Now	1933 South Broadway, Suite 101	Los Angeles	CA	90007
Adamm's American Crafts	1426 Fourth St.	Santa Monica	CA	90401
Anniglass Eyecandy	110 Cooper Street Ste.F	Santa Cruz	CA	95060
Art for the Soul	210 Marine Ave., Ste. A	Balboa Island	CA	92662
Artful Eye, The	8910 Jeannette Ave	Sebastopol	CA	95472
Artful Soul	1237-C Prospect St.	La Jolla	CA	92037
Artisan's	111 W. 7th St.	Hanford	CA	93230
Backroads Contemp.Craft Gallery	2180 Old Creamery Rd., Box 16	Harmony	CA	93435
Bella Cosa	250 Harvard Ave.	Claremont	CA	91711
Blue Oak Gallery	Via La Circula	Redondo Beach	CA	90277
By the Bay Gallery	910 Embarcadero	Morro Bay	CA	93442
Cedanna	1925 Fillmore Street	San Francisco	CA	94115
Chambers Gallery	755 B Main Street	Cambria	CA	93428
Christensen Heller Gallery	5831 College Ave	Oakland	CA	94618
Coast Galleries	P. O. Box 223519	Carmel	CA	93922
Coda Gallery	73-151 El Paseo	Palm Desert	CA	92260
Contemporary Center	2630 West Sepulveda Boulevard	Torrance	CA	90505
Corbin Gallery	407 Townsend Dr.	Aptos	CA	95003
Corrie Glass	37683 Niles Blvd.	Fremont	CA	94536
Crystal Fox Gallery	381 Cannery Row	Monterrey	CA	93940
Crystal Reflections	425 San Anselmo Ave.	San Anselmo	CA	94960
Culture Shop Gallery	1221 Abbot Kinney Blvd.	Venice	CA	90291
D. P. Fong Gallery	383 S. First St.	San Jose	CA	94113
De Novo	250 University Ave	Palo Alto	CA	94301
Del Mano Gallery	11981 San Vincente Boulevard	Los Angeles	CA	90049
Destiny	4210 Bridge Street	Cambria	CA	93428
Dollerious Delights	1544 Locust St.	Walnut Creek	CA	94596
Dovetail Collection	407 Healdsburg Ave	Healdsburg	CA	95448
Dune Mehler Gallery	337 Mirada Road	Half Moon Bay	CA	94019
Eileen Bremen Gallery	619 N. Harbor Blvd.	Fulerton	CA	92832
Elizabeth Fortner Gallery	1114 State St. #9	Santa Barbara	CA	93101
F. Dorian Gallery	388 Hayes St.	San Francisco`	CA	94102
Fire and Rain Gallery	705 Sutte Street	Folsom	CA	95685
Flax	240 Valley Drive	Brisbane	CA	94005

Top Craft Galleries

Folk Tree Collection	199 South Fair Oaks Ave.	Pasadena	CA	91105
Food For Thought	31760 Camino Capistrano, Ste. C	San Juan Capistrano	CA	92675
Freehand	8413 West Third Street	Los Angeles	CA	90048
Gallery Alexander	7925 Girard Ave.	La Jolla	CA	92037
Gallery Eight	7464 Girard Avenue	La Jolla	CA	92037
Gallery House	320 California Ave.	Palo Alto	CA	94396
Gallery Judaica	1312 Westwood Blvd	Los Angeles	CA	90024
Gallery of Functional Art	2525 Michigan Ave. E-3	Santa Monica	CA	90404
Gallery One	209 Western Avenue	Petaluma	CA	94952
Gatsby's	381 Cannery Row Suite N.	Monterrey	CA	93940
Gump's	135 Post	San Francisco`	CA	94108
Hands Gallery	777 Higuera Street	San Luis Obispo	CA	93401
Hardy Diagnostics	1439 McCoy Lane	Santa Maria	CA	93455
Harvest Moon	13251 S. Hwy 101 Ste 1	Hopland	CA	95449
Highlight Gallery	45052 Main St.	Mendocino	CA	95460
Hirzel Fine Jewelry	728 Santa Cruz Ave.	Menlo Park	CA	94025
Human Arts	310 East Ojai Ave	Ojai	CA	93023
Humboldt's Finest	417 2nd Street	Eureka	CA	95501
Huntington Library Gift Shop	1151 Oxford Road	San Marino	CA	91108
Jessel Miller Gallery	1019 Atlas Peak Rd.	Napa	CA	94558
John Natsoulas Gallery	140 F. St.	Davis	CA	95616
Ken McMaster	P. O. Box 223519	Calpine	CA	96124
L.H. Selman Ltd.	123 Locust St. Suite OL	Santa Cruz	CA	95060
Legion of Honor Museum Store	34th Avenue and Clement Street	San Francisco	CA	94121
Lily Rock Gallery	54245 Circle Dr. Ste. 7-C	Idyllwild	CA	92549
Luna	4928 East 2nd Street	Long Beach	CA	90803
Mackenzies Gallery of Am. Style	2766 East Bidwell, Ste. 600	Folsom	CA	95630
Main Element	1000 Main Street #10	Napa	CA	94559
Main Street Gallery	106 Main Street	Murphys	CA	95247
Mateel Art Cooperative Gallery	773 Redwood Dr.	Garberville	CA	95542
Meadowlark Gallery	317 Corte Madera Town Center	Corte Madera	CA	94925
Melting Pot, The	Main and Lansing Streets	Mendocino	CA	95460
Michael's	118 West Washington Boulevard	Crescent City	CA	95531
Mill Valley Sculptor Garden	219 Shoreline Hwy.	Mill Valley	CA	94941
Mingei Int. Museum Gift Store	P. O. Box 553	La Jolla	CA	92038
Mixt	1722 South Catalina Avenue	Redondo Beach	CA	90277
Moonstones Gallery	4070 Burton Dr.	Cambria	CA	93428
Museum of Contemporary Art Shop	250 Grand Avenue	Los Angeles	CA	90012
Museum of the American West	4700 Western Heritage Way	Los Angeles	CA	90027
New Stone Age	8407 W. Third St.	Los Angeles	CA	90048
Nina Gerety	1704 Tiburon Blvd.	Tiburon	CA	94920
North Bay Gallery	6525 Washington Street 2nd Flr	Yountville	CA	94599
Not Only Baja!	306-312 Oak Street	Brentwood	CA	90049
Oakland Museum Store	1000 Oak Street	Oakland	CA	94607
Objects	1187 Coast Village Rd.	Montecito	CA	93108
Olive Hyde Art Gallery	123 Washington Boulevard	Fremont	CA	94537
Palo Alto Art Center	1313 Newell Rd.	Palo Alto	CA	94301
Panache	45110 Main St.	Mendocino	CA	95460
Plaza Design	808 G. St.	Arcata	CA	95521
Positively Fourth Street	628 4th Street	Santa Rosa	CA	95404
Raw Style	1511 Montana Avenue	Santa Monica	CA	90403

Top Craft Galleries

Name	Address	City	State	Zip
Red Envelope	149 New Montgomery St. Gd. Fl.	San Francisco	CA	94105
Regent Jewelry and Gifts	6525 Washington St.	Yountville	CA	94599
Renaissance Solvang	486 First Street. #L	Solvang	CA	93463
Rookie T. Gallery	14300 Highway 128	Boonville	CA	95415
San Diego Natural History Museum	1788 El Prado	San Diego	CA	92101
San Francisco Craft and Folk Art	Building A, Fort Mason Center	San Francisco	CA	94123
Sculpture to Wear	9638 Brighton Way	Beverlee Hills	CA	90210
Seekers Collection and Gallery	4090 Burton Dr.	Cambria	CA	93428
SF Museum of Modern Art Store	151 Third Street	San Francisco	CA	94103
Shalom House	19740 Ventura Boulevard	Woodland Hills	CA	91364
Sherwood Gallery	460 S. Coast Hwy	Laguna Beach	CA	92651
SJ Museum of Art Store	110 South Market Street	San Jose	CA	95113
Solarium	815 Grant Ave.	Novato	CA	94945
Solomon Dubnick Gallery	2131 Northrop Ave.	Sacramento	CA	95825
Spirals	7906 Girard Ave.	La Jolla	CA	92037
Studio 41	700 First St.	Benecia	CA	94510
Studio Forty Two Gallery	23 North Santa Cruz Avenue	Los Gatos	CA	95030
Summer House	21 Trockmorton	Mill Valley	CA	94941
Teller Galleries	16055 Ventura Blvd. #635	Encino	CA	91436
Tercera	534 Ramona St.	Palo Alto	CA	94301
The Artery	207 G Street	Davis	CA	95616
The Gold Rush	P. O. Box 1143	Graeagle	CA	96103
The Last Straw	4540 Irving St.	San Francisco	CA	94122
The Vault	1339 Pacfic Avenue	Santa Cruz	CA	95060
The Zetter Collection	3261 Celinda Dr.	Carlsbad	CA	92008
Tops	23410 Civic Center Way	Malibu	CA	90265
Trios Gallery	130 South Cedros Ave.	Solana Beach	CA	92075
Twig Gallery of American Crafts	2163 Union St.	San Francisco	CA	94123
Two Babes in the Woods	55750 S. Circle Drive Box 3256	Idyllwild	CA	92549
Velvet Da Vinci	508 Hayes ST.	San Francisco	CA	94102
Ventura County Museum Store	100 East Main Street	Ventura	CA	93001
Verdigris-The Cannery	2801 Leavenworth St.	San Francisco	CA	94115
Village Artisans	2315 Honolulu Ave.	Montrose	CA	91020
Village Gallery	22651 Lambert #103	Lake Forest	CA	92630
Virginia Brier Gallery	3091 Sacramento St.	San Francisco	CA	94115
Visions Gallery	201 N. Mt. Shasta Blvd	Mt. Shasta	CA	96067
Zosaku Fine Arts	1782 4th Street	Berkeley	CA	94710
Abloom	9433 S. University Blvd.	Highlands Ranch	CO	80126
Art Mart	1222 Pearl	Boulder	CO	80302
Artisans Gallery	2757 E. Third Ave.	Denver	CO	80206
Artistic Judaic Promotions	4990 S. Lafayette Lane	Englewood	CO	80110
Blue Zebra	1404 Larimer	Denver	CO	80202
Boulder Arts & Crafts Cooperative	1421 Pearl St. Mall	Boulder	CO	80302
Camera Obscura Gallery	1309 Bannock St.	Denver	CO	80204
Clay Pigeon, The	601 Ogden Street	Denver	CO	80218
Colorado Collection	19111 East Garden Place	Aurora	CO	80015
Culture Clash	101 North F Street	Salida	CO	81201
Evergreen Fine Art	3092 Evergreen Pkwy.	Evergreen	CO	80439
Fire Ice Gallery	8100 West Tenth Ave.	Lakewood	CO	80215
Foya	10497 Centennial Rd.	Littleton	CO	80125
Gallery 150	150 W. First St.	Salida	CO	81201

Top Craft Galleries

Georgetown Gallery	612B Sixth Street, P.O. Box 402	Georgetown	CO	80444
Human Touch Galleries	8 Canon Ave.	Manitou Springs	CO	80829
J. Cotter Gallery	234 Wall Street	Vail	CO	81657
Luma -- The Broadmoor Hotel	1 Lake Ave.	Colorado Springs	CO	80906
Mackin Katz Gallery	2041 Broadway	Boulder	CO	80302
Middle Fish	1500 Pearl St.	Boulder	CO	80302
Might as Well	P. O. Box 603	Littleton	CO	80160
Mountain Spirit Gallery	201 F Street	Salida	CO	81201
Original Accents	P. O. Box 627	Grand Junction	CO	81502
Pismo Galleries	235 Fillmore St.	Denver	CO	80206
RAF	6913 W. Lakeside Dr.	Littleton	CO	80125
Rare Things	106 Main St.	Creede	CO	81130
Redstone Art Closet	364 Redstone Blvd.	Redstone	CO	81623
Show of Hands	210 Clayton Street	Denver	CO	80206
Smith-Klein Gallery	1116 Pearl	Boulder	CO	80302
Steamboat Art Company	903 Lincoln Avenue	Steamboat Springs	CO	80487
Stonehenge	504 Sixth Street, P.O. Box 636	Georgetown	CO	80444
Taminah Gallery, Gifts and Frame	414 Pagosa Street, P. O. 4487	Pagosa Springs	CO	81157
Termer Gallery	780 Main Avenue	Durango	CO	81301
The Evergreen Gallery	P.O. Box 431	Evergreen	CO	80437
The Johnson Building Gallery	124 North Main	Gunnison	CO	81230
The Watersweeper and the Dwarf	717 Grande Ave.	Glenwood Springs	CO	81601
Waterfall Hope	307 S. Mill Street	Aspen	CO	81611
West SouthWest	257 Fillmore St.	Denver	CO	80206
An Artisian's Marketplace	120 East Street	Plainville	CT	06062
Artists Market	163 Main Street	Norwalk	CT	06851
Brookfield Craft Center, Inc.	286 Whisconier Road	Brookfield	CT	06804
Company of Craftsmen	43 West Main Street	Mystic	CT	06355
Engleman Gallery	1014A Chapel Street	New Haven	CT	06510
Evergreen Fine American Crafts	21 Boston St.	Guilford	CT	06437
Fair Haven Woodworks	72 Blatchley Ave.	New Haven	CT	06513
Fisher Gallery Shop	Farmington Valley Arts Center	Avon	CT	06001
Florence Griswold Museum Shop	96 Lyme Street	Old Lyme	CT	06371
Gallery 12	29 Whitfield St.	Guilford	CT	06437
Guilford Handcrafts, Inc	411 Church Street	Guilford	CT	06437
Heron American Craft Gallery	16 N. Main St.	Kent	CT	06757
Honore Gallery	995 B Farming Avenue	West Hartford	CT	06107
Hoot Inc., The	East Brook Mall	Willimantic	CT	06226
J. C. Glassworks	990 Main Street	Branford	CT	06405
Mattatuck Museum	144 West Main Street	Waterbury	CT	06702
Sculpture to Wear	11 Salt Meadow Ln	Madison	CT	06443
Swanton of Essex	One Griswald Square	Essex	CT	06426
The Green Fox Gallery	15 Water Street	Torrington	CT	06790
The Ironwood Gallery	Box 449	Ridgefield	CT	06877
The Museum Shop	600 Main St.	Hartford	CT	06103
The Silo	44 Upland Road	New Milford	CT	06776
Tresor Gallery	951A Farmington Ave.	West Hartford	CT	06107
Wave	107 Main Street	New Canaan	CT	06840
American Hand Plus	2906 M Street, NW	Washington	DC	20007
apartment zero	406 7th St. N.W.	Washington	DC	20004

Top Craft Galleries

Appalachian Spring	1415 Wisconsin Ave. N.W.	Washington	DC	20007
Art & Soul	225 Pennsylvania Ave. S.E.	Washington	DC	20003
As Kindred Spirits	Reagan National Airport Term. B	Washington	DC	20001
Beadazzled	1507 Connecticut Ave. N.W.	Washington	DC	20036
Folger Museum Shop	201 East Capital Street SE	Washington	DC	20003
Jackie Chalkley Gallery	5301 Wisconsin Avenue NW	Washington	DC	20015
Lbrary of Congress Museum Store	101 Independence Ave, SE	Washington	DC	20540
Maurine Littleton Gallery	1667 Wisconsin Ave. N.W.	Washington	DC	20007
National Cathredral Museum Store	3101 Wisconsin Ave. NW	Washington	DC	20016
Renwick Gallery, Smithsonian	MRC 510, P. O. Box 37012	Washington	DC	20013
The Magical Animal	3222 M Street NW	Washington	DC	20007
Wake Up Little Suzie	3409 Connecticut Ave. NW	Washington	DC	20008
Beyond Dimensions	59 South Governor's Ave.	Dover	DE	19904
Blue Streak Gallery	1721-1723 Delaware Ave.	Wilmington	DE	19806
Creations Fine Woodworking Gallery	451 Hockessin Corner	Hockessin	DE	19707
Delaware Art Museum	2301 Kentmere Parkway	Wilmington	DE	19806
Down By the Bay	205 Second St.	Lewes	DE	19958
Ellen Rice Gallery	103 Atlantic Ave	Ocean View	DE	19970
Grassroots Gallery	93 East Main St.	Newark	DE	19711
Panache	129 B. Rehobeth Ave.	Rehobeth Beach	DE	19971
Winterthur Museum Gift Shop	Route 52	Winterthur	DE	19735
A Mixed Bag	8912 Laurel Dr.	Pinellas Park	FL	33782
Art Center	719 Central Ave.	St. Petersburg	FL	33701
Artisan's Gallery	5402 NW 8th Ave.	Gainesville	FL	32605
Arts and Antiques Gallery	702 Centre St.	Fernandina Beach	FL	32034
Artsiphartsi	2717 W. Kennedy Blvd.	Tampa	FL	33609
Atlantic Beach Potters	400 Levy Rd.	Atlantic Beach	FL	32233
Avalon Gallery	425 E. Atlantic Ave.	Delray Beach	FL	33483
B. Hock Gallery	5810 Sunset Drive	Miami	FL	33143
Bayfront Gallery	713 S. Palafox	Pensacola	FL	32501
Brooke Pottery	223 North Kentucky Avenue	Lakeland	FL	33801
Crystal Mirage Gallery	800 Second Avenue NE	St. Petersburg	FL	33701
Dali Museum Gift Store	1000 Third Street South	St. Petersburg	FL	33701
Deborah and Friends	P. O. Box 1491	Mt. Dora	FL	32754
Dennison-Maran Gallery	696 5th Avenue. South	Naples	FL	34102
DreamWeaver	364 St Armands Cir	Sarasota	FL	34236
First Street Gallery	216 B First St.	Neptune Beach	FL	32266
Florida Craftsmen Gallery	501 Central Ave.	St. Petersburg	FL	33701
Funky Monkey	12199 Indian Rocks Rd.	Largo	FL	33774
Galeria of Sculpture	11 Via Parigi	Palm Beach	FL	33480
Gallery Five	387 Tequesta Drive	Tequesta	FL	33469
Gallery Morada	81610 Overseas Highway	Islamorada	Fl	33036
Gene Brenner Pottery	104 N. Circle	Seabring	FL	33870
Gingerbread Square Gallery	1207 Duval Street	Key West	FL	33040
Glass Reunions of Key West	825 Duval St.	Key West	FL	33040
Glisco Visions	P.O. Box 25217	Sarasota	FL	34277
Grass Roots Gallery	411 W. Dearborn St.	Englewood	FL	34223
Habatat Galleries	608 Banyan Trail	Boca Raton	FL	33431
Harmony Isle Gallery	902 NE 19th Ave	Fort Lauderdale	FL	33304
Heartworks Gallery	820 Lomax	Jacksonville	FL	32204
High Springs Gallery	115 N. Main St.	High Springs	FL	32643

Top Craft Galleries

Hodgell Gallery	46 South Palm Avenue South	Sarasota	FL	34236
Home Shopping Club	1 HSN Drive	St. Petersburg	FL	33729
Hoypoloi Gallery	1502 E. Buena Vista Drive	Lake Buena Vista	FL	32830
Inside Out Gallery	7400 Gulf Blvd.	St. Pete Beach	FL	33706
Ioma Art	6000 Glades Rd. #1206A	Boca Raton	FL	33431
Island Treasure	10709 Gulf Boulevard	Treasure Island	FL	33706
Justines	81904 Overseas	Islamorada	FL	33036
Kravis Center Gallery	701 Okeechobee Blvd	W. Palm Beach	FL	33408
La Store	223 N. 12th Street	Tampa	FL	33602
Laughing Dog Gallery	23 Royal Palm Pointe #1A	Vero Beach	FL	32960
Lighting Solutions	11780 B. Metro Pkwy	Fort Meyers	FL	33912
Mosaica	2020 Hollywood Blvd.	Hollywood	FL	33020
Nancy Markoe Fine Crafts Gallery	3112 Pass-a-Grille Way	St. Pete Beach	FL	33706
Newbill Collection by the Sea	P. O. Box 4809 309 Ruskin Pl.	Seaside	FL	32459
Nicholson House	2223 N. Westshore Blvd.	Tampa	FL	33607
Norton Museum Store	1451 S. Olive Avenue	West Palm Beach	FL	33401
On a Whim Gallery	12000 SE Dixie Highwayt	Hobie Sound	FL	33455
Peace Creek Trading Company	4204 S. Florida Avenue	Lakeland	FL	33813
Polk Museum of Art Store	800 East Palmetto Street	Lakeland	FL	33801
Prickly Pear	3251 SW Winding Way	Palm City	FL	34990
Seldom Seen Gallery	817 East Las Olas Blvd.	Ft. Lauderdale	FL	33301
Shapiro Studio & Gallery	538 Central Ave.	St. Petersburg	FL	33701
Sign of the Dolphin	652 Maderia Beach Causeway	Madeira Beach	FL	33708
Stage Right Interiors	924 N. Flagler Dr.	Fort Lauderdale	FL	33304
Suwannee Triangle Gallery	491 Dock Street	Cedar Key	FL	32625
The Giving Tree	5 North Blvd of the Presidents	Sarasota	FL	34236
Thornbrook Gallery	2441 NW 43rd St. Ste 6D	Gainesville	FL	33606
Timothys Gallery	236 N. Park Ave.	Winter Park	FL	32789
Traditions	19575 Biscayne Blvd.	Aventura	FL	33180
Tumbleweed	14611 Balgowan Rd. #104	Miami Lakes	FL	33016
Unique Boutique	1185 3rd St. S	Naples	FL	34102
Artrages Gallery	6035 Sandy Springs Cir. NE	Atlanta	GA	30328
By Hand South	112 E. Ponce de Leon Ave.	Decatur	GA	30030
Gallery 209	209 E. River Street	Savannah	GA	31401
High Museum of Art Shop	1280 Peachtree Street Ne	Atlanta	GA	30309
Labaire Pottery	35 South Peachtree Street	Norcross	GA	30071
Main Street Gallery	51 N. Main St.	Clayton	GA	30525
Mainstreet Art Company	21 South Main Street	Alpharetta	GA	30004
Mucklow's Fine Jewelry	552 Crosstown Road	Peachtree City	GA	30269
Out of the Woods Gallery	22-B Bennett Street NW	Atlanta	GA	30309
Raiford Gallery	1169 Canton Street	Roswell	GA	30075
Signature Shop and Gallery	3267 Roswell Rd. N. W.	Atlanta	GA	30305
Smith Jewelers	130 W. Jackson St	Dublin	GA	31021
Soho	5482 Chamblee Dunwoody Rd.	Atlanta	GA	30338
Wildcat on a Wing	10061 Ball Ground Highway	Ball Ground	GA	30107
Biasa Rose Boutique	104 Hana Hwy. Box 97	Paia, Maui	HI	96779
Bishop Museum Shop Pacifica	1525 Bernice Street	Honolulu	HI	96817
Chelsea	2752 Woodlawn, Ste 5-110	Honolulu	HI	96822
Elizabeth Doyle Galleries	119 Bay Drive	Lahaina	HI	96761
Hawaii Craftsmen	P O Box 22645	Honolulu	HI	96823

Top Craft Galleries

Jeff Chang Pottery and Fine Crafts	45-523 Kiani St.	Kanoehe	HI	96744
Kahn Galleries	3129 Pelike St.	Lihue	HI	96766
Kebanu, A Gallery	3440 Poipu Rd	Koloa	HI	96756
Kii Gallery	P. O. Box 791189	Paia	HI	96779
Lavender Moon Gallery	79-7404 Mamalohoa Highway	Kealakekua	HI	96750
Martin & Macarthur Whaler's	2435 Kaanapali Pkwy #A-4	Lahaina	HI	96761
Nohea Galleries	5000 Kahala Ave.	Honolulu	HI	96816
Reflections of the Heart	4211 Waialae Ave #C8	Honolulu	HI	96816
Volcano Arts Center	P. O. Box 129	Volcano Village	HI	96785
Volcano Gallery	Box 699	Volcano Village	HI	96785
Woodshop Gallery	P. O. Box 280	Paauilo	HI	96776
Agora Arts	104 E. Water St., Ste. 1	Decorah	IA	52101
AKAR	257 E. Iowa Ave.	Iowa City	IA	52240
Arts on Grand	408 North Grand Ave.	Spencer	IA	51301
Campbell Steele	1064 7th Ave.	Marion	IA	52302
Charles Mac Nider Museum	303 2nd St. Southeast	Mason City	IA	50401
CornerHouse Gallery and Frame	2753 First Ave., SE	Cedar Rapids	IA	52402
Henry Myrtle Gallery	915 West 23rd St.	Cedar Falls	IA	50613
JK Creative Wood and Gifts	2410 105th St	Kalona	IA	52247
Laree's	306 First East Street	Independence	IA	50644
M.C. Ginsberg	110 East Washington St.	Iowa City	IA	52240
Sticks	3631 Southwest 61st St.	Des Moines	IA	50321
Anne Reed Gallery	620 Sun Valley Road, Box 597	Ketchum	ID	83340
Boise Art Museum Store	670 Julia Davis Drive	Boise	ID	83702
R. Grey Gallery	818 W. Idaho St.	Boise	ID	83702
Roland Gallery	Box 221	Ketchum	ID	83340
Tara-James Gallery	200 S. Main Street	Pocatello	ID	83204
Whitetail Butte Gallery	5549 Gleason McAbee Road	Priest River	ID	83856
Ancient Echoes	1003 W. Armitage	Chicago	IL	60614
ArtFX	1629 2nd Ave	Rock Island	IL	61201
Artisan Shop & Gallery	248 Robert Parker Coffin Road	Long Grove	IL	60047
Artisan Shop and Gallery	1515 Sheridan Road	Wilmette	IL	60091
Artists' Works	32 West Chicago Avenue	Naperville	IL	60540
Arts & Artisans	108 South Michigan Avenue	Chicago	IL	60603
Best Art Shop and Gallery	4 East Jefferson	Naperville	IL	60540
Chairoscuro	700 North Michigan Ave.	Chicago	IL	60611
Citywoods	651 Central Ave.	Highland Park	IL	60035
Coveny Lane	30 East Burlington Street	Riverside	IL	60546
Function + Art	1046 West Fulton Market	Chicago	IL	60607
Gallery of Precious Objects	113 S. 3rd St.	Geneva	IL	60134
Gallimaufry Gallery	4712 N. Lincoln Ave.	Chicago	IL	60625
Ginkgo Tree Bookshop	951 Chicago Avenue	Oak Park	IL	60302
Greenleaf Gallery	1760 Sunset Lane	Bannockburn	IL	60015
Illinois State Museum Gift Shops	Spring and Edwards Streets	Springfield	IL	62706
Jane Miller	2626 N. Lakeview Ave.	Chicago	IL	60614
Lindsey Gallery	111 N. Oak Park	Oak Park	IL	60301
Lockport Street Gallery	503 W. Lockport St.	Plainfield	IL	60544
Lotton Gallery	900 N. Michigan Ave., Level 4	Chicago	IL	60611
Marx Gallery	230 West Superior	Chicago	IL	60610
Menshenables Judaica	1173 McHenry Road	Buffalo Grove	IL	60089
Mindscape Adornments	2114 Central Street	Evanston	IL	60201

Top Craft Galleries

Northern Possessions	900 N. Michigan Ave.	Chicago	IL	60611
Oriental Institute Museum Store	1155 East 58th Str.	Chicago	Il	60637
Pieces Gallery	644 Central Ave	Highland Park	IL	60035
Poopsie's	107 South Main St.	Galena	IL	61036
Prestige Art Gallery	3909 West Howard Street	Skokie	IL	60076
Priveleges	1618 North Alpine Road	Rockford	IL	61107
Riverview Gallery	588 Latham Dr. Ste 9	Bourbannais	IL	60914
Robie House Bookshop	5757 S. Woodlawn Avenue	Chicago	IL	60637
Sawbridge Studios	153 West Ohio St.	Chicago	IL	60610
Sawbridge Studios	1015 TOWER CT	Winnetka	IL	60093
Schneider-Bluhm-Loeb Gallery	230 W. Superior	Chicago	IL	60610
SoTish	23 S. La Grange Rd.	La Grange	IL	60525
The Art Stop	5 South La Grange Road	La Grange	IL	60525
Unusual Accents	3137 Dundee Rd.	Northbrook	IL	60062
Vale Craft Gallery	230 W. Superior St.	Chicago	IL	60610
Verve on Third	113 South Third Street	Geneva	IL	60134
Woodbine Glass Museum	Rt. 20	Woodbine	IL	61085
Woodstock Gallery	904 Green Bay Road	Winnetka	IL	60093
Aquarius Custom Jewelry	286 Island Drive	Lowell	IN	46356
Argentum Jewelry	P. O. Box 1221	Bloomington	IN	47402
Art Hand Crafts	P. O. Box 123	Zionsville	IN	46077
Art IN Hand Gallery	211 S. Main St.	Zionsville	IN	46077
Artifacts Gallery	6327 Guilford Ave.	Indianapolois	IN	46220
Artists' Den	203 Jefferson St.	Valpariso	IN	46383
Arts in Harmony	1488 East 86th Street	Indianapolis	IN	46236
Artworks Gallery	301 S. Walnut St. Ste 101	Muncie	IN	47305
Details	8663 River Crossing Blvd.	Indianapolis	IN	46240
Heart to Heart Gallery	921 Ridge Rd	Munster	IN	46321
Lake Street Gallery	613 S. Lake Street	Gary	IN	46403
NIAA Gift Shop	1040 Ridge Road	Munster	IN	46321
Red Dot Gallery	6734 Dorchester Court	Indianapolis	IN	46214
Shimmery	1622 Santa Ana Ct.	Munster	IN	46321
The Stuart Group	100 East Main	Nashville	IN	47448
Trilogy Gallery	120 E. Main St.	Nashville	IN	47448
Baker Arts Center	624 N. Pershing	Liberal	KS	67901
Bearden's Stained Glass	7600 Metcalf	Overland Park	KS	66204
Courtyard Gallery	125 N. Main St.	Lindsborg	KS	67456
Frame Woods Gallery	819 Massachusetts St.	Lawrence	KS	66044
Gallery at Hawthorne Plaza	4845 West 119th St.	Overland Park	KS	66209
Glass Expressions	1250 SW Oakley Ave #100	Topeka	KS	66604
Harris Gallery	South Hwy. 95	Elkhart	KS	67950
Silver Works and More	715 Massachusetts St.	Lawrence	KS	66044
Tiger Lily	117 South Main St.	Ulysses	KS	67880
Adath Jeshurun	2401 Woodbourne Ave.	Louisville	KY	40205
Artique	410 W. Vine St.	Lexington	KY	40507
Edenside Gallery	1422 Bardstown Rd.	Louisville	KY	40204
Glassworks Gallery	815 West Market St.	Louisville	KY	40202
Heike Pickett Gallery	110 Morgan St.	Versailles	KY	40383
Home and Hearth Gallery	215 Adams St.	Berea	KY	40403
Huneysuckle Vine	Broadway and Depot	Berea	KY	40403
Images	624 W. Main St.	Louisville	KY	40202

Top Craft Galleries

Name	Address	City	State	Zip
Lionheart Gallery	313 S. 4th St.	Louisville	KY	40202
Log House Craft Gallery	Cpo 2145, Berea College	Berea	KY	40404
Loudoun House Gallery	209 Castlewood Drive	Lexington	KY	40505
Morris Fork Crafts	930 Morris Fork Road	Booneville	KY	41314
Museum American Quilter's	215 Jefferson St.	Paducah	KY	42002
Promenade Gallery	204 Center St.	Berea	KY	40403
Shaker Village of Pleasant Hill	3501 Lexington Road	Harrodsburg	KY	40330
Swanson Cralle Gallery	1377 Bardstown Rd.	Louisville	KY	40204
Vardens	509 Main St.	Paris	KY	40361
Anton Haardt Gallery	2858 Magazine St.	New Orleans	LA	70130
Ariodante Craft Gallery	535 Julia Street	New Orleans	LA	70130
Bedazzled	635 Saint Peter Street	New Orleans	LA	70116
Body Art	3414 Hessmer Ave.	Metairie	LA	70002
Caffery Gallery	4016 Government Street	Baton Rouge	LA	70806
Cezar Magi	234 Charres St.	New Orleans	LA	70130
Earthworks	1424 Ryan St.	Lake Charles	LA	70601
Interiors and Extras	324 Metairie Road	Metairie	LA	70005
Louisiana Pottery	6470 Hwy. 22	Sorrento	LA	70778
Rhino Contemporary Crafts Co.	333 Canal St. Level 3	New Orleans	LA	70130
Thomas Mann Gallery	1804 Magazine St.	New Orleans	LA	70130
Uniquely Yours	5827 Youree Drive	Shreveport	LA	71105
William and Joseph Gallery	713 Royal Street	New Orleans	LA	70116
Alianza	154 Newbury Street	Boston	MA	02116
Art Effects	10 Church St.	Northborough	MA	01532
Art of Framing	2 South Main St.	Middleton	MA	01949
Artful Hand Gallery	36 Copley Place	Boston	MA	02116
Artful Image	16A Walden St.	Concord	MA	01742
Artisans Gallery	150 Main St.	Northampton	MA	01060
Bhadon Gallery	1075 Pleasant Street	Worcester	MA	01602
Busy Beaver Gift Shop	7 Brockton Avenue	Abington	MA	02351
By-the-Bay Designs	1073 Main Street	Brewster	MA	02631
Cambridge Artist Cooperative	59A Church Street	Cambridge	MA	02138
Ceruttis	373 Commercial St.	Provincetown	MA	02657
Choices	365 Boston Post Rd.	Sudbury	MA	01776
Choices Gallery	11 Pleasant Street	Newbury Port	MA	01950
Craftworks	102 Circuit Avenue	Oak Bluffs	MA	02557
Crafty Yankee, The	1838 Massachusetts Avenue	Lexington	MA	02173
DeCordova Museum Gift Shop	51 Sandy Pond Road	Lincoln	MA	01773
Divinity's Splendor-Glow	311 Broadway	Arlington	MA	02174
Don Muller Gallery	40 Main St	Northampton	MA	01060
Evergreen Contemporary Crafts	291 Main Street	Great Barrington	MA	01230
Fellerman & Raabe Glassworks	362 Shunpike Rd.	Sheffield	MA	01257
Ferrin Gallery	179 Main St.	Northampton	MA	01060
Fire Opal	7 Pond St.	Jamaica Plain	MA	02130
Fireburst	R. F. D. #2	Orange	MA	01364
Five Crows	8 Court St.	Natick	MA	01760
Frame-It Studio and Gallery	588 Randolf Avenue	Milton	MA	02186
Fruitlands Museum Store	102 Prospect Hill Road	Harvard	MA	01451
Glass Eye, The	Main Street Mercantile	North Eastham	MA	02651
Grey Goose	95 Chapel Street	Needham	MA	02492
Habatat Galleries	117 State Road Route 7	Great Barrington	MA	01230

Top Craft Galleries

Name	Address	City	State	Zip
Handcraft House	3966 Route 8A	Brewster	MA	02631
Handworks Gallery	161 Great Road	Acton	MA	01720
Hartstone Gallery	25 Washington Street	Nonwell	MA	02061
Holsten Galleries	Elm Street	Stockbridge	MA	01262
Impulse	188 Commercial Street	Provincetown	MA	02657
Joie de Vivre	1792 Massachusetts Avenue	Cambridge	MA	02140
Jubilation	91 Union Street	Newton	MA	02159
Lacoste Gallery	25 Main St.	Concord	MA	01742
L'Attitude Gallery	218 Newbury St.	Boston	MA	02116
Left Bank Gallery	8 Cove Road	Orleans	MA	02653
Left Bank Gallery	3 West Main Street	Wellfleet	MA	02667
Light Hunter	One Cottage Street	East Hampton	MA	01027
Limited Editions, Inc.	1176 Walnut Street	Newton Highlands	MA	02161
Muse's Window Gallery	1656 Massachusetts Ave.	Lexington	MA	02420
Museum of Fine Arts Boston Shop	465 Huntington Avenue	Boston	MA	02115
Ocmulgee Pottery and Fine Crafts	26 Market Street	Ipswich	MA	01938
Old Spouter Gallery	118 Orange St.	Nantucket	MA	02554
Old Sturbridge Village Mus. Shop	1 Old Sturbridge Village Road	Sturbridge	MA	01566
Paper Tiger Inc	P. O. Box 1768	Vinyard Haven	MA	02568
Ralph Jordan's	254 Great Rd.	Acton	MA	01720
Silverscape Designs	1 King Street	Northhampton	MA	01060
Skera Contemporary Crafts	221 Main St.	Northampton	MA	01060
Society of Arts and Crafts	175 Newbury St	Boston	MA	02118
Sparrow House Pottery	32 Summer Street	Plymouth	MA	02630
Spectrum of American Artists	369 Old Kings Highway	Brewster	MA	02631
Susi's Gallery For Children	348 Huron Ave.	Cambridge	MA	02138
Terra Firma	49 Leonard St.	Belmont	MA	02478
The Gatehouse	110 Commonwealth Ave.	Concord	MA	01742
The Gifted Hand	32 Church Street	Wellesley	MA	02482
The Navigator Shop	294 ELM ST.	South Dartmouth	MA	02748
The Potted Geranium	188 Main Street	West Harwich	MA	02671
The Silver Ribbon	15 Columbia Road Route 53	Pembroke	MA	02359
The Wells Emporium	175 Merrimack Street	Lowell	MA	01852
Valleries Gallery	12 State Street	Newburyport	MA	01950
Vinyard Lights	39 Circuit Ave	Oak Bluffs	MA	02557
W. O. W.	32 Needham St.	Newton Highlands	MA	02461
WA Gallery	184 Commercial St.	Provincetown	MA	02657
Walter Family Judaica Shop	125 Pond St.	Sharon	MA	02067
Wayside Gallery	512 Main Street	Chatham	MA	02633
Whippoorwill Crafts	126 Market Blvd.	Boston	MA	02109
Wild Goose Chase	1431 Beacon St.	Brookline	MA	02446
Winstanley-Roark Fine Arts	601 Main St. Route 6A	Dennis	MA	02638
Worchester Center for Crafts	25 Sagamore Rd.	Worcester	MA	01605
Yankee Ingenuity	525 Main Street	Chatham	MA	02633
2910 on the Square	2910 O'Donnell Street	Baltimore	MD	21224
American Craftworks Collection	189 B. Main Street	Annapolis	MD	21401
Annapolis Pottery	40 State Circle	Annapolis	MD	21401
Appalachian Spring	1641 Rockville	Rockville	MD	20852
Artcraft Collection	8600 Foundry Street	Savage	MD	20763
As Kindred Spirits	1611 Rockville Pike	Rockville	MD	20852
Balcony Gallery	12 Broad St.	Berlin	MD	21811

Top Craft Galleries

Name	Address	City	State	Zip
Baltimore Clayworks Gallery	5707 Smith Ave.	Baltimore	MD	21209
Calico Cat	2137 Gywnn Oak Avenue	Baltimore	MD	21207
Craft Concepts	Green Spring Station	Lutherville	MD	21093
Easy Street Gallery	8 Francis Street	Annapolis	MD	21401
Gallery 44	9469 Baltimore National Pike	Ellicott City	MD	21029
Gazelle	5100 Falls Road	Baltimore	MD	21210
Globe Theatre Gallery	12 Broad Street	Berlin	MD	21811
Hardwood Artisans	12266 Rockville Pike	Rockville	MD	20852
J Fish Studio and Fine Crafts	P. O. Box 1218	Berlin	MD	21811
Jurus Ltd.	5618 Newury Street	Baltimore	MD	21209
Kokopelli	1436 Columbia Mall	Columbia	MD	21044
La De Da	10126 River Rd.	Potomac	MD	20854
Main Street Gallery	486 Main Street	Prince Frederick	MD	20678
Meredith Gallery	805 North Charles Street	Baltimore	MD	21201
Mind's Eye Gallery	103 S. Talbot St.	St. Michaels	MD	21663
Mu d and Metal	813 W. 36th St.	Baltimore	MD	21211
Paper & Ink	3 N.Second St	Woodsboro	MD	21798
Paper Rock Scissors	1111 W. 36th St.	Baltimore	MD	21211
Red Orchard	10217 Old Georgetown Road	Bethesda	MD	20814
Rosenthal Collection, Inc.	4210 Howard Ave.	Kensington	MD	20895
Sansar	4805 Bethesda Ave.	Bethesda	MD	20814
Tomlinson Craft Collection	711 West 40th Street	Baltimore	MD	21211
Village Gem	4317 Ebenezer Road	Baltimore	MD	21236
Water From the Moon	217 Albemarle St.	Baltimore	MD	21202
Windrush Gallery	720 Morris Ave.	Friendsville	MD	21513
Zyzyx!	10301A Old Georgetown Rd.	Bethesda	MD	20814
ARTFX	49 West Street	Annapolis	MD	21401
Garden Architects	115 West St	Annapolis	MD	21403
National Gallery of Art Store	2000B South Club Drive	Landover	MD	20785
Abacus	44 Exchange Street	Portland	ME	04101
Bluen Heron Gallery	22 Church St.	Deer Isle	ME	04627
Compliments	Dock Square, P. O. Box 567 A	Kennebunkport	ME	04046
Eclipse Gallery	12 Mount Desert St.	Bar Harbor	ME	04609
Edgecomb Potters	727 Boothbay Road	Edgecomb	ME	04556
Farnsworth Museum Store	16 Museum Street	Rockland	ME	04841
Hole in the Wall Studioworks	1544 Roosevelt Trail Rte 302	Raymond	ME	04071
Panache Gallery	U. S. Route 1	Ogunquit	ME	03907
Portland Museum of Art Store	Seven Congress Square	Portland	ME	04101
Pottery By Celia	Rt. 114, P. O. Box 4116	Naples	ME	04055
Stein Gallery	195 Middle Street	Portland	ME	04101
Swamp John's	Oamweed Road, Perkins Cove	Ogunquit	ME	03907
West Island Gallery	37 Bay Point Road	Georgetown	ME	04548
16 Hands Gallery	216 South Main	Ann Arbor	MI	48104
Ariana Gallery	119 S. Main Street	Royal Oak	MI	48067
Biddle Gallery	2840 Biddle Avenue	Wyandotte	MI	48192
Bier Art Gallery	17959 Ferry Rd.	Charlevoix	MI	49720
Castle Park Gallery	8 East 8th Street	Holland	MI	49423
Czarina's Treasure	403 Water St., Box 1168	Saugatuck	MI	49453
Detroit Gallery of Contemp. Craft	104 Fisher Building	Detroit	MI	48202
Elements	107 Bridge Street	Charlevoix	MI	49720
EUC Gallery	812 Saginaw Street	Bay City	MI	48708

Top Craft Galleries

Gallery	Address	City	State	Zip
Gallery on the Alley	611 Broad Street	St. Joseph	MI	49085
Good Goods	106 Mason St.	Saugatuck	MI	49453
Harbor Muse	19135 W. US 12	New Buffalo	MI	49117
John McMartin Jewelry Arts Gallery	440 N. Main	Milford	MI	48381
Le Flair	5763 28th St. SE	Grand Rapids	MI	49546
Les Sirena Galerie D'Art	338 S. Main St.	Frankfort	MI	49635
Mackerel Sky Gallery	217 Ann St	East Lansing	MI	48823
Margot's Gallery and Frame	5 South Washington	Oxford	MI	48371
Moynihan Gallery & Framing, Inc.	28 East 8th Street	Holland	MI	49423
Mullay's 128 Studio & Gallery	128 River Street Box 5	Elk Rapids	MI	49629
Northwood Gallery	144 E. Main	Midland	MI	48640
Novus Art Gallery	15200 E. Jefferson Ave.	Grosse Pointe Park	MI	48230
Saginaw Art Museum	1126 N. Michigan Ave	Saginaw	MI	48602
Sandra Collins Gallery	1114 Lakeside Dr.	Birmingham	MI	48009
Selo/Shevel Gallery	301 S Main St	Ann Arbor	MI	48104
Silver Crow	201 S. Front Street	Marquette	MI	49855
The Muse, a Fine Craft Gallery	408 S. Main Street	Plymouth	MI	48170
The Secret Garden	4321 Cherry Hill Dr.	Empire	MI	48864
Twisted Fish Gallery	10284 S. Bayshore Dr.	Elk Rapids	MI	49629
Whistling Moose Gallery	273 East Main St.	Harbor Springs	MI	49740
Yaw Gallery	550 N. Woodward Ave.	Birmingham	MI	48009
Bibelot Shops, The	1082 Grand Avenue	St. Paul	MN	55105
Douglass Baker Gallery	601 2nd Ave S. #100A	Minneapolis	MN	55402
Gallery at the Clay Coyote	17614 240th Street	Hutchinson	MN	55350
Judith McGrann and Friends	4615 Excelsior Blvd	Minneapolis	MN	55416
Lizzards II	36 East Superior St.	Duluth	MN	55802
Mealey's Gift	124 N. Central Ave.	Ely	MN	55731
Minneapolis Inst. of the Arts Shop	2400 Third Avenue South	Minneapolis	MN	55404
Northern Clay Centery	2424 Franklin Ave. East	Minneapolis	MN	55406
Recollections from the Inn	14709 Maple Inn Road SE	Mentor	MN	56736
Rourke Art Gallery	523 South Fourth St.	Moorehead	MN	56560
SEMVA Art Gallery	16 First St. SW	Rochester	MN	55902
Steppingstone Gallery	50 Main Street South	Hutchinson	MN	55350
Three Rooms Up	3505 GALLERIA	Edina	MN	55435
Walker Art Center Store	725 Vineland Place	Minneapolis	MN	55403
Americana Gallery	Corner of Walnut & Ferry Street	Augusta	MO	63332
Art St. Louis Craft Gallery	917 Locust St.	St. Louis	MO	63101
Barucci Gallery	8101 Maryland Avenue	St. Louis	MO	63105
Craft Alliance	6640 Delmar Blvd.	St. Louis	MO	63130
Eclectics Gallery	7015 Oak St.	Kansas City	MO	64113
Gallery North	2105 Burlington	North Kansas City	MO	64116
Kemper Museum of Contemp. Art	4420 Warwick Blvd.	Kansas City	MO	64111
Limited Additions	2644 Metro Blvd.	Maryland Heights	MO	63043
Lisa Frick Gallery	2840 Bus. Hwy 54	Lake Ozark	MO	65049
Michael Anton Bruckdorfer	Walnut and Ferry Streets	Augusta	MO	63332
Poppy	914 East Broadway	Columbia	MO	65201
Small Indulgences	1045 South Big Bend Boulevard	St. Louis	MO	63117
Tobiason Studio	515 Felix	St. Joseph	MO	64501
Waverly House Gifts/Gallery	2031 S. Waverly	Springfield	MO	65804
A Gallery	512 Main Street	Hattiesburg	MS	39401
Baycrafts	107 North Beach Blvd.	Bay St. Louis	MS	39520

Top Craft Galleries

Name	Address	City	State	Zip
Chimneyville Crafts Gallery	1150 Lakeland Drive	Jackson	MS	39216
Goldring Instite Gift Shop	P. O. Box 16528	Jackson	MS	39236
Hillyer House	207 East Scenic Avenue	Pass Christian	MS	39571
Southern Breeze Gallery	4500 1-55 North Ste. 160	Jackson	MS	39211
Southside Gallery	150 Courthouse Square	Oxford	MS	38655
Artworks Gallery	123 West Main St.	Bozeman	MT	59715
Basin Creek Pottery and Gallery	82 E. Basin St.	Basin	MT	59631
Noice Studio and Gallery	127 Main St.	Kalispell	MT	59901
Riecke's Bayside Gallery	482 Electric Ave.	Bigfork	MT	59911
Sutton West Gallery	121 West Broadway	Missoula	MT	59101
Toucan Gallery	2505 Montana Ave.	Billings	MT	59101
2Sisters Gallery	2002 New Garden Road	Greensboro	NC	27410
Accipiter	2046 Clark Ave.S	Raleigh	NC	27605
Alta Vista	2839 Broadstone Rd.	Valle Crucis	NC	28691
American Folk	64 Biltmore Ave.	Asheville	NC	28801
Bellagio	7 Boston Way	Asheville	NC	28803
Blue Heron Gallery	1780-10A Chandlers Lane	Sunset Beach	NC	28468
Blue Moon Gallery	1387 Highway 705 S.	Seagrove	NC	27341
Blue Spiral One	38 Biltmore Avenue	Asheville	NC	28801
Browning Artworks Ltd	P. O. Box 275	Frisco	NC	27936
Carolina Creations	321 Pollock Street	New Bern	NC	28560
Carolina Moon	P. O. Box 1060, Nags Head Stn	Nags Head	NC	27959
Cedar Creek Gallery	1150 Fleming Road	Creedmoor	NC	27522
City Art Works	PMB 315 7804 Fairview Rd.	Charlotte	NC	28226
Continuity, Inc	P. O. Box 999, Market Square	Maggie Valley	NC	28751
Crabtree Meadows Store	Milespost #339	Little Switzerland	NC	28749
Earthworks	21 N. Main St.	Waynesville	NC	28786
Favorite Designs	P. O. Box 467	Mebane	NC	27302
Fine Lines	304 South Stratford Road	Winston-Salem	NC	27103
Gallery Mia Tyson	217 N. Front Street	Wilmington	NC	28401
Gallery of the Mountains	290 Macon Avenue	Asheville	NC	28814
Greenleaf Gallery	6917 S. Croatan Hwy.	Nags Head	NC	27959
Grovewood Gallery	111 Grovewood Road	Asheville	NC	28805
Hands Craft Gallery	542 W. King St.	Boone	NC	28607
Handscapes Gallery	410 Front Street	Beaufort	NC	28516
Jewels That Dance	63 Haywood Street	Asheville	NC	28801
Julia Rush Fine Crafts	216 Union Square	Hickory	NC	28601
Lick Log Mill Store	4321 Dillard Road S. R. 106	Highlands	NC	28741
Little Art Gallery	432 Daniels Street Center	Raleigh	NC	27605
Maddi's Gallery	1530 East Boulevard	Charlotte	NC	28203
Midland Crafters	2176 Midland Rd. P. O. Box 100	Pinehurst	NC	28370
Mint Museum Shop	220 North Tryon Street	Charlotte	NC	28202
Moondance Gallery	603 Meadowmont Village Circle	Chapel Hill	NC	27517
Morning Glory	102 Caledon Ct.	Greenville	NC	29615
New Elements Gallery	216 North Front Street	Wilmington	NC	28401
New Morning Gallery	7 Boston Way	Asheville	NC	28803
Ocean Annie'	815A Ocean Trail	Corolla	NC	27927
Peak Experience	P. O. Box 834	Highlands	NC	28741
Red Sky Gallery	4705 Savings PL #108	Charlotte	NC	28210
Sandy Bay Gallery	Highway 12, P. O. Box 538	Hatteras	NC	27943
Seven Sisters Gallery	117 Cherry Street	Black Mountain	NC	28711

Top Craft Galleries

Silent Poetry	120 West Main Street	Burnsville	NC	28714
Silver Bonsai Gallery	905 Hwy. 64 East	Manteo	NC	27954
Skillbeck Gallery	248 South Sharon Amity Road	Charlotte	NC	28211
SOLO Art Gallery	33 Miller St.	Winston-Salem	NC	27104
Somerhill Gallery	3 Eastgate, E. Franklin St.	Chapel Hill	NC	27514
Southern Hands	1 Wright Square P. O. Box 1827	Highlands	NC	28741
Spectrum Gallery	1121-B Military Cutoff Road	Wilmington	NC	28405
Stewart's Village Gallery	116 McDonald St.	Waxhaw	NC	28173
Summit One Gallery	4152 Cashiers Road, Hwy 64	Highlands	NC	28741
Twigs & Leaves Craft Gallery	98 North Main Street	Waynesville	NC	28786
Twisted Laurel Gallery	333 Locust Ave.	Spruce Pine	NC	28777
Village Galleries Arts and Crafts	Historic Biltmore Village	Asheville	NC	28803
Vitrum Gallerie	10 Lodge Street	Asheville	NC	28803
Wickwire Fine Art/Folk Art	330 North Main Street	Hendersonville	NC	28792
Wildwoods Gallery	1345 Poplar Grove Rd. South	Boone	NC	28607
Wilkes Art Gallery	913 C St.	North Wilkesboro	NC	28659
Artsplace	1110 Second Ave. North	Grand Forks	ND	58203
Latitudes Gallery, Framing & Gifts	107 N. Fifth St.	Bismarck	ND	58501
ND Museum of Art Gift Store	P. O. Box 7305	Grand Forks	ND	58202
Spirit Room Gallery	111 Broadway	Fargo	ND	58102
Artists' Cooperative Gallery	405 South 11th St.	Omaha	NE	68102
Borsheim's	120 Regency Pkwy.	Omaha	NE	68114
Noyes Art Gallery	119 South Ninth St.	Lincoln	NE	68508
Strategic Air Museum Store	28210 West Park Highway	Ashland	NE	68003
White Crane Gallery	1032 Howard Street	Omaha	NE	68102
ARTISAN'S WORKSHOP	P. O.B 124	New London	NH	03257
Casual Cat	112 Rte. 101A	Amherst	NH	03031
Cordwainer Gallery	176 Rt. 101	Bedford	NH	03110
Country Artisans	53 Main St.	Keene	NH	03431
Detailed Stained Glass	51 South Main Street	Concord	NH	03301
Finn and Co.	29 Congress St.	Portsmouth	NH	03801
gallery 205	205 N. Main St.	Concord	NH	03301
N.W.Barrett Gallery	53 Market St	Portsmouth	NH	03801
NJM Gallery	57 Bow Street	Portsmouth	NH	03801
North Gallery at Tewksbury	RR101	Peterborough	NH	03458
Oglethorpe Fine Arts & Crafts	312 D.W. Highway, Ste.#3	Meredith	NH	03253
Pierce Designs	41 Glen Road	West Lebanon	NH	03784
Worldly Goods	37 Congress Street	Portsmouth	NH	03801
Yikes! American Craft Gallery	Main Street and Route 25	Center Harbor	NH	03226
A Mano Galleries	36 North Union St.	Lambertville	NJ	08530
Accent Gallery	956 Ashbury Avenue	Ocean City	NJ	08226
Accent Studio	207 Kings Hwy E.	Haddonfield	NJ	08033
American Craft Gallery	163 South St.	Morristown	NJ	07960
Armadillo	31 West 22nd Street	Avalon	NJ	08202
Arrivee	15 Broad Street	Red Bank	NJ	07701
Beautiful Things	1038 East Second Street	Scotch Plains	NJ	07076
Bloom's	114 Raritan Ave.	Highland Park	NJ	08904
Blue Tulip	100 Overlook Center 2nd Floor	Princeton	NJ	08540
By Hand Fine Craft Gallery	142 Kings Highway East	Hardonfield	NJ	08033
Capital City Craft Studio	117 South Warren Street	Trenton	NJ	08608
Catch the Wind	23 South Main Street	Medford	NJ	08055

Top Craft Galleries

CBL Fine Art	459 Pleasant Valley Way	West Orange	NJ	07052
Church Door Gallery	P. O. Box 207/ 103 Philhower Ave	Califon	NJ	07830
Dexterity, Ltd.	26 Church Street	Montclair	NJ	07042
Drew Chryst Gallery	14 Winona Parkway	Sparta	NJ	07871
Eco Galleria	500 Cedar Lane	Teaneck	NJ	07666
Frick and Frack	1480 Route 23 North	Wayne	NJ	07470
Frog Hollow Gallery	31 Maple St.	Summit	NJ	07901
Gallery of American Craft	1501 Glasstown Rd.	Millville	NJ	08332
Grey Dove, The	159 South Livingston Avenue	Livingston	NJ	07039
Horsefeathers West	200 E. Ridgewood Ave	Ridgewood	NJ	07450
Jewel Spiegel Gallery	30 North Dean Street	Englewood	NJ	07631
Kornbluth Gallery	7-21 Fairlawn Ave.	Fair Lawn	NJ	07410
Limited Editions	2200 Long Beach Blvd.	Surf City	NJ	08008
Louisa Melrose Gallery	41 Bridge Street	Frenchtown	NJ	08825
Masterpiece Craft Gallery	968 Route 73 South	Marlton	NJ	08053
Michael Roth & Co.	67 Nassau St	Clark	NJ	07066
N. K. Thaine Gallery	150 Kings Highway East	Haddonfield	NJ	08033
Oceanside Gallery	1010 Main Street	Belmar	NJ	07719
Off the Wall Craft Gallery	42 S. Main Box 128	Allentown	NJ	08501
Ooh La La	13211 Long Beach Blvd.	Beach Haven	NJ	08008
Peters Valley Craft Store	19 Kuhn Rd	Layton	NJ	07851
Quest	50 Main St.	Chester	NJ	07930
Ru Crafts	P. O. Box 4352	Cherry Hill	NJ	08034
Solaris Gallery	P. O. Box 522/56 Main Street	Califon	NJ	07830
The Flying Carp	743 Ashbury Ave.	Ocean City	NJ	08226
The Mendham Art Gallery	13 West Main Street	Mendham	NJ	07945
The Quest	38 MAIN ST	Chester	NJ	07930
Trendz-OT & Company	209 96th Street	Stone Harbor	NJ	08247
Wheaton Village	The Gallery of American Craft	Millville	NJ	08332
Wheaton Village Museum of Glass	1501 Glasstown Rd.	Millville	NJ	08332
Wortendyke Gallery	211 Greenwood Ave.	Midland Park	NJ	07432
Zecca Gallery	450 Main Street	Metuchen	NJ	08840
Zephyr Gallery	The Market Fair, 3535 US Rte 1	Princeton	NJ	08540
Abiquin Inn	P.O. Box 120	Abiquiu	NM	87510
Arlene Siegel Gallery	102 East Water St.	Santa Fe	NM	87501
Bryans Gallery	121 Kit Carson Rd.	Taos	NM	87571
Casa de Avila	5001 Ellison NE	Albuquerque	NM	87109
Chalk Farm Gallery	330 Old Santa Fe Trail	Santa Fe	NM	87501
Desert Star	2044 South Plaza	Albuquerque	NM	87102
Georgia O'Keefe Museum Shop	217 Johnson Street	Santa Fe	NM	87501
Karen Melfi Collection	225 Canyon Rd.	Santa Fe	NM	87501
Las Comadres Gallery	228A Paseo del Pueblo Norte	Taos	NM	87571
Lew Allen Contemporary	129 W. Palace Ave.	Santa Fe	NM	87501
M.S. Franco Gallery	1107 S. First St.	Clayton	NM	88415
Mariposa Gallery	3500 Central Ave. SE	Albuquerque	NM	87106
Millicent Rogers Museum Gift Shop	Millicent Rogers Museum Rd.	Taos	NM	87571
Ortega's On The Plaza	101 W. San Francisco St.	Santa Fe	NM	87501
Patina Gallery	131 West Palace Avenue	Santa Fe	NM	87501
Purple Sage	110 Don Gaspar	Santa Fe	NM	87501
Santa Fe Pottery	323 S. Guadeloupe St.	Santa Fe	NM	87501
Santa Fe Weaving Gallery	124 1/2 Galisteo	Santa Fe	NM	87501

Top Craft Galleries

Gallery	Address	City	State	Zip
Shidoni Gallery	Bishop Lodge Rd.	Tesuque	NM	87574
Southwest Mercado Gallery	121 Romero NW	Albuquerque	NM	87104
Susan Wilder Gallery	119 Kit Carson Rd.	Taos	NM	87571
The Rare Vision Gallery	2935 D Louisiana, N E	Albuquerque	NM	87110
The Taos Company	124 John Dunn/Bent St.	Taos	NM	87571
Thirteen Moons Gallery	652 Canyon Road	Santa Fe	NM	87501
Variant Gallery	135 North Plaza	Taos	NM	87571
Weaving Southwest	216B Pueblo Norte	Taos	NM	87571
Weyrich Gallery	2935-D Louisiana Blvd. N.E.	Albuquerque	NM	87110
Fiddlesticks	1229 Arizona St.	Boulder City	NV	89005
Gene Speck's Silver State Gallery	719 Plumas St.	Reno	NV	89509
Infinite Ideas	527 California Ave	Reno	NV	89509
Just Write	8050 W. Charleston #108	Las Vegas	NV	89117
Mandalay Bay Resort	3950 Las Vegas Blvd South	Las Vegas	NV	89119
Paper and Gold Gallery	Ceasar's Tahoe Hotel and Casino	Stateline	NV	89449
Richardson Gallery of Fine Art	3670 S. Virginia St.	Reno	NV	89502
15 Steps	171 The Commons	Ithaca	NY	14850
Aaron Faber Gallery	666 5th Ave.	New York	NY	10019
Adirondack Artworks	Route 3, Box 324	Natural Bridge	NY	13665
Adirondack Craft Center	93 Saranac Ave	Lake Placid	NY	12946
Adrein Linford	1320 Madison Avenue	New York City	NY	10128
Albright-Knox Gallery	1285 Elmwood Avenue	Buffalo	NY	14222
Altamira	541 Main St.	Islip	NY	11751
American Artisan	790 Seventh Ave.	New York	NY	10019
American Craft Museum Shop	40 West 53rd. St.	New York	NY	10019
An American Craftsman	P. O. Box 480	Slate Hill	NY	10973
Ann Kolb Gallery	46 Mian Street	East Hampton	NY	11937
Artcrafters Gallery	472 Elmwood Avenue	Buffalo	NY	14222
Artisans Alley	1897 W. River Rd.	Grand Island	NY	12072
Brooklyn Artisans Gallery	221A Court St.	Brooklyn	NY	11201
Brooklyn Museum of Art Store	200 Eastern Parkway	Brooklyn	NY	11238
Clay Pot	162 7th Ave.	Brooklyn	NY	11215
Clouds Gallery	1Mill Hill Rd.	Woodstock	NY	12498
Craft Company No. 6	785 University Ave.	Rochester	NY	14607
Crafts People	262 Spillway Road	West Hurley	NY	12491
Creative Spirit	5111 Route 213	Olivebridge	NY	12461
Creator's Hands, The	336 Arnett Boulevard	Rochester	NY	14619
Cross Harris Fine Crafts	45 E. 72nd St. #3C	New York	NY	10021
Designers Studio	492 Broadway	Saratoga Sprin	NY	12866
Dr. Livingston's Finds	234 Broadway #2	Monticello	NY	12701
Eclectic Collector	215 Katonah Ave	Katonah	NY	10536
Enchanted Forest, The	P. O. Box 20215	New York	NY	10014
Eureka Crafts	210 Walton St.	Syracuse	NY	13202
For Decor	1458 Plum Lane	East Meadow	NY	11554
Freewheel Pottery, The	7 Tinker Street	Woodstock	NY	12498
Gallery M	308A Main St.	Greenport	NY	11944
Galmer Silversmiths	5-19 47th Ave	Long Island City	NY	11101
Garth Clark Gallery	24 West 57 St.	New York	NY	10019
Goldsmith, The	49 Court Street	Binghampton	NY	13901
Guggenheim Museum Store	1071 Fifth Avenue (at 89th Street)	New York	NY	10128
Hand of Man	Main Street	Old Forge	NY	13420

Top Craft Galleries

Handcrafters, The	57 Main Street	Chatham	NY	12037
Handmade and More	6 North Front Street	New Paltz	NY	12561
Handwork	102 West State Street	Ithaca	NY	14850
Hudson Valley Arts Center	337 Warren St.	Hudson	NY	12534
Imagine	8 East Genesee Street	Skaneateles	NY	13152
Intrepid Sea-Air-Space Museum	Pier 86 12th Ave and 46th Street	New York	NY	10036
Jenss	4230C Ridge Lea Road Ste.1	Amherst	NY	14226
Judaica Art Is....	80-12 Surrey Place	Jamaica Estates	NY	11432
Julie's Artisan's Gallery	762 Madison Ave.	New York	NY	10021
Kate's Paperie	561 Broadway	New York	NY	10012
Klay Gallery	65 South Broadway	Nyack	NY	10960
Landing Gallery	71 East Main Street	Smithtown	NY	11787
Lee Gallery	49 Main St.	Southhampton	NY	11968
Loveed Assoc.	575 Madison Avenue	New York	NY	10022
Metropolitan Museum of Art Store	1000 Fifth Avenue at 82nd Street	New York	NY	10028
Mill Cottage Gallery	Main St.	Rensselaerville	NY	12147
Moon Tree Design	22 Main St	Lake Placid	NY	12946
Museum Of Jewish Heritage	18 First Pl.	New York	NY	10280
Museum of Modern art Store	11 W. 53rd Street	New York	NY	10019
NCH Studio	201 Court Street	Brooklyn	NY	11201
Northport Crafters Gallery	106 Main Street	Northport	NY	11768
Offerings	59 Katonah Ave.	Katonah	NY	10536
Originals	582 Westbury Ave.	Carle Place	NY	11514
Sedoni Gallery	304-A New York Ave.	Huntington	NY	11743
Surroundings Art Gallery	73 East Main St.	Westfield	NY	14787
SweetHeart Gallery	8 Tannery Brook Road	Woodstock	NY	12498
Symmetry	348 Broadway	Saratoga Springs	NY	12866
Temple Beth Am Gift Shop	4660 Sheridan Drive	Williamsville	NY	14221
The AptGallery.com, Inc.	900 West End Avenue	New York City	NY	10025
The Collector	2067 Merrick Rd.	Merrick	NY	11566
The Eclectic Collector	215 Katonah Ave.	Katonah	NY	10536
The Gift Cupboard	104 Lafayette Avenue	Suffern	NY	10901
The Painted Garden	4138 Lakeville Groveland Rd	Geneseo	NY	14454
The River Gallery	39 Main Street	Irvington	NY	10533
Union Square Ceramic Center	7 East 17th Street 8th floor	New York	NY	10003
Whitney Mus. of American Art Store	945 Madison Avenue at 75th St.	New York	NY	10021
Cameo Gallery	772 North High Street	Columbus	OH	43215
Century House of Glendale	3 Village Square	Cincinnati	OH	45246
Cleveland Museum of Art Store	11150 East Boulevard	Cleveland	OH	44106
Creative Elements Furniture Studio	24186 Front St.	Grand Rapids	OH	43522
Don Drumm Studios and Gallery	437 Crouse St.	Akron	OH	44311
Finishing Touch Gallery	115 S Front Street	Fremont	OH	43420
Fiori-Omni Gallery	2072 Murray Hill Rd.	Cleveland	OH	44106
Gallery 143	1840 Town Park Blvd.	Uniontown	OH	44685
Gallery in the Vault	105 E. Liberty St.	Wooster	OH	44691
Ginko Gallery & Studio	19 South Main Street	Oberlin	OH	44074
Harris Stanton Gallery	2301 W. Market St.	Akron	OH	44313
Helen Winnemores	150 E Kossuth St	Columbus	OH	43206
Lazar's Art Gallery	2940 Woodlawn Ave.	Canton	OH	44708
Murray Hill Art & Craft	2188 Murray Hill Road	Cleveland	OH	44106
Off The Wall-Ohio	26450 Bernwood Road	Cleveland	OH	44122

Top Craft Galleries

Ohio Historical Society Store	1982 Velma Ave.	Columbus	OH	43211
PM Gallery	726 N. High St.	Columbus	OH	43215
Rutlage Gallery	1964 N. Main St.	Dayton	OH	45402
Standing Rock Gallery	5194 Darrow Road	Hudson	OH	44236
Taft Museum of Art Store	316 Pike Street	Cincinnati	OH	45202
The American Gallery	6600 Sylvania Ave.	Sylvania	OH	43560
The Sassy Cat	88 N. Main St.	Chagrin Falls	OH	44022
Verne Collection	2207 Murray Hill Rd.	Cleveland	OH	44106
Zig Zag Gallery	101 E. Alex Bell Rd. #172	Dayton	OH	45459
American Furnishings	1409 West 3rd Avenue	Columbus	OH	43212
Bebe's	6480 Avondale/Nichols Hills Pl.	Oklahoma City	OK	73116
Eleanor Kirkpatrick Gallery	3000 General Pershing Blvd.	Oklahoma City	OK	73107
Firehouse Art Center	444 S. Flood Ave.	Norman	OK	73069
Gallery 107	107 North Main Street	Sand Springs	OK	74063
M. A. Doran Gallery	3509 South Peoria	Tulsa	OK	74105
Terra Bijou	201 West Oklahoma #234	Guthrie	OK	73044
Tribes Gallery	307 E. Main St.	Norman	OK	73069
Ashland Harwood Gallery	17 North Main St.	Ashland	OR	97520
Breach the Moon Gallery	434 SW Bay Blvd	Newport	OR	97365
Bullseye Connection Glass Gallery	300 NW Thirteenth Ave.	Portland	OR	97209
Butters Gallery	520 N.W. Davis	Portland	OR	97209
Contemporary Crafts Gallery	3934 SW Corbett Ave.	Portland	OR	97201
Faith Mountain Art Gallery	50095 Highway 25	John Day	OR	97845
Forrest Gallery	10767 Butte St. NE	Aurora	OR	97002
Freed Gallery	6119 S.W. Highway 101	Lincoln City	OR	97367
Gallery 33	1400 NW Everett St.	Portland	OR	97209
Hoffman Gallery Shop	8245 SW Barnes Rd.	Portland	OR	97225
Illahe Tileworks Studio	695 Mistletoe Rd. #F	Ashland	OR	97520
La Bella Casa	121 NE 5th Street	Mcminnville	OR	97128
Lawrence Gallery	Box 187, Hwy. 18	Sheridan	OR	97378
Mary Lou Zeek Gallery	335 State Street	Salem	OR	97301
Mole Hole	11787 SW Beaverton	Beaverton	OR	97005
Nimbus	25 East Main Street	Ashland	OR	97520
Oceanic Arts	444 SW Bay Blvd	Newport	OR	97365
Rare Discovery	148 N. Hemlock Box 1000	Cannon Beach	OR	97110
Real Mother Goose	901 S.W. Yamhill	Portland	OR	97205
Salem Art Association	600 Mission St. S.E.	Salem	OR	97302
Soaring Crane Gallery	33105 Cape Kiwanda Dr.	Pacific City	OR	97135
Sticks and Stones	512 Cascade Avenue	Hood River	OR	97031
Sunbird Gallery Inc.	916 N.W. Wall St.	Bend	OR	97701
The Real Mother Goose	901 S W Yamhill	Portland	OR	97205
Triad Gallery	5667 NW Highway 101	Seal Rock	OR	97376
Twisted Laurel Gallery	30 NW 23rd Pl.	Portland	OR	97210
White Bird Gallery	Box 502 No. Hemlock St.	Cannon Beach	OR	97110
Widney Moore Gallery	202 NW 13th Ave	Portland	Or	97209
Wood Gallery	818 S.W. Bay Blvd.	Newport	OR	97365
20th Century Glass, Pottery	23 Phillip Drive	Kirkwood	PA	17536
A Mano Gallery	128 South Main Street	New Hope	PA	18938
Accents & Images	Peddler's Village Route 263	Lahaska	PA	18931
AIA Bookstore	117 South 17th St.	Philadelphia	PA	19103
Allegheny Country	503 Anderson Road	Schellsburg	PA	15559

Top Craft Galleries

Name	Address	City	State	Zip
Ambitious Endeavors	11 Union Avenue	Bala Cynwyd	PA	19004
American Pie	327 South Street	Philadelphia	PA	19147
An American Gallery	101 E. Pittsburg St.	Greensburg	PA	15601
Antiques and Handcrafts	1712 Chester Road	Bethlehem	PA	18017
Art Effects Gallery	350 Montgomery Ave	Merian	PA	19066
Artery	210 Broad St.	Milford	PA	18337
Artisans Gallery	Box 133 Peddlers Village	Lahaska	PA	18931
Artisans Three	The Village Center	Spring House	PA	19477
Baubles and Beads	25 West King Street	Lancaster	PA	17603
Black Cat, The	3424 Sansom Street	Philadelphia	PA	19104
Boutique To Go	1119 Bell Ave	Allentown	PA	18103
Box Heart Gallery	4523 Liberty Ave.	Pittsburgh	PA	15224
Campbell Pottery Gallery	25579 Plank Road P. O. Box 246	Cambridge Springs	PA	16403
Cenzia Arts and Gifts	121 West State Street	Kennett Square	PA	19348
Chestnut House	25 W. King Street	Lancaster	PA	17603
Circa 2000-Fine American Crafts	2932 Conestoga Road	Glenmoore	PA	19343
Clay Place, The	5416 Walnut Street	Pittsburg	PA	15232
Cleo's Silversmith Gallery	21 E. Third Street	Bethlehem	PA	18015
Creative Hands	P. O. Box 284	Furlong	PA	18925
Dandelion	6609 Springbank Street	Philadelphia	PA	19119
Design Interiors	134 West Main St.	Leola	PA	17540
Douglas Albert Gallery	107 McAlister Alley Walkway	State College	PA	16801
DragonFly Gallery	29 South High St.	West Chester	PA	19382
Earth and State	23 W. State St.	Media	PA	19063
Earthworks Pa	233 Haverford Ave	Narberth	PA	19072
Equinox Jewelry and Gifts	120 West State St.	Kennett Square	PA	19348
From the Heart	105 Pine Haven Drive	Somerset	PA	15501
G Squared Gallery & Gardens	212 E Main St.	Ligonier	PA	15658
Galan	100 Evergreen Dr. #113	Glen Mills	PA	19380
Gallerie 500	3205 Scotts Lane Ste 303	Philadelphia	PA	19129
Gallery 61	1380 Pottsville Pike	Shoemakersville	PA	19555
Gallery At Cedar Hollow	2447 Yellow Springs Rd.	Malvern	PA	19355
Gallery at Forest Hall	101 West Hartford Street	Milford	PA	18337
Gallery at Liztech	95 Crystal St. 1st Floor	East Stroudsburg	PA	18301
Gallery Chiz	5831 Ellsworth Ave.	Pittsburgh	PA	15232
Golden Fish Gallery	307 Broad Street	Milford	PA	18337
Hearts Afire	28 South Main Street	New Hope	PA	18938
Home and Garden Culture	908 East Baltimore Pike	Kennett Square	PA	19348
J R Weldon Company	415 Wood Street	Pittsburgh	PA	15222
Jewish Cntr. Little Shop	400 W. Ellet St.	Philadelphia	PA	19119
Keller Charles	2413 Federal Street	Philadelphia	PA	19146
Langman Gallery	Willow Grove Park # 1118	Willow Grove	PA	19090
Latitudes Gallery	4325 Main Street	Philadelphia	PA	19127
Lavender Rose	317 South State Street	Newtown	PA	18940
LL Pavorsky Jewels and Gifts	707 Walnut Street	Philadelphia	PA	19106
Magpie Gallery	400 Market St.	Lewisburg	PA	17837
Mark Williams, Goldsmith	111 West 3rd Street	Williamsport	PA	17701
Morgan Contemp. Glass Gallery	5833 Ellsworth Ave	Pittsburgh	PA	15232
Otter Creek Store, The	106 South Diamond Street	Mercer	PA	16137
Our American Heritage	17114 East Lancaster Avenue	Paoli	PA	19301
Owen/Patrick Gallery	4345 Main Street	Philadelphia	PA	19127

Top Craft Galleries

Name	Address	City	State	Zip
Pennsylvania Museum Store	3260 South Street	Philadelphia	PA	19104
Philadelphia Art Museum	26th & Parkway	Philadelphia	PA	19101
Philadelphia Museum of Art Store	Benjamin Pkwy and 26th Street	Philadelphia	PA	19130
Pittsburgh Center for the Arts	6300 Fifth Ave.	Pittsburgh	PA	15232
Route 5	380 Wayne Avenue	Chambersburg	PA	17201
Show of Hands	1006 Pine Street	Philadelphia	PA	19107
Simple Pleasures	22 South High St.	West Chester	PA	19382
Sisterhood Gift Shop	944 Second St. Pike	Richboro	PA	18954
Snyderman Gallery	303 Cherry St.	Philadelphia	PA	19106
SOTA Spirit of the Artist	1022 Pine St.	Philadelphia	PA	19107
Susan's Treasures	W. S. Farmers Market #8 Upstairs	Lemoyne	PA	17043
The Works	303 Cherry St.	Philadelphia	PA	19106
This Little Gallery	617 West Ave	Jenkintown	PA	19046
Topeo Gallery	35 N Main St	New Hope	PA	18938
Turning Point Gallery	34 West State St.	Media	PA	19063
Unique by Design	1000 Mansion View	West Chester	PA	19382
Village Artisans Gallery	321 Walnut Street	Boiling Springs	PA	17007
Vitetta	4747 S. Broad Street	Philadelphia	PA	19112
William Ris Gallery	2208 Market Street	Camp Hill	PA	17011
Woodburners	11 North Market St.	Hatfield	PA	19440
Youghiogheny Glass	900 W. Crawford	Connellsville	PA	15425
Collaga	25 Bowens Wharf	Newport	RI	02840
Juleez Artique's	10 Phillips Street	Wickford	RI	02852
Mixed Media	Box 271	Block Island	RI	02807
OOP! contemporary gift gallery	297 Thayer St.	Providence	RI	02906
Sun Up Gallery	95 Watch Hill Road	Westerly	RI	02891
American Originals Gallery	153 East Bay Street	Charleston	SC	29401
ArtWare	1203A Main Street Village	Hilton Head	SC	29926
Carol Saunders Gallery	922 Gervais Street	Columbia	SC	29201
Clay Works Gallery	285 Meeting House Rd.	Charleston	SC	29401
Llyn Strong	119 North Main St.	Greenville	SC	29601
Michael McDunn Gallery	741 Rutherford Rd.	Greenville	SC	29609
Nash Gallery	2 H Harbourside	Hilton Head	SC	29928
Portfolio Art Gallery	2007 Devine St.	Columbia	SC	29205
Smith Galleries	Village at Wexfort Ste.	Hilton Head	SC	29928
Bear Rock Art	RR-1 Box 19-A	Custer	SD	57730
Prarie Edge	606 Main St.	Rapid City	SD	57701
American Artisan	4231 Harding Rd.	Nashville	TN	37205
Atelier	8400 Highway 100	Nashville	TN	37221
Babcock Gifts	P. O. Box 241028	Memphis	TN	38124
Bennett Gallery	5308 Kingston Pike	Knoxville	TN	37919
Enchanted Décor	41 W. Broad St.	Cookeville	TN	38501
Finer Things Gallery	1898 Nolenville Rd.	Nashville	TN	37210
Hanson Gallery	5607 Kingston Pike	Knoxville	TN	37919
James-Ben: Studio and Gallery	129 North Main ST.	Greenvile	TN	37743
Jay Etkin Gallery	409 South Main St.	Memphis	TN	38103
Jonesborough Art Glass Gallery	101 E. Main St.	Jonesborough	TN	37659
Liz-Beth & Co.	9211 Park West Boulevard	Knoxville	TN	37923
Nouveau Classics	2104 Crestmoor Rd.	Nashville	TN	37215
River Gallery	400 Second Street	Chattanooga	TN	37403
River Gallery-Tennessee	400 East Second Street	Chattanooga	TN	37403

Top Craft Galleries

Name	Address	City	State	Zip
Signature Designs	508 South Main Street #101	Memphis	TN	38103
Spirit of the Hand	545 E. Meeting St.	Dandridge	TN	37725
Twisted Vessel Contemporary Craft	3335 Old Mill St.	Pigeon Forge	TN	37863
Allie - Coosh	6726 Snider Plaza	Dallas	TX	75205
Art Alley	14072 Memorial Dr.	Houston	TX	77079
Art in the City	3601 W. Alabama, Suite 101	Houston	TX	77027
Artistic Home	P. O. Box 1209	Crosby	TX	77532
Artworks	1214 West 6th St.	Austin	TX	78703
Ashley Averys	12707 North Fwy Ste 330	Houston	TX	77060
Austin Presence	3736 Beecave Road #5	Austin	TX	78746
Carlyn Galerie	6137 Luther Lane	Dallas	TX	75225
Center Gallery	300 Augusta	San Antonio	TX	78205
Clarksville Pottery and Galleries	4001 N. Lamar	Austin	TX	78756
Dreidels	1465 West Campbel Road	Richardson	TX	75080
Escape	713 Main St.	Georgetown	TX	78626
Gallery Vetro! Creative Art Glass	600 North Presa St.	San Antonio	TX	78205
Great Ideas	3144 Oak Hills Rd	Carollton	TX	75007
Gregory's	P. O.B 588/ 2 Main St	Saledo	TX	76571
Hanson Galleries	1101-10 Uptown Park Blvd.	Houston	TX	77056
Hill Country Weavers	1701 South Congress	Austin	TX	78704
Illuminata	700 Town & Cntry Blvd. Ste.2460	Houston	TX	77024
J Matthias Galleries	3739 FM 1960 Road West	Houston	TX	77068
Kittrell/Riffkind Art Glass	5100 Beltline Road #820	Dallas	TX	75240
Laurie Ltd.	P. O. BOX 671098	Dallas	TX	75367
Mirrors and Light	2309 Clearspring Dr, S	Irving	TX	75063
Monte Wade Fine Arts	514 Paseo De La Villita	San Antonio	TX	78205
Off Mainstreet Gallery	420 South Main	Grapeville	TX	76051
Originals	10225 Research #100	Austin	TX	78759
Positive Images	1118 West 6th Street	Austin	TX	78703
Screen Porch Art	2422 Rice Blvd.	Houston	TX	77005
The Artful Hand	6248 Camp Bowie Rd.	Fort Worth	TX	76116
The Ole Moon	3016 GreenVille Ave.	Dallas	TX	75206
Uncommon Angles	1616 S. University, Ste. 303	Fort Worth	TX	76107
Ursuline Sales Gallery	300 Augusta	San Antonio	TX	78205
Village Gallery	502 La Villita	San Antonio	TX	78205
Village Weavers	418 La Villita #8	San Antonio	TX	78205
A Gallery	1321 S, 2100 E,	Salt Lake City	UT	84108
Artworks	461 Main St.	Park City	UT	84060
Canyon Offerings	933 Zion Park Blvd.	Springdale	UT	84767
CODA Gallery	804 Main Street	Park City	UT	84060
E. Street Gallery	82 E. Street	Salt Lake City	UT	84103
Finch Lane Gallery	54 Finch Lane	Salt Lake City	UT	84102
Q Street Fine Crafts	88 Q St	Salt Lake City	UT	84103
Red Canyon Indian Store	3279 Hwy. 12	Panguitch	UT	84759
Appalachian Spring	102 W. Jefferson St.	Falls Church	VA	22046
Appalachian Spring	11877 Market St/Town Center	Reston	VA	20190
Art Craft Collection	123 King Street	Alexandria	VA	22314
Artemis Gallery	1601 W. Main St.	Richmond	VA	23220
Artisans	1368 Chain Bridge Rd.	MacLean	VA	22101
Arts Afire Gallery	102 North Fayette St.	Alexandria	VA	22314
As Kindred Spirits	1101 South Joyce Street #B8	Arlington	VA	22202

Top Craft Galleries

Name	Address	City	State	Zip
Blue Skies Gallery	26 S. King St.	Hampton	VA	23669
Crafter's Gallery	Route 10, Box 97	Charlottesville	VA	22903
Creative Classics	111 S. Alfred St.	Alexandria	VA	22314
Crystal Galleria	7951 L Tysons Corner Center	McLean	VA	22102
Elder Crafters of Alexandria	405 Cameron St.	Alexandria	VA	22314
Electric Glass Company	1 East Melon Street	Hampton	VA	23663
Hudson Bay Jewelry	1860 Laskin Rd.	Virginia Beach	VA	23454
Imagine Artwear	1124 King St.	Alexandria	VA	22314
J. Fenton Gallery	110 S. Henry St.	Williamsburg	VA	23185
Kane Marie Fine Arts Gallery	2865 Lynnhaven Drive Suite C-3	Virginia Beach	VA	23451
Lane Sanson Home Eclectique	3423 W. Cary St.	Richmond	VA	23221
Leaping Lizard	4408 Shore Drive	Virginia Beach	VA	23455
Mabry Mill Store	266 Mabry Mill Rd. SE	Meadows of Dan	VA	24120
Piedmont Arts Association	215 Starling Ave.	Martinsville	VA	24112
Riverview Gallery	1 High Street	Portsmouth	VA	23704
Signet Gallery	212 5th Street NE	Charlottesville	VA	22902
Spirited Collections	125 Mill Street #9	Occoquan	VA	22125
Spruce Creek Gallery	1368 Rockfish Valley Hwy Bx 434	Nellysford	VA	22958
Sully Framing and Art	6 Wickham Court	Sterling	VA	20165
Sussex Gallery	9563 Braddock Rd.	Fairfax	VA	22032
Touch of Earth	P. O. Box 346	Lightfoot	VA	23090
Touch of Earth	6580 Richmond Rd.	Williamsburg	VA	23188
Vivian's Art to Wear	301 E. MAIN ST.	Charlottesville	VA	22902
Windrush Gallery	12186 Fairfax Town Center	Fairfax	VA	22033
Designer's Circle	52 Church Street	Burlington	VT	05401
Fiddlehead at Four Corners	338 Main St.	Bennington	VT	05201
Garden Gallery	4367 Main Street	Manchester	VT	05254
Little River Hot Glass Studio	P. O. Box 1504	Stowe	VT	05672
Stowe Craft Gallery	55 Mountain Road	Stowe	VT	05672
Unicorn	15 Central St.	Woodstock	VT	05091
Vermont Artisan Designs	106 Main St.	Brattleboro	VT	05301
Vermont State Craft Center	85 Church St.	Burlington	VT	05401
Young & Constantin Gallery	Ten South Main St., Box 882	Wilmington	VT	05363
Afishionado Gallery	1900 W. Nickerson	Seattle	WA	98119
American Art Company	1126 Broadway Plaza	Tacoma	WA	98402
Art by Fire	5465 Leary Way NW	Seattle	WA	98107
Art Concepts on Broadway	924 Broadway Plaza	Tacoma	WA	98402
Art Stop	940 Broadway	Tacoma	WA	98402
Artists' Gallery of Seattle	902 First Ave. S.	Seattle	WA	98134
Bainbridge Arts and Crafts	151 Winslow Way E	Bainbridge Island	WA	98110
Crow Valley Pottery	2274 Orcas Road	Eastsound	WA	98245
Design Concern	1420 5th Avenue #201	Seattle	WA	98101
EarthenWorks	713 First Street	La Conner	WA	98257
Earthenworks Galleries	702 Water St.	Port Townsent	WA	98368
Elements Gallery	10500 NE 8th St.	Bellevue	WA	98004
Fireworks Gallery	210 First Ave.	Seattle	WA	98104
Flying Shuttle	607 First Avenue	Seattle	WA	98104
Folk Art Gallery	4138 University Way NE	Seattle	WA	98105
Glasshouse Studio	311 Occidental Ave. S.	Seattle	WA	98104
Global Art Venue	314 1st Ave. S.	Seattle	WA	98104

Top Craft Galleries

Holiday Gift & Craft Shop	526 19th Ave. E.	Seattle	WA	98112
La Tienda Folk Art Gallery	2050 NW Market St.	Seattle	WA	98107
Lakeshore Gallery	107 Park Lane	Kirkland	WA	98033
Meloy & Company Gallery	1208 Harris AVe.	Bellingham	WA	98225
Northwest Craft Center and Gallery	Seattle Center	Seattle	WA	98109
Phoenix Rising Gallery	2030 Western Ave.	Seattle	WA	98121
The American Art Company	1126 Broadway Plaza	Tacoma	WA	98402
The Legacy LTD	1003 First Avenue	Seattle	WA	98104
The Woodcarver Gallery	12652 Wilson St	Leavenworth	WA	98826
Watermark	1115 A ST	Tacoma	WA	98402
William Traver Gallery	110 Union St., 2nd floor	Seattle	WA	98101
Artisan Gallery	6858 Paoli Road	Paoli	WI	53508
Artisan Woods	2935 S. Fish Hatchery Rd.	Madison	WI	53711
Blue Dolphin House	10320 N. Water St.	Ephraim	WI	54211
Cornerstone Gallery	101 Fourth St.	Baraboo	WI	53913
Edgewood Orchard Galleries	4140 Peninsula Players Rd.	Fish Creek	WI	54212
Fanny Garver Gallery, The	230 State Street	Madison	WI	53703
Fine Line Designs Gallery	10376 Highway 42	Sister Bay	WI	54234
Flying Colors	608 New York Avenue	Sheboygan	WI	53081
Gift Itself	125 North Broadway	Green Bay	WI	54303
John Red's	N70 W6340 Bridge Road	Cedarburg	WI	53012
Johnston Gallery	245 High St	Mineral Point	WI	53565
Katie Gingrass Gallery	241 N. Broadway	Milwaukee	WI	53202
Kohler/Art Space	P. O. Box 489	Sheboygan	WI	53082
Milwaukee Art Museum Store	700 N. Art Museum Drive	Milwaukee	WI	53202
Newell Gallery	315 East Main Street	Waunakee	WI	53597
Racine Art Museum	441 Main Street	Racine	WI	53403
The Potters Shed	260 Industrial Blvd.	Shell Lake	WI	54871
Turtle Ridge Gallery	11736 Mink River Rd.	Ellison Bay	WI	54210
Two Fish Gallery	244 E. Rhine St.	Elkhart Lake	WI	53020
Water Street Gallery	522 W. Water St.	Princeton	WI	54968
Art Company of Davis	Box 452	Davis	WV	26260
Little Kanawha Craft House	113 Ann Street	Parkersburg	WV	26101
MorningStar FolkArts	US Route 219 North	Hillsboro	WV	24946
Mountain Laurel Crafts	101 N. Washington St.	Berkeley Springs	WV	25411
MountainMade	P O Box 660 100 Douglas Rd Cir	Thomas	WV	26292
Simple Gifts	120 Fairfax St.	Berkeley Springs	WV	25411
Tamarack	One Tamarack Park	Beckley	WV	25801
Earth, Wind and Fire Galleries	216 S. 2nd St.	Laramie	WY	82070
Wyoming Arts Council Gallery	2320 Capitol Ave.	Cheyenne	WY	82002
Wyoming Classics	546 Greybull Ave	Reybull	WY	82426

Conclusion

As a skilled craftsperson, you will always have a source of income, because the public will always appreciate the beautiful things that you make. You have only to educate the customer as to why your locally handmade jewelry is worth more money than the global counterparts (cheap imports.) The heart-felt appreciation by the customer for the craftsperson who is committed to quality and uniqueness makes the sacrifices and uncertainties of this unique lifestyle worthwhile.

In writing this book and software, we hope we have given you some new insights into how to improve your craft business, and shown you how a computer and spreadsheet can help you. We know you will find a use for many of the tips, addresses, and spreadsheets. The ones you don't use today may be helpful to you in the coming years as you modify your approach to marketing your craft products.

This book and software is updated with every new printing, so if you have any comments, corrections, sources, ideas for new forms, or criticisms, please take a moment to write or email us at eagleab@aol.com.

Columbus Arts Festival, Columbus, Ohio

Index

AAA, 36, 37
AARP, 36, 76
Abstracta, 39, 40, 75
ACC, 53
advertising, 103, 114, 116
alarm, 38
Allstate, 37
American Craft Council, 49, 53
American Express, 30, 31
American Style, 58
AOL, 64
Application Organizer, 84
application process, 11
applications, 125
Armstrong Products, 29
Art Fair SourceBook, 9
awning, 26
bamboo rollups, 28
banner, 26, 27
booth shot, 16
Booth sign, 42
brochure, 98
business plan, 110, 114
C. O. D., 56
Caravan, 21, 26
cash box, 45
checklist, 42
clip art, 122
collapsible water carrier, 40
commission, 96
computer, 88, 181
concrete blocks, 40
Concrete blocks, 23
consignment, 60, 103, 104
Consignment Agreement, 103
Contico, 39, 45
Copyright, 2, 71
copyright notice, 55, 71

craft fair applications, 125
craft fair guides, 9
craft fairs, 90
Craft Fairs, 84, 86
Craft Gallery, 98, 156, 157, 160, 164, 165, 168, 169, 170, 171, 179
Craft Huts, 23
Craft Pricing, 82
craftspeople, 77, 103
craftsperson, 103
Creative Energies, 22, 75
credit, 101
Credit Application, 101, 102
credit card, 17, 29, 30, 31, 32, 33, 45, 56, 57, 62, 70, 92
Credit Cards, 31
customer, 7, 11, 19, 27, 28, 29, 30, 31, 32, 33, 34, 43, 44, 55, 56, 57, 62, 63, 64, 66, 73, 81, 92, 108, 181
Customer List, 92
customers, 92, 101, 110, 112, 114
database, 98
deadline, 84
deduction, 90
Delivery Confirmation, 66
digital camera, 13, 15, 17
directory, 81
Discover Card, 30
dog stakes, 23
domain name, 63
Dome book, 69, 70
Dreamweaver, 62
eBay, 15, 62, 65, 66
EIN, 70
Elements, 14, 17, 63, 168, 170, 174, 179
employee identification number, 70
environmental aspects, 34, 116
Equipment List, 88

Index

Excel, 77, 78, 79, 81, 88, 92, 98, 101, 106
exclusivity, 57
Expense Report, 90
fax, 90
festivalnet.com, 9
Filtering Data, 98
Finding Information, 101
Five-Year Goal, 110
Flamort, 29
flea market, 8, 44, 62
fluorescent, 15
Flying, 38, 39, 172, 179, 180
forms, 77, 78, 79
galleries, 98
George Little Management, 50, 53
gift shops, 58, 60, 97, 98
Good Sam Club, 37
Google, 9, 64
gradient paper, 14
Halogen lamps, 20
Hang tags, 42
Hap Sakwa, 76
Health, 46
Home Occupation, 70
hostexcellence.com, 63
income, 90, 106, 110
Indoor booths, 19
ink jet printer, 79
instructions, 81
insurance, 88, 90, 103
Internet Service Provider, 63
inventory, 112
invoice, 108
JPEG, 14
jumper cables, 36
jury, 12, 18, 46
key words, 34
Keyboard Shortcuts, 103
letterheads, 118
letters, 77, 79, 118
Light Dome, 22

light tent, 15
Lipman, 31
macro, 15, 65
Mail List, 98
mailing labels, 92
mailing list, 11, 32, 44, 53, 54, 58, 69, 77, 78, 98, 124, 125
mapquest.com, 36
marketing plan, 114
MasterCard, 30, 31
metatags, 64
Monthly Accounting, 106
Novus, 30, 77, 168
Office, 19, 57, 69, 71, 77, 78, 79, 81, 106, 122
order form, 55, 57, 62
packtrack.com, 59
partnership, 110
past due invoices, 57
patent, 71
paypal, 64, 66
Pedestals, 29
photography, 13, 76
Photoshop, 14, 17, 63
plastic water cans, 25
portable battery pack, 32
postcards, 53, 54, 72, 156
press release, 72, 116
price, 82, 96, 110
priceline.com, 39
print, 79, 81, 88, 106, 116, 118
profit, 82
promoter, 7, 9, 11, 12, 36, 42, 54, 90, 125
Publisher, 2, 72, 78, 122, 156
PVC tube, 25
QVC, 61
records, 90, 106
rep, 82, 96
Resizing Excel, 101
rest stops, 35
resume, 120
retail, 82, 94, 96

Index

Rosen, 53
Rubbermaid, 24
Sale, 44, 127, 136, 146
Sales, 33, 52, 96, 97, 104, 178
sales receipts book, 57
sales rep, 52, 58, 97
sales representative, 96
sales tax, 45, 71, 106
seconds, 18, 31, 44, 54
shipping labels, 123
Shortcuts, 96
show special, 55
shows, 81, 82, 86, 96, 110, 112
slides, 12, 13, 14, 16, 17, 18, 27, 28, 84
Social Security, 106
software, 2, 181
sort, 84
statement, 108
store, 28, 52, 53, 54, 55, 56, 57, 60, 75, 82, 103, 104, 116
tablecloths, 29
tax included, 106
templates, 77, 78
terms, 55, 57, 101, 110
Tips, 90
trade show, 52, 53, 55, 60, 90, 94, 101
trailer, 38
travel agent, 39
travelocity.com, 39
Trimline, 23
truck stop, 35
Turbo Lister, 65
Uline, 76
VISA, 30, 31, 34, 42
web page, 65
wholesale, 82, 96, 101, 106
wholesale line sheet, 55
word processor, 118, 124
Works, 79
Zapplication, 17, 18
Zippy Mats, 54

Reveille by John C. Reiger

live again!
an' ready to show
Winter's over
I'm rarin' to go

Goodbye to the boredom
dull staring at walls
Now I am Faire-bound
off to the Malls.

Ol' Bertha is flying
past princes and prole's
Filled to the sunroof
with pitchers and bowls

So scatter before me
you freeway turtles
I am a Red Streak
bounding hurdles.

Friends and Fortune
beckon ahead.
Bright lights, warm smiles,
and plenty of bread.

I come once again
to hear the praise,
Puffs, and purchases
for three or four days.

Unless, of course
the show's for the birds,
And all that attend
are lookers and nerds.

But it's my life
This "Doing the shows."
How I survive it,
nobody knows.

"Hope springs eternal"
so optimists say.
I guess I agree,
I welcome today.

www.ingramcontent.com/pod-product-compliance
Lightning Source LLC
Chambersburg PA
CBHW080544170426
43195CB00016B/2680